Sight and Blindness in Luke-Acts

Biblical Interpretation Series

VOLUME 94

Sight and Blindness in Luke-Acts

The Use of Physical Features in Characterization

By
Chad Hartsock

BRILL

LEIDEN • BOSTON
2008

This book is printed on acid-free paper.

Library of Congress Catalogin-in-Publication Data

A C.I.P. record for this book is available from the Library of Congress

ISBN 0928-0731
ISBN 978 90 04 16535 9

PRINTED IN THE NETHERLANDS

CONTENTS

CHAPTER ONE

INTRODUCTION

This book is a literary study of the biblical texts, and specifically of Luke-Acts. It is a literary study that seeks to understand what an ancient audience might have heard when reading these texts. Specifically, this book is a literary study in characterization, particularly the use of physical descriptions as a means of characterization. In the ancient world, people often thought in terms of "physiognomics." Physiognomy is a pseudo-science that claims that the inner, moral character of a person can be known by studying the outward, physical features. That is, it was believed that there was a direct correlation between appearance and character such that the body reflected the character and the character could be discerned by careful physical examination. In fact, entire handbooks were devoted to this study, handbooks that provide a kind of index to these physical markers. In the modern world, we are not accustomed to thinking in these ways. In fact, such an approach would be dismissed or even condemned as stereotyping or even racial profiling. Nonetheless, if such a study was common in the ancient world, then one can expect authors to make use of these physiognomic conventions, and one can expect that an audience would hear in such physical descriptions a corresponding set of moral traits. In short, we in the modern world are missing an entire means of characterization when we fail to recognize that physical descriptions have moral freight.

Within the larger rubric of physiognomics, this book will study one specific physical marker in particular—blindness. As we study the ancient sources, we actually find something of a literary *topos* for the blind character that begins to emerge. That is to say that whenever a character in ancient literature is described as "blind," a certain set of assumptions about the person's character would likely be made by the audience. Ultimately, this book argues that blindness serves as an interpretive principle that is programmatic for Luke-Acts, and this book seeks to bring that element of the narrative to the forefront.

Within these same texts, blindness is also often used in a completely metaphorical sense. That is, a physically blind character would be considered spiritually blind, but that physical conclusion also began to take on a life of its own such that someone with perfectly healthy eyesight can be labeled "blind" in order to talk about his spiritual condition. The metaphorical usage is widespread and commonly used in both the ancient world as well as the modern world, and it is probable that the metaphorical usage takes its meaning from the physiognomic world. While it is recognized that the physiognomic use of blindness and the metaphorical use of blindness are at times different things, both will be treated together here because in terms of their literary function both accomplish the same goals when it comes to characterization.

Methodology

The methodology of this study is an audience-oriented literary criticism. The method is literary in that we are looking specifically at characterization and the ways in which a story finds meaning in the way that story is told. Specifically though, the method is audience-oriented. We are not interested in a kind of modern reader-response that asks what these texts mean to the *modern* reader, however. Instead, we are interested in how an ancient auditor would have heard these texts. Audiences understand texts as they are filtered through shared cultural assumptions. Physiognomic conventions were so prevalent in the ancient world that they indeed permeated the culture and were by no means limited to the educated elite. Elizabeth Evans has expertly demonstrated that the "physiognomic consciousness" extends to all genres of literature in the Greco-Roman world, and she argues that the ancient world would have been thoroughly familiar with physical descriptions as a means of describing one's character.[1] Based on the widespread familiarity with these conventions in the ancient world, we can expect that an audience would be conditioned to hear statements about a person's character implicit in the person's physical description. Thus, the method of this study is to come to an understanding of how an ancient audience would have thought about blindness as a physical description, and then to read the biblical text in light of those assumptions.

[1] See Elizabeth C. Evans, *Physiognomics in the Ancient World* (Transactions of the American Philosophical Society 59; Philadelphia: The American Philosophical Society, 1969). In the appendix to her work, she counts more than two thousand references in which she sees physiognomy at work. The term "physiognomic consciousness" is also hers, and it is a term that will be employed extensively here.

In order to articulate those specific cultural assumptions, methodologically we must triangulate the biblical text with at least two bodies of works—the physiognomic handbooks which prescribe the proper practice of physiognomy, and the body of Greek literature which puts those conventions into practice. Four physiognomic handbooks have survived, and they will be described in more detail in the first chapter. Likewise, the secondary literature concerning physiognomy will be treated as we come to each handbook. The oldest, dating to the third century B.C.E., is *Physiognomonica* by Ps.-Aristotle. We know that Ps-Aristotle's is not the first handbook on physiognomy, for in the opening section of his work he refers to "previous physiognomists" (805a) and proceeds to critique their work, but his is the oldest that has survived. The second physiognomic handbook comes from Polemo of Laodicea, a highly influential rhetorician in the era of Hadrian. His handbook, *De Physiognomonica*, was composed in the second century C.E.[2] Surviving only in Arabic translation, Polemo's text is important as it gives witness to the use of physiognomics as a means of encomium and invective. Two other treatises on physiognomy have survived, and they are largely dependant upon Polemo. One work dates to the fourth-century and is written by an otherwise unknown Adamantius the sophist. The other work is a fourth-century anonymous Latin handbook (generally cited as "Anonymous Latin").

These four handbooks offer the prescribed practice of physiognomy. They must be read in conversation with physiognomy in practice in ancient literature, beginning even as early as Homer. As Evans demonstrates, the presence of physiognomic descriptions spans all major genres of literature, and these various sources give us an idea of how physiognomics was used in literature as a means of characterization. The handbooks and the literature live in a symbiotic relationship, each helping to inform the other. By reading these two bodies of work in conversation with each other, one can then read the biblical text with a good idea of how an ancient audience would have heard the text. Thus, our method is to try to approximate what an ancient auditor familiar with these physiognomic conventions would have understood about a character based on these descriptions, and we get at such an

[2] Polemo, "Polemonis: De Physiognomonia Liber Arabice et Latine," in *Scriptores Physiognomonici Graeci et Latini* (2 vols; ed. Richardus Foerster; Leipzig: Teubner, 1893), 93–294. Foerster's volume has collected all of the physiognomic handbooks, with the exception of Ps-Aristotle.

interpretation by using both the physiognomic handbooks as well as the larger body of literature that puts these conventions in practice.

Outline of Chapters

This project will move forward is five chapters. We begin by introducing the topic of physiognomy, and then we proceed through the various bodies of literature that are relevant to our study. We begin with Greco-Roman sources, move through Jewish sources, then turn to early Christian material before finally turning to Luke-Acts.

Chapter two introduces the study of physiognomics. That chapter will give definition to the term and will examine the pervasiveness of physiognomics throughout the Greco-Roman literature. We will begin by examining the history of the pseudo-science, including the major handbooks that serve as our primary sources. Then we will explore the methods employed by the physiognomists, using plenty of examples in order to make those methods clear. Finally, the chapter will conclude with a number of examples from various genres of literature. The purpose of this chapter is to introduce the reader to physiognomics and the techniques employed, and to give the reader enough concrete examples to make the practice clear.

Chapter three turns attention to the eyes as a specific subset of physiognomics. All of the physiognomists agree that there is no more important physical marker than the eyes, as the eyes are the proverbial "window to the soul." After examining the study of the eyes in general, we will turn attention specifically to blindness. A number of examples of blind characters in Greco-Roman literature will be examined. When studying all of these examples as a whole, a literary *topos* begins to emerge. That is, there are certain stereotypical things that are associated with a character that is blind. This *topos* will be established as a kind of guiding heuristic as we read further examples of blindness in the biblical literature.

Chapter four begins our study of the biblical literature. This chapter will explore examples found in the Old Testament and in the literature of Second Temple Judaism. As we explore the Jewish literature, we find that the same kinds of physiognomic assumptions that were found in the Greco-Roman literature are also found in the Jewish literature. The chapter has two major sections. First, the chapter explores examples of physiognomics in general. It considers examples such as Saul who is "head and shoulders above the rest," Ehud who is left-handed, hairy and ruddy Esau, and long-haired Absalom. These examples help establish that physiognomic descriptions are indeed employed in the Jewish literature. The second part of the chapter will examine examples of blindness specifically, including examples of those who have dim eyesight in old age. Examples in this section will include the likes of Eli, Samson, and Tobit, to name only a few. It will also treat blindness as a metaphor as is frequently found in the prophets. We find that those who are blind in the Jewish literature function consistently with what one would expect from the *topos* outlined in chapter two.

In the fifth chapter we turn attention to the early Christian literature. That chapter explores examples found in the rest of the New Testament apart from Luke-Acts, as well as in other early Christian literature that makes up the early Christian milieu. The goal is to demonstrate that the early Christians, like their larger Greco-Roman and Jewish cultures, are often thinking in physiognomic terms. That chapter will also move forward in two sections. The first section will deal with physical descriptions, including the *Acts of Paul* and Ambrose's *On the Duties of the Clergy*, and this section will speak to the striking absence of physical descriptions in most of the canonical Christian literature. While physiognomic descriptions are largely absent from the canon, blindness is certainly widespread. The second section of the chapter will treat examples of blindness, including Bartimaeus, the man born blind in John 9, and the use of Isaiah's descriptions of blindness in the NT.

Finally, the last chapter turns attention specifically to Luke-Acts. A recent work by Mikeal Parsons[3] has already treated physiognomics in Luke-Acts, and his work is the only full-length work in the field of New Testament scholarship devoted to the topic of physiognomy. His work will be summarized as we look at examples of physical descriptions in Luke-Acts, including Zacchaeus who is short, the bent woman of Luke 13, the lame man of Acts 3, and the Ethiopian eunuch. The majority of this chapter, however, is devoted specifically to blindness in Luke-Acts. Luke begins the public ministry of Jesus by having Jesus read from the scroll of Isaiah a passage declaring that the gospel will bring, among other things, sight to the blind. Acts ends with a similar statement, with Paul quoting from Isaiah regarding the blindness of the

[3] Mikeal C. Parsons, *Body and Character in Luke and Acts: The Subversion of Physiognomy in Early Christianity* (Grand Rapids: Baker Academic Press, 2006).

people to the message of God. In between, we find characters such as Saul of Tarsus who finds himself blinded when he encounters Christ. Throughout Luke-Acts, the *topos* of the blind character is maintained and offers valuable insights as to how to interpret these passages. It will bc argued in that chapter that blindness becomes something of an interpretive guide or heuristic that, as it were, opens the eyes of the reader to the message and mission of Christ.

Let us begin our study, and we begin it with an introduction to the methods and practice of physiognomics.

CHAPTER TWO

AN INTRODUCTION TO PHYSIOGNOMY

Chapters two and three of this work are devoted to an examination of the practice of physiognomy in the Greco-Roman world. This chapter will examine the practice of physiognomy in general in order to establish the pervasiveness of these conventions in the ancient world. This first major section will define the history and practice of physiognomy, establish the physiognomic handbooks as source material, and explore the methods used by the physiognomists. The final part of this chapter will demonstrate physiognomy at work in Greek literature with a number of helpful examples. The next chapter will then turn attention to the eyes specifically as a significant subset of physiognomic markers. We begin with an introduction to physiognomics in general.

Physiognomy Defined: Its History and Practice

Physiognomy is an ancient pseudo-science in which one seeks to know something of a person's moral character by observing certain physical features.[1] A tractate falsely attributed to Aristotle (hereafter referred to as Pseudo-Aristotle) defines the thesis of the physiognomist succinctly: "Dispositions follow bodily characteristics and are not in themselves unaffected by bodily impulses."[2] Later, the author states that "the physiognomist draws his data from movements, shapes and colours, and

---

[1] The most important recent work on this topic is Elizabeth C. Evans, *Physiognomics in the Ancient World* (Transactions of the American Philosophical Society 59; Philadelphia: The American Philosophical Society, 1969). But see also A. MacC. Armstrong, "The Methods of the Greek Physiognomists," *Greece and Rome* 5 (1958): 52–56; Tamsyn S. Barton, *Power and Knowledge: Astrology, Physiognomics, and Medicine Under the Roman Empire* (Ann Arbor: University of Michigan Press, 1994); Robert Garland, *The Eye of the Beholder: Deformity and Disability in the Graeco-Roman World* (Ithaca, N.Y.: Cornell University Press, 1995); and Maud W. Gleason, *Making Men: Sophists and Self-Presentation in Ancient Rome* (Princeton, Princeton University Press, 1995).

[2] Aristotle, *Physiognomics*, 805a. All subsequent references to Ps-Aristotle are taken from Aristotle, *Physiognomics* in *Minor Works* (trans. W. S. Hett; LCL 307; Cambridge: Harvard University Press, 1963), 84–137. Translations follow this Loeb volume unless otherwise noted, and all subsequent references will appear as parenthetical references within the text.

from habits as appearing in the face, from the growth of hair, from the smoothness of the skin, from voice, from the condition of the flesh, from parts of the body, and from the general character of the body" (806a). The following anecdote is illustrative here, in which Pythagoras is said to have "physiognomized" potential students:

> It is said that the order and method followed by Pythagoras, and afterwards by his school and his successors, in admitting and training their pupils were as follows: At the very outset he "physiognomized" the young men who presented themselves for instruction. That word means to inquire into the character and dispositions of men by an inference drawn from their facial appearance and expression, and from the form and bearing of their whole body. Then, when he had thus examined a man and found him suitable, he at once gave orders that he should be admitted to the school and should keep silence for a fixed period of time; this was not the same for all, but differed according to his estimate of the man's capacity for learning quickly. But the one who kept silent listened to what was said by others; he was, however, religiously forbidden to ask questions, if he has not fully understood, or to remark upon what he had heard. Now, no one kept silence for less than two years, and during the entire period of silent listening the were called ἀκουστικοί or "auditors." But when they had learned what is of all things the most difficult, to keep quiet and listen, and had finally begun to be adepts in that silence which is called ἐχυμυθία or "continence in words," they were then allowed to speak, to ask questions, and to write down what they had heard, and to express their own opinions (*Noct. att.*, 1.9.1–6).

It is not entirely certain where and with whom the study of physiognomy actually began. The famed doctor Hippocrates is generally credited with founding physiognomy as a discipline—Galen claims as much, and there is no reason to doubt the claim. The study of the body seems a natural fit with the practice of medicine and medical diagnosis. The oldest extant use of the term φυσιογνωμονέω is found in Hippocrates' *Epidemics*, 2.5.1 where it appears as the subtitle of the section, and in that treatise the Hippocratic school appears to use physiognomy as a science.[3] Later in this tractate, he uses some brief physiognomic elements such as a large head, black eyes, or stammering speech in his diagnosis (2.6.1). So it is probably best to speak of the study of physiognomics as a kind of science as originating with Hippocrates.

---

[3] Hippocrates uses this term numerous times in this tractate, and the term can be found in various other works in the Hippocratic corpus. On Hippocrates as the originator of physiognomy, see Barton, *Power and Knowledge*, 101, and Armstrong, "The Methods of the Greek Physiognomists," 52.

We, however, must also be aware that physiognomy was practiced, even if not studied systematically, in the Greek-speaking world at least as far back as the time of Homer,[4] who long predates any of the extant physiognomic handbooks by several generations. Thus we must realize that the notion that one's physical features say something about one's inner character is an idea that far predates any attempt to outline systematically those characteristics and what they might mean. In the words of Evans, "it is these theorists who set down in orderly fashion what had long been informally observed and practiced."[5] It is crucial, particularly in studying early writers like Homer, that we understand first that the practice of physiognomy was pervasive in the ancient world, and second, that the practice long predates any attempt to systematically record the "rules" for its practice. It is that informal practice that helps to make up the pervasive physiognomic consciousness in the ancient world.

Hippocrates is by no means alone, however, and some ancient sources date the systematic practice of physiognomy prior to him. According to Hippolytus and others, Pythagoras is to be credited with the invention of physiognomy (although Hippolytus calls it "physiogony").[6] Still others in the ancient world credited the beginning of the practice of physiognomy to a certain Zopyrus. According to Cicero, a Syrian magician named Zopyrus was the first to practice physiognomy in Athens by physiognomizing Socrates. He writes, "Zopyrus, who claimed to discern every man's nature from his appearance, accused Socrates in company of a number of vices which he enumerated, and when he was ridiculed by the rest who said they failed to recognize such vices in Socrates, Socrates himself came to his rescue by saying that he was naturally inclined to the vices named, but had cast them out of him by the help of reason" (*Tusc.* 4.37.80).[7] It is interesting to note in this case that the practice of reading a person's character from his physical features is being done by a non-Greek, which probably indicates that such practice was by no means limited to the Greek-speaking world.

[4] Examples in Homer are numerous, and several will be discussed in the section of examples below.

[5] Evans, *Physiognomics in the Ancient World*, 6.

[6] Hippolytus, *Haer.* 1.2 (*ANF* 5). Pythagoras is also credited in Porphyry *Vit. Pyth.* 13 and in Iamblichus *Vit. Pyth.* 17.

[7] Cf. Diogenes Laertus 2.45, citing Aristotle; also Cicero, *Fat.* 5.10, relaying the same story.

Also, it is important to note that the practice in this case was closely tied to magic and divination.

Nevertheless, the most common—and most likely correct—way to speak of the beginning of physiognomy as a systematic practice of diagnosing character is to talk about it in connection with the medical practices of Hippocrates. It is not until roughly the third century B.C.E. with Ps-Aristotle that one finds a full physiognomic treatise being written down and preserved. While that work claims to know of previous writings, none of those have survived antiquity. While the handbook traditions offer us a concrete entry point and a stable handle on physiognomic practice, especially since they date very closely to the time of the New Testament, they do not monopolize the history and traditions of this pseudo-science. Therefore, a history of the physiognomic tradition would be remiss to omit a discussion of the ways the tradition develops in the second and third centuries C.E. and beyond. Before turning to the handbooks themselves, let us first look at the medical practice of Galen.[8]

Chronologically, Galen the physician follows shortly after Polemo, the famed rhetorician and author of a major physiognomic handbook in the second century C.E. (discussed below). Polemo spent a great deal of his career teaching in Smyrna, and it is here that Galen gains fame as well, shortly after the death of Polemo. Galen actually began his study of medicine at the temple of Asclepius in Pergamum before moving to the highly respected school at Smyrna. Galen's approach to physiognomy is based primarily on the humors—the ancient scientific belief that the human body was a composite of four fluids or humors: blood, phlegm, black bile, and yellow bile. The particular combination of these humors determines everything from one's appearance to one's demeanor and temperament to one's health and/or illnesses. Whereas the physiognomic handbooks of both Ps-Aristotle and Polemo identify physical features that correspond to various character traits, neither examines why this correspondence is so. Galen, though not a physiognomist proper, attempts to explain *why* people behave the way they do, and the answer for him lies in the humors and their combinations

[8] On Galen as a practitioner of physiognomics, see especially Evans, "Galen the Physician as Physiognomist," *TAPA* 76 (1945): 287–98.

within a person.[9] Galen, then, seeks to make use of the conventions of physiognomics as a means of diagnosing and treating patients.

With the physiognomists using physical features to "diagnose" character, and Galen using physical features to diagnose illnesses, it is no surprise that eventually the conventions of physiognomy would be used to "diagnose" the future. Eventually, in this way the study of physiognomics bleeds into astrology. Thus Barton, who links physiognomy and astrology closely together, defines physiognomy as "the discipline that seeks to detect from individuals' exterior features their character, disposition, *or destiny*."[10] This bleeding of physiognomy and astrology was, as best as we can tell, later in the tradition. Though certainly hints can be found of physical characteristics being used for the purpose of divination, it seems that such a practice is rare before about the third century C.E., and since it is that era that Barton primarily has in view, the inclusion of "destiny" in the definition of physiognomy is to be expected. Barton considers physiognomy to be a poorly developed pretender that had far less influence compared to astrology, and by the third century C.E. and beyond, she may well be correct. However, that conclusion appears to be incorrect prior to the third century, an observation which is important to the study of the biblical writings. Significantly to the Christian tradition, this bleeding together of physiognomy and astrology may also account for why physiognomics falls out of favor with so many (though certainly not all) of the Church Fathers.

To complete the overview of the history of the practice of physiognomy, it is important to note that physiognomy has made something of a resurgence in the past few centuries. This resurgence is often associated with the Swiss physiognomist Lavater, Freudian psychology, and especially phrenology—the study of the face and head. A simple search on any internet search engine or library catalogue for "physiognomy" will produce numerous hits, nearly all of them dating from the Enlightenment era to the present. It is important for the reader to note that the modern study and practice of physiognomy is considerably different from the Greco-Roman practice of physiognomy, and

[9] For an brief but excellent description of Galen's theory of the humors, see Evans, "Galen the Physician as Physiognomist," 290–92. For Galen's own explanation, see Galen, *Mixt* 1.8ff.

[10] Tamsyn S. Barton, *Power and Knowledge*, 95, emphasis mine.

while the modern study is interesting in many ways, it is almost entirely irrelevant to this project.[11]

Lastly, a word is in order concerning the practice of physiognomy and the arts. While this paper is primarily concerned with physiognomy as a literary practice, it may well be the case that much of what occurs in art, especially in sculptures of people, may likewise reflect physiognomic conventions. Such an investigation lies beyond the scope of this project, but suffice it to say that the practice probably took place. Take for example the claim of Lyssipus, who claims that while others sculpted people "as they are", he is able to portray them "as they appeared."[12] Apparently, he thinks he is able to depict the character of the subject in addition to and along with the physical appearance. His claim was supported by Plutarch, who states that "Lyssipus was the only one who revealed in bronze the *ethos* of Alexander and who at the same time expressed his virtue along with his form."[13]

Introducing the Sources—Handbooks on Physiognomy

With the practice of physiognomy pervasive in the ancient world, there eventually sprang up a series of handbooks and treatises on the subject. There are four significant handbooks that are extant, each of which will be discussed in this section. In reading the handbooks, it is again helpful to note that these handbooks are both descriptive and prescriptive in nature. They are descriptive in that the handbooks by no means invent the practice of physiognomics; rather they give testimony to what had been informally practiced for generations. They are prescriptive in that once the handbooks are written, they in many ways help to set the terms of discussion, or at least to set some boundaries and establish some controls. Thus one should not expect the handbooks to be entirely

---

[11] To give just one example from the modern world, see Evan Marshall, *The Eyes Have It: Revealing Their Power, Messages, and Secrets* (New York: Citadel Press, 2003). This book is a modern study of what can be known of a person—both their character as well as their transient, momentary emotions—by simply observing the eyes.

[12] Pliny the Elder, *Nat.* 34.65.

[13] Plutarch, *Alex. fort.* 2.2, also found in *Mor.* 335B. Along those lines, some studies do exist that deal with the presence of physiognomic conventions in art. See for example Piers D. G. Britton, "The Signs of Faces: Leonardo on Physiognomic Science and the 'Four Universal States of Man,'" *The Society for Renaissance Studies* 16 (2002): 143–62. This article also gives a trail of good bibliography for those interested in pursuing physiognomy in art.

consistent with one another—two handbooks can certainly read the same physical marker in two very different ways—although there is a remarkable consistency between them nonetheless. Let us describe the four major handbooks in chronological order—Ps-Aristotle, Polemo, Adamantius, and the *Anonymous Latin* tractate.

Ps-Aristotle

The oldest *extant* physiognomic handbook is one that is falsely attributed to Aristotle, called *Physiognomonica*. The treatise dates to the third century B.C.E. and was most likely composed by a student or students of Aristotle, or at least by someone strongly influenced by Aristotle's writings. It is widely believed that this handbook as we have it now is a compilation of two originally independent works, but antiquity has combined and preserved them as complementary in a single volume. We know that Ps-Aristotle's handbook is not the first handbook on physiognomy, for in the opening section of his work he refers to "previous physiognomists" (805a) and proceeds to critique their work. Whoever these "previous physiognomists" may have been, their writings have not survived, and thus our only window into their writings is through Ps-Aristotle. As it stands now, Ps-Aristotle is the oldest and, therefore, most significant handbook on physiognomy that survives. This handbook also remains as the only written index of physiognomic conventions for some three hundred years.

The first half of the handbook—or, more properly, the first of the two treatises that have been combined to form the handbook—states its method at the outset: "Dispositions follow bodily characteristics and are not in themselves unaffected by bodily impulses" (805a). The author then explores and critiques the work of his predecessors. He writes,

> Now previous physiognomists have attempted three methods in the science of physiognomics. For some base the science on the genera of animals, assuming for each genus one form and disposition for the animal. On these grounds they have supposed one type of body for the animal and then have concluded that the man who has a body similar to this will have a similar soul. A second class have pursued the same method, but have not based their conclusions entirely on animals, but upon the genus man itself, dividing him into races, in so far as they differ in appearance and in character... A third class have made a collection of superficial characteristics, and the dispositions which follow each. (805a)

After a thorough critique of these methods, he lists the markers from which the physiognomist takes his information: "movements, shapes and colours, and from habits as appearing in the face, from the growth of the hair, from the smoothness of the skin, from voice, from the condition of the flesh, from parts of the body, and from the general character of the body" (806a). He briefly explores these signs individually, though he ultimately concludes that, "generally speaking, it is foolish to put one's faith in any one of the signs; but when on finds several of the signs in agreement in one individual, one would probably have more justification for believing the inference is true" (806b–807a). This first half of the handbook then concludes by exploring various character types or types of men. That is, the author lists the physical markers of the brave man, the coward, the insensitive man, the shameless man, the orderly man, the effeminate, the hot-tempered, the gentle man, and so forth (807a–808b).

The second half of the handbook—or, more properly, the second treatise—begins again, stating a new but similar thesis: "It seems to me that soul and body react on each other; when the character of the soul changes, it changes also the form of the body, and conversely, when the form of the body changes, it changes the character of the soul" (808b). The remainder of the work is particularly attuned to the zoological method of reading the body. That is, the characteristics of animals are used in diagnosing the character of humans, since the essential character of an animal is consistent as a species, lacking individual personality like humans. The author first divides the animal kingdom into two basic animals—the lion, who most perfectly typifies the ideal male, and the panther, who most perfectly typifies the human female (809b–810a). After these two examples, the rest of the handbook is an exploration of bodily signs, moving in general from the feet upwards through the rest of the body. As each body part is described, possible character traits are explored. The corresponding character traits are generally based upon comparisons to the animal kingdom. Let us consider just one example to illustrate the point, that of the nose:

> Those that have thick extremities to the nostrils are lazy; witness cattle. Those that have a thickening at the end of the nose are insensitive; witness the boar. Those that have a sharp nose-tip are prone to anger; witness the dog. Those that have a circular nose-tip, but a flat one, are magnanimous; witness the lions. Those that have a thin nose-tip are bird-like; but when it is somewhat hooked and rises straight from the forehead they are shameless; witness ravens; but those who have an aquiline nose with a marked separation from the forehead are magnanimous; witness the eagle. Those who have a hollow nose, rounded where it rises from the forehead, and the rounded part standing above, are salacious; witness

> cocks. But the snub-nosed are also salacious; witness deer. Those whose nostrils are spread are passionate; this refers to the affection which occurs in the temper. (811a–b)

After the index of signs, the handbook concludes with the suggestion that the reader consider all bodily signs but prefer those signs "that appear in the most favourable position" (814b), namely, those signs which appear around the eyes and the face. The further one gets from the face, the less clear the sign. Noteworthy to this project is the preferential treatment given to the eyes.

Polemo of Laodicea

The second physiognomic handbook comes from Polemo of Laodicea (sometimes known as "Polemon" instead). Polemo was a highly influential rhetorician in the era of Hadrian. His handbook, *De Physiognomonica*, was composed in the second century C.E.[14] While physiognomy was certainly in practice during the centuries between the handbooks of Ps-Aristotle and Polemo, Polemo is largely responsible for triggering a large-scale renewal of interest and fascination with the pseudo-science. We know a great deal about the person Polemo,[15] yet the text of the handbook itself is problematic. Polemo was born sometime around 88 C.E. in Laodicea and died around 145 C.E. As a youth, Polemo was trained in rhetoric in Smyrna, one of the leading educational cities of the Greco-Roman world at that time. As an adult he spent time in various other places practicing his skills in a number of capacities, but he eventually returned to Smyrna as a teacher. He became a leader of the New Sophistic School at Smyrna, where he eventually even had a

---

[14] Polemo, "Polemonis: De Physiognomonia Liber Arabice et Latine," in *Scriptores Physiognomonici Graeci et Latini* (2 vols; ed. Richardus Foerster; Leipzig: Teubner, 1893), 93–294. Foerster's volume has collected all of the physiognomic handbooks and is the only modern source where any of the handbooks can be found, with the exception of Ps-Aristotle. Unfortunately, only Ps-Aristotle has been translated into English, as Foerster's volume is Greek or Arabic on one side of the page and a Latin translation on the opposite side. References to the text of Polemo in this book will be to the appropriate page number in Foerster's edition. A forthcoming translation of Polemo is forthcoming by a group of scholars headed by Simon Swain. The title of the work is *"Seeing the Face, Seeing the Soul": Physiognomy from Classical Antiquity to Medieval Islam*. Unfortunately, the volume will not be available in a published form in time for this project.

[15] For an excellent summary of the life and work of Polemo, see the first chapter of William W. Reader, *The Severed Hand and the Upright Corpse: The Declamations of Marcus Antonius Polemo* (SBLTT 42; Atlanta: Scholars Press, 1996). See also Gleason, *Making Men*, esp. chapter 2, "Portrait of Polemo."

statue built in his honor. As a high-profile teacher in Smyrna, Polemo managed to catch the eye of the emperor and was even befriended by Hadrian. Hadrian appointed Polemo as something of the court rhetorician, a position he would eventually use to become one of the giants of all of Roman learning, but especially in the practice of rhetoric. He was still very active and influential during the reign of Marcus Aurelius as well. Without a doubt, Polemo was one of the greatest minds of his era, well-learned in numerous fields. Physiognomy was one of his many fields of interest, finding in physiognomics a potent tool for rhetorical practice—particularly when it came to discrediting his opponents.

Though Polemo wrote a widely influential handbook on physiognomy, the preservation of that text through antiquity is mercilessly problematic. Though Polemo originally wrote in Greek, only a few phrases of the Greek text have survived, likely having been destroyed in the numerous wars and invasions that were soon to befall the Roman Empire. Fortunately, Polemo was much adored by the Arabic-speaking peoples, and they translated and preserved most of his works into Arabic. What survives from Polemo's physiognomic handbook now is only an Arabic version of the text that is mostly complete. The surviving manuscript, which represents centuries of recopying, dates to the 1300s. No English translation yet exists of Polemo's handbook; what we instead have is the Latin translation in Foerster. Foerster, near the end of the 19th century, collected the four extant handbooks. In each case, a Latin translation of the text is provided on one page to accompany the Greek or Arabic (in Polemo's case). Thus the student of Polemo is riddled with a translation problem, as the student must track backwards through multiple retranslations. Unless otherwise noted, all translations in this book are my own English translations of Foerster's Latin, which is a translation of the surviving Arabic manuscript, which is based however distantly on the Greek original. Nevertheless, one can have more confidence in the translation than it appears, since the other two physiognomic handbooks do name Polemo's handbook as a source, thus giving the student a corollary source to aid in the reading of Polemo.

While a systematic outline of the handbook is not really necessary since this particular handbook is intended to be used in a more episodic way, it is nonetheless helpful to know something of the larger structure of Polemo's work. In the case of Polemo, the larger structure is particularly noteworthy since he is such a skillful rhetorician, and thus one would expect him to have a careful and deliberate arrangement. Polemo spends the first one-third of his handbook talking primarily about the signs to be found in the eyes. The clear conclusion for the reader to draw, then, is that given the length of the discussion of the eyes along with the fronting of this discussion in the handbook, the eyes are the most telling marker for the physiognomist to study. The eyes are, of course, the famed "window to the soul," and all of the physiognomists believe that while other character markers on the body may be disguised, the eyes are the most difficult to mask. Thus Polemo devotes nearly one-third of his book to the exegesis of the eyes.

Next, he presents a zoological section in which he lists character traits of more than ninety animals, though he does not specifically link those traits to corresponding human traits in the way that Ps.-Aristotle had done. In the final section of his handbook, he undertakes a section that indexes the signs of each part of the body, more or less moving from the bottom of the body to the top, from the feet to the head and facial features. Included in this discussion is an ethnographic section that explores the character of various people based on their place of origin—northern races, southern races, oriental and western races, and finally what he calls "the pure race of the Greeks". His work concludes with a treatment of body movement, gait, gestures, and voice. Once again, it is notable that the eyes are not discussed in this section on the exploration of the body but are instead fronted and given a lengthy discussion at the beginning of the handbook.

Polemo, a connoisseur of all sorts of knowledge and learning, found in physiognomics a powerful rhetorical tool, and thus by reviving the formal study of physiognomics, Polemo made an important shift. For Polemo, physiognomy was not simply a science to be studied objectively. Rather, physiognomy could be used rhetorically as a weapon—a means of belittling and discrediting his opponents in the public square, or in Barton's words, "a new resource for attacking rivals and enemies."[16] The widespread use of physiognomics in ancient rhetoric gives witness to the effectiveness with which Polemo and others were able to use physiognomy to empower friends and demonize opponents.[17]

[16] Tamsyn S. Barton, *Power and Knowledge: Astrology, Physiognomics, and Medicine Under the Roman Empire* (Ann Arbor: University of Michigan Press, 1994), 113.

[17] As an example of Polemo using physiognomy as a rhetorical weapon, take the example of the man from Qwyryn, who has been identified by some scholars as Lusius Quietus, one of the men who plotted against Hadrian. See Josef Mesk, "Die Biespiele in Polemons Physiognomonik," *Wiener Studien* 50 (1932): 51–67 and A. von Premerstein, "Das Attentat Der Konsulare auf Hadrian im Jahre 118 n. Chr.," *Klio Beiheft* 8 (1908): 46–71.

Generally, Polemo is using physiognomics as invective. The only clear encomium is of the eyes of Hadrian. He writes, "Certainly Hadrian's eyes were... gleaming, filled with beautiful light, sharp in their gaze. No man was ever seen with a more luminous eye."[18] Hadrian, of course, was the emperor to whom Polemo owed so much. Therefore it is not surprising that Polemo would paint the emperor in a favorable light. Throughout the rest of Polemo's handbook, however, his examples are rather clearly invectives. The scholarly consensus is that while Polemo rarely names the person whom he is attacking, he often tends to have a single person in mind when he vilifies an entire group (such as the Celts or the Corinthians, for example).[19] Barton argues that for Polemo, then, "physiognomical theory served as a classificatory grid to contain his political and intellectual opponents," and that "with physiognomics he constructed their [his opponents'] bodies so as to destroy their character. And destroying the ἦθος of a rival deprived him of the moral claim to persuade."[20] In summary, Polemo revives the formal study of physiognomy, writing a handbook that serves in large part to strike his and his emperor's opponents. To use the conventions of physiognomy as a weapon, then, becomes a common use for the physical description.

Adamantius and Anonymous Latin

Two other treatises on physiognomy have survived, though both are essentially a popularization of Polemo's second-century handbook. Consequently, their greatest value is generally for the purposes of comparison with Polemo's text as well as for filling in the missing pieces of Polemo's text. Both works follow the methodology of Ps-Aristotle and essentially paraphrase Polemo.[21]

---

[18] Foerster 1.148, lines 6–9.

[19] On Polemo as invective, see Barton, *Power and Knowledge*, 96–97. See also Evans, *Physiognomics in the Ancient World*, 12, who writes, "It is quite clear, likewise, that he could make use of physiognomy for the purpose of encomium and invective" and gives several examples. Evans also gives several examples in an earlier article, "The Study of Physiognomy in the Second Century A.D.," *TAPA* 72 (1941): 97–98.

[20] Barton, *Power and Knowledge*, 96–97.

[21] Both because of the later date of these two treatises and because of their heavy dependence upon the two earlier works, this book will generally only refer to the works of Ps-Aristotle and Polemo. Both Adamantius and the *Anonymous Latin* tract can be found in Foerster. Jacques André has also produced a critical edition of *Anonymous Latin*. See Jacques André, *Anonyme Latin: Traité de Physiognomonie* (Paris: Les Belles Lettres, 1981).

One work dates to the fourth-century C.E. and is written by an otherwise unknown Adamantius the sophist. One tradition holds that he is a Jewish physician that fled from Alexandria during a Jewish-Christian conflict, later converted to Christianity, then returned to Alexandria,[22] but there are several people in antiquity bearing this name and we lack sufficient evidence to safely identify our author as any one of them. Adamantius's handbook falls into two parts. The first part deals exclusively with the eyes, and here he is closely following Polemo. The second part deals with other parts of the body on an individual basis, again following closely the work of Polemo. Adamantius also abbreviates Polemo's work, leaving out a number of Polemo's discussions and examples. This editing may indicate that Adamantius has in mind a more popular audience, whereas Polemo, as a great rhetorician working for the emperor, has in mind a more elite audience. This, too, is conjectural.

The other work is a fourth-century anonymous Latin handbook that bears the title *Physiognomonia Latina* but which is generally known as *Anonymous Latin*. This handbook is often falsely attributed to Apuleius,[23] but it almost certainly belongs to the fourth century C.E. instead, since it is clearly so heavily dependant on the other handbooks. The author states at the outset that his work is a compilation of the "medicine of Loxus, the philosophy of Aristotle, and the declamations of Polemo."[24] This work of Loxus is otherwise unknown, but it is presumably a handbook of some sort that has not survived. Loxus himself, aside from this citation in *Anonymous Latin*, is also known from a passing reference in Origen: "And if there be any truth in the doctrine of the physiognomists, whether Zopyrus, or Loxus, or Polemon, or any other who wrote on such a subject, and who profess to know in some wonderful way that all bodies are adapted to the habits of the souls..." (*Cels* 1.33). Here we find Origen listing Loxus among two known practitioners of physiognomy.[25]

---

[22] Evans, *Physiognomics in the Ancient World*, 15 relays this story, though she is not favorably disposed toward this attribution. She also lists a number of people bearing the name Adamantius in the ancient world, along with the corresponding references. Since we cannot do better than speculation on the identity of this author, I have not reproduced those references here.

[23] See Evans, *Physiognomics in the Ancient World*, 16 for this argument.

[24] Foerster 2.3.

[25] For more on Loxus, see Geneva Misener, "Loxus, Physician and Physiognomist," *CP* 18 (1923): 1–22. Misener seeks to reconstruct the treatise of Loxus by pulling apart

The author of *Anonymous Latin* is particularly fond of the signs surrounding the complexion, showing a definitive mixing of the medical theory of the humors with the practice of physiognomics. The emphasis on the complexion is probably the only significant material that occurs in detail in this handbook that is not found in this kind of detail in any of the other three extant handbooks. Such an emphasis on the humors is probably also to be attributed to the handbook of Loxus.[26]

Thus the two handbooks—that of Adamantius along with *Anonymous Latin*—are evidence that the fourth century brought another renewal of interest in the study of physiognomy similar to the renewal in the time of Polemo. It is not surprising, then, that in this same era many of the Church Fathers (Ambrose, Gregory of Nazianzus, and Eusebius, for example) take interest in the subject as well. However, shortly after its revival in the fourth century, physiognomy fell out of grace with many of the Church Fathers, almost certainly because it became too closely tied to astrology and other practices of divination.

The Methods of the Physiognomists

The physiognomists use a variety of methods in order to ascertain the character of individuals. Ps-Aristotle, in fact, engages in a lengthy discussion of the methods used by the previous physiognomists. He offers substantial criticism of those methods, although he makes use of those methods himself, even if it is a chastened use. Before exploring examples of physiognomy at work in the literature of the Greco-Roman world, it is first necessary to understand the methods used and the assumptions made by the physiognomists, particularly as those methods are found in the handbooks. There are three major methods for doing physiognomy: the zoological method, the racial method, and the method of physical features or the expression method. Each will be treated in turn.

The Zoological Method

The first method for doing physiognomy is the zoological method. In this method, a person's character can be derived from the person's

---

Anonymous Latin. That is to say that if *Anonymous Latin* is a compilation of Aristotle, Polemo, and Loxus, and we have the works of two of the three, then it stands to reason that whatever else is left belongs to the handbook of Loxus.

[26] Loxus is a doctor, so claims Barton, *Power and Knowledge*, 98.

similarity to this or that kind of animal. That is, one considers the general appearance of a person along with the general appearance of various animals. Whenever commonalities exist (such as a similar kind of nose or hair), it can be concluded that the person and the animal share similar character traits. While humans often seek to mask their true inner character, it is supposed, animals make no such pretentious attempts. Instead, the character of a type of animal is considered fixed for the entire species and open for all to see. Thus one finds that, for example, all deer and hares are timid, all lions are courageous, and all foxes are effeminate and wily. One method for the physiognomist, then, is to identify physical characteristics of the deer (or lion, or fox, etc.), and then to look for the same characteristics in the human. Any human sharing the physical features of the deer, lion, and so forth can be said to share the corresponding nature of that animal. In the words of Ps-Aristotle, "some base the science on the genera of animals, assuming for each genus one form and disposition for the animal. On these grounds they have supposed one type of body for the animal and then have concluded that the man who has a body similar to this will have a similar soul" (805a).

Ps-Aristotle criticizes this method on two grounds: first, nobody looks exactly like any animal but only shares certain features similar to that of the animals; second, animals have very few features that are peculiar to their species and not found in others.[27] In other words, Ps-Aristotle considers the zoological method, when it takes a single physical marker of a single species, to be imprecise and overly subjective. For example, it may be true that the lion is broad-shouldered, but so are a number of other animals, and thus it is not possible to say which animal a broad-shouldered man is most similar too. Ps-Aristotle instead argues that we must eliminate from consideration those characteristics that are common to multiple and diversely-behaving animals. Instead, the physiognomists should "make our selection from a very large number of animals, and from those that have no common characteristic in their disposition other than that whose character we are considering" (806a). With these criticisms in place, however, Ps-Aristotle proceeds to make frequent use of this method of physiognomy, drawing numerous comparisons between the human and the animal kingdoms. Polemo makes even more extensive use of this method, citing some ninety animals in

---

[27] For Ps-Aristotle's criticisms, see *Physiognomics*, 805b–806a.

his handbook and offering a couple of sentences to the explanation of the character of each. He notes the same animals as Ps-Aristotle—such as the lion, panther, wolf, bull, dog, and so forth—but he adds plenty of others, including some exotic animals like the elephant, rhinoceros, crocodile, hippopotamus, dolphin, whale, frog, fly, and even as specific as the magpie.[28]

One of the primary uses of the zoological method is in understanding the general character of male and female. As mentioned above, Ps-Aristotle uses the lion and the panther as his two fully-developed examples of the male and female type. He writes, "the lion of all animals seems to have the most perfect share of the male type" (809b). He describes the lion as follows:

> Its mouth is very large, its face is square, not too bony, the upper jaw not overhanging but equally balanced with the lower jaw... bright deep-set eyes, neither very round nor very narrow, of moderate size, a large eyebrow, a square forehead,... hair sloping outwards like bristles, a head of moderate size, a long neck, with corresponding thickness... his shoulders are strong and his chest powerful. His frame is broad with sufficiently large ribs and back; the animal has lean haunches and thighs; his legs are strong and muscular, his walk is vigorous, and his whole body is well-jointed and muscular, neither very hard nor very moist. He moves slowly with a long stride, and swings his shoulders as he moves. These then are his bodily characteristics; in character he is generous and liberal, magnanimous and with a will to win; he is gentle, just, and affectionate towards his associates. (809b)

If the lion is the ideal representation of the male, the panther is the animal counterpart to the human female. Ps-Aristotle writes,

> Among the animals reputed to be brave the panther is more female in appearance except in the legs; with these he achieves and accomplishes mighty deeds. For he has a small face, a large mouth, small eyes rather pale, hollow and somewhat flat; the forehead is rather long, rather rounded than flat about the ears; the neck is over long and light, the chest is narrow, the back long, the haunches and thighs are fleshy, while the parts about the flanks and belly are flatter; the skin is mottled and the body as a whole is badly jointed and imperfectly proportioned. This is the shape of the body, and its character is petty, thieving and, generally speaking, deceitful.

[28] For a complete list of Polemo's animals, see his second chapter, Foerster 170–198.

The lion and the panther are the only animals that Ps-Aristotle explains in detail, and he categorizes them as being of the male and female type. Polemo chooses several other examples from other genera of animals, labeling representatives of the male and female type in each group. For example, when he discusses birds, he labels the eagle and the partridge as male and female in type, respectively. Among the reptiles, he labels the dragon as the masculine form and the viper as the feminine.[29] While Ps-Aristotle offers a robust paragraph on the lion and the panther, Polemo's tendency is to offer merely a sentence or two for each of his ninety animals.

Noting the weight given to the zoological method, it is easy to imagine that a person who heard a comparison between a human and an animal in the ancient world would readily assume some sort of relationship in their character. For now, let us point to only a couple of examples from the plays of Aristophanes. In *Clouds* (line 444) Strepsiades refers to the one who can argue in court as the "cleverest, slyest fox," invoking a zoological comparison between a rhetorician in court and the fox—whose characteristics include especially slyness and deceit,[30] and what Ps-Aristotle will generally refer to as "bad character" (812a). Likewise, in his *Lysistrata* (lines 1014–15), the Men's Leader states, "There is no beast more stubborn than a woman, and neither fire nor leopard is more ruthless." Here we find the stereotype of the leopard as ruthless, but we also find the stubborn animals in general (of which the mule is chief among the physiognomists) applied to the character of women in general. The Latin word for leopard is *panthera*, and Polemo describes this animal with phrases like "malicious," loving to do what is necessary to conquer the opponent, and "not gentle nor tamable" (Foerster 172). Clearly Polemo and Aristophanes have the same characterization in mind. Aristophanes, then, employs the commonly-held stereotypes of animals in order to characterize the participants in the play. Later, as we move to the biblical material, these same sorts of comparisons are frequent. One might think especially of Herod, whom Jesus calls "that fox," the Pharisees, whom John the Baptist calls a "brood of vipers," Esau when he is called "a wild ass of a man," or perhaps even the imagery of the lamb and the dragon in Revelation.

---

[29] For Polemo's discussion of these particular birds and reptiles, along with the lion and panther, see Foerster 194–98.

[30] See, for example, Polemo's description of the fox in Foerster 174.

One might also consider the example of Plato involving the transmigration of the soul. One particular example finds a myth in which souls get to choose their next life, but it must be different from the first. The soul chooses the next life largely based on zoological reasons. The soul of Orpheus chooses the life of a swan because he detests females and does not want to be born from a woman; Ajax chooses the life of a lion; Agamemnon chooses an eagle; and Thersites chooses the life of an ape, a move very much in keeping with his character as we will see below in the examples from Homer.[31]

The Racial or Ethnographical Method

The second method of physiognomy is the racial method, also commonly known as the ethnographical method. This method is little more than the zoological method applied to people groups. Ps-Aristotle explains it this way: "A second class have pursued the same method, but have not based their conclusions entirely on animals, but upon the genus man itself, dividing him into races, in so far as they differ in appearance and in character (for instance Egyptians, Thracians, and Scythians), and have made a corresponding selection of characteristics" (805a).[32] In this method, then, one considers the collective behaviors of a race and ties those behaviors to their distinctive physical features. In other words, the physiognomist looks for characteristics in a person that resemble those of a race whose character as a whole is already known. Common examples in the ancient world would include such widespread stereotypes as "all Cretans are liars" or "all Corinthians are sexually promiscuous."

Generally, it would seem that this method had two purposes, though nowhere is it directly explained as such: first, to elevate the "pure race" of the Greeks (and later, the Romans), and second, to vilify the barbarians that surrounded them. Polemo in particular devoted a good bit of attention to the latter goal, spending several chapters on the racial characteristics of the people groups surrounding—and in some cases, threatening—Rome.[33] The Greek or Roman body, of which one

---

[31] All of these examples can be found in Plato, *Resp.* 10.620a–d.

[32] It is noteworthy that the racial method is the method used least by Ps-Aristotle. He critiques it in the same way as the zoological method, since they are quite similar, but whereas he makes widespread use of the zoological method throughout the handbook, one finds only passing references to the racial method at work.

[33] Specifically, Polemo devotes five full chapters to the races: the nations of the

would see multiple examples every day, was considered common and normative. The further one ventured from the center of the mainland, however, the more one could expect to find increasingly different, and in some cases frightening, variations in racial appearances. Unfamiliarity, then, bred fear of that which was different. Consequently, it is no surprise that in mythology the place where one encounters monsters, giants, and various deformed creatures is inevitably in a land far, far away. The further one gets from the "center" of the world, the stranger the races and creatures become.

With Polemo we find a good example of how the Greek is considered the ideal type. He assumes that Greece is the center of the world, and then divides the world north, south, east, and west from there. He describes people based on their geographical relationship to Greece (e.g., a section on western peoples, etc.), but the assumption is that the Greeks are at the center. The further one gets from Greece, of course, the most exaggerated the deviation from the norm.

The linking of this method with science may go back to Hippocrates. His "De Aere, Aquis, Locis," which is later quoted often by Galen, talks about the influences of geography and climate on temperament and the body. It is this work which some scholars believe may give the foundation for doing the racial method of physiognomy.[34] In fact, it is this ethnical study that peaks the interest of Galen in physiognomics as well. According to the theory of humors, certain peoples have characteristic mixtures of fluids based on geography and thus have common characteristics as a people. If one's particular location on the globe helps determine one's particular mix of humors and thus one's temperament and characteristics, then the racial method of physiognomy has a legitimate place among the ancient sciences.[35]

Examples of this method abound throughout the ancient world, not only in Greek culture, but in any culture that perceives itself as different from other peoples. To return to the comedies of Aristophanes, we can

world, the northern races, the southern races, the eastern (oriental) and western races, and the pure race of the Greeks. See chapters XXXI–XXXV in Foerster, 236–240. In addition to these specific chapters, Polemo also makes numerous appeals to racial physiognomy throughout the rest of his handbook.

[34] See especially Misener, "Loxus, Physician and Physiognomist," 1 and Evans, *Physiognomics in the Ancient World*, 19.

[35] See Evans, "Galen the Physician as Physiognomist," 296–97 for a good discussion of the supposed racial characteristics and their basis is Galen's exposition of the humors.

find numerous examples in any single play of racial types. This method is particularly clear in *Lysistrata* in the ways Aristophanes portrays some specific Greek sub-groups, particularly the Beotians, Corinthians, and Spartans throughout the play. Each is inferior to the Athenians, in varying degrees, and is portrayed as such on stage. The Spartans, not surprisingly, are disparaged the most, speaking in such a dialect that is only barely recognizable as Greek. In the case of Aristophanes, these types are employed for satirical purposes—unfortunately, the Greek world often used these stereotypes in more sinister ways.

One important note on the racial method is in order regarding the description of the African people by the Greeks. It is important to note that the African people are often referred to in general terms by Greek authors using the term "*Aithiopes*" (Ethiopians), which literally means "burnt-faced people." In the Greek system for classifying people groups, Ethiopians were considered the darkest people on the spectrum.[36] They are also the most woolly-haired people according to Herodotus,[37] who also tries to draw a distinction between two kinds of Ethiopians, making it clear that he has two rather different African peoples in mind.[38] "Ethiopian", then, is probably less of a geographical designation than a racial one—that is, "Ethiopian" is often used to refer to any number of African people, not just to the specific people of Ethiopia, the southern neighbor of Egypt.[39]

This type of physiognomy is for the modern reader a particularly sensitive issue, since, of course, it amounts to little more than racial stereotyping. It goes without saying that this current study and its author neither condone the methodology nor advocate its use in the modern world. Certainly our own American history reminds us that we do not wish to return to such a time. Yet despite our modern sensibilities, it is important to realize that the Greeks did not share our racial concerns, and if we are to read the Greek literature correctly, we must be aware that racial typing was a common practice. Here it is important to remind the reader that our goal in reading ancient literature, and

[36] "The Ethiopians stain the world and depict a race of men steeped in darkness"; Manilius, *Astronomica* 4.723–24.

[37] Herodotus, *Hist.* 7.70.

[38] Cf. Ps-Aristotle 812b.

[39] See especially Frank M. Snowden, Jr., "The Physical Characteristics of Egyptians and Their Southern Neighbors: The Classical Evidence," in *Africa in Egypt* (ed. Theodore Celenko; Indianapolis: Indianapolis Museum of Art: 1996) 106–08.

specifically the texts most sacred to the Christian faith, is to understand the text as its ancient auditors would have understood it, even when that means we must momentarily drop our modern sense of the evils of racial divisions.

The Expression Method, or the Method of Physical Features

The third method used is that of studying individual physical features. The physiognomist, for example, looks for certain facial features (such as a scowl or a furrowed brow) and then identifies the corresponding emotion behind the expression. Then, whenever the expression is encountered again on a different person, the corresponding character trait can be assumed. Ps-Aristotle criticizes this method on two grounds. He writes,

> Those who proceed in their science entirely by characteristics are wrong; first of all, because some men, who are in no sense alike, have the same facial expressions (for instance the brave and the shameless man have the same expressions), but are widely different in disposition; secondly, because at certain times they do not have the same expressions but different ones; for the low-spirited sometimes spend a happy day and assume the facial expression of the high-spirited, and conversely the high-spirited may be suffering grief, so that the expression in the face changes. (805b)

Since some men who are very different can mislead the physiognomists by virtue of sharing common expressions, and since expressions change to reflect one's transient mood, then expressions are not a reliable gauge of one's permanent moral character. A more trustworthy method is to study those physical features that do not change as the expressions change. Thus, one is better served to look at static features—height, hairiness, shape of the nose or eyes, and things of that sort. Interestingly, Ps-Aristotle believed that if one of these static physical features changed, so did the character, and vice versa:

> It seems to me that the soul and body react on each other; when the character of the soul changes, it changes also the form of the body, and conversely, when the form of the body changes, it changes the character of the soul.... This becomes most clear from the following considerations. Madness appears to be an affection of the soul, and yet physicians by purging the body with drugs, and in addition to these by prescribing certain modes of life can free the soul from madness. By treatment of the body the form of the body is released, and the soul is freed from its madness. Since, then, they are both released simultaneously, their reactions evidently synchronize. (808b)

All of the physiognomists rely most heavily on this third method, though they all try to place the most emphasis on permanent physical characteristics rather than transient facial features.

Ps-Aristotle prefers a combination of the all three methods—zoological, racial, and expression—although throughout his work it is clear that the third method is the dominant one for him. Nevertheless, he partakes in a steady diet of the zoological method, less of the racial method. Polemo follows a similar path, showing a clear preference for the latter of the three methods, although in his case he makes much more extensive use of the zoological and racial method than did his predecessor.

After listing the best regions of the body from which to draw information, Ps-Aristotle offers this caution: "Generally speaking, it is foolish to put one's faith in any one of the signs; but when one finds several of the signs in agreement in one individual, one would probably have more justification for believing the inference true" (806b). This is how the methodology of the physiognomists proceeds as outlined by Ps-Aristotle and as followed by Polemo and the others. It is important to remember that Ps-Aristotle is both criticizing his predecessors as well as systematizing what had to that point been a rather amorphous physiognomic consciousness. With the handbooks of the physiognomists in mind, let us now turn to an exploration of a good number of examples of physiognomics in practice in ancient literature.

Physiognomy in Practice: Examples in Ancient Literature

To this point, we have explored the definition and history of the study of physiognomics, the handbooks used as a guide in that study, as well as the methods by which the physiognomists operated. What remains now is an exploration of examples drawn from various genres of ancient literature. The examples are important to note for many reasons. First, we need to take note of the number of examples and the vastness of the way these examples spread across all kinds of Greco-Roman literature. Such notice is important because it demonstrates just how common the use of physiognomics was, and if the use of physiognomics is so common, one would expect the reader of the biblical text to hear the text with ears attuned to physical features as a guide to character. Second, it is important to note the examples because the commonness of these examples demonstrates that physiognomics was by no means limited to a few handbooks and a few practitioners; rather, most authors who use physical features in their writings do so as a means of characterization without any formal explanation of what they are doing. Again, this demonstrates that both author and audience are well-steeped in a culture that has a highly sensitive physiognomic consciousness. Third, in order to exegete the meaning of physical characteristics in the biblical text, it is best to consider the meaning of a particular characteristic in *both* the handbooks as well as in the broader scope of literature in general. Fourth—and, admittedly, methodologically quite distant from the aforementioned reasons—the examples are fascinating. Perhaps it is because the use of physiognomics is so foreign to modern culture, these examples from antiquity are interesting, and thus I have included the text of the examples in most cases.

The list of examples that follows is by no means exhaustive.[40] Instead, it is hoped that the list is sufficient to demonstrate the widespread use of physiognomics in the ancient literature. The list that follows includes several categories. The list begins with a series of examples that demonstrate clearly that physiognomics was in use, with particular attention given to examples where the author overtly states as much. Second, we will examine the most important of Greek texts, the epics of Homer. Homer provides a number of examples of physiognomics in practice several centuries before a handbook exists, and since Homer is foundational for Greek education and literature to follow and is also widely known in the first century, Homer is a good baseline for understanding the use of physiognomics in the Greco-Roman world. Third, we will explore examples from the place where one might most obviously expect to find physiognomics in practice—ancient biographies. Let us, then, begin with some introductory examples.

Introductory Examples

Perhaps because the use of physical markers for the purpose of illustrating moral character is so common in the ancient world, relatively few authors state overtly that this is what they are doing. Nevertheless, such self-aware statements can be found in several places. The purpose of

[40] For a much more nearly exhaustive list, see the appendices in Evans, *Physiognomics in the Ancient World*, where she catalogues several thousand examples that range across every maj[illegible]e of literature. There is no reason to reproduce all of those examples here, and [illegible]discussion would span multiple volumes.

these examples is to demonstrate *that* authors made use of physiognomics, and that they were self-consciously aware of what they were doing. Take for example Origen in *Cels.* 1.33, where he names physiognomists and is himself interested in the topic.[41] So also Dio Chrysostom *Or.* 33,[42] which talks about physiognomy being common in his era. He lists several features that "reveal their true character and disposition", and he includes voice, glance, posture, hair, gait, eyes, the tilt of the neck, and gestures like an upturned palm (*Or.* 33.52). He even continues by telling a story of a physiognomist who studied a particular person who had eluded the diagnosis of the physiognomist. Eventually, though, the person sneezed, at which point the physiognomist immediately diagnosed the man as a catamite (*Or.* 33.53–54). Dio Chrysostom is keenly aware of the practice of physiognomy in his world.

Though mentioned above, it bears noting again here that it is said that Pythagoras "physiognomized" his students (the full quote can be found at the beginning of this chapter). So also Socrates is said to have done a similar thing in choosing his students.[43] Also mentioned above, Zopyrus comes physiognomizing Socrates, and Socrates does not reject the practice, but instead agrees that the diagnosis is correct but claims to have mastered his bad character traits through the power of reason (*Tusc.* 4.37.80).

At other times, it is the masses that are said to have examined their leaders. Take the example of Julian being sized up by the people: "Gazing long and earnestly on his eyes, at once terrible and full of charm, and on his face attractive in its usual animation, they divined what manner of man he would be, as if they had perused those ancient books, the reading of which discloses from bodily signs the inward qualities of the soul."[44] Here we find awareness of physiognomic handbooks, and the practice of physiognomics is projected upon the crowds. Clearly the author is aware of the practice of physiognomy and invokes its conventions as Julian is described.

In many other examples, the physical attribute is listed and the corresponding character trait(s) is subsequently explained in the text. Take for example Archilochus's description of his ideal general: "I love not a tall general nor a straddling, nor one proud of his hair nor one part-

---

[41] Cf. Philostratus *Vit Soph* 2.618 where he talks about physiognomists as well.
[42] *Oration 33* = *First Tarsic Discourse*. Both titles are acceptable.
[43] Cf. Apuleius, *De Dogmate Platonis* I.I.
[44] Ammianus Marcellinus 15.8.16 (LCL).

shaven; for me a man should be short and bowlegged to behold, set firm on his feet, full of heart."[45] In this example, we find the explicit linking of the physical marker—being bowlegged—and the corresponding character trait—being set firm on one's feet. One can easily see the logical progression here in the mind of the physiognomist—since bowed legs provide a sturdy base physically, the physiognomist can infer that the moral character of the one who possesses bowed legs is sturdy and firm as well.

Consider also the example of Seneca, who opens *De Ira* with descriptions of the calm man and the angry man using physical markers:

> But you have only to behold the aspect of those possessed by anger to know that they are insane. For as the marks of a madman are unmistakable—a bold and threatening mein, a gloomy brow, a fierce expression, a hurried step, restless hands, an altered colour, a quick and more violent breathing—so likewise are the marks of the angry man; his eyes blaze and sparkle, his whole face is crimson with the blood that surges from the lowest depths of the heart, his lips quiver, his teeth are clenched, his hair bristles and stands on end, his breathing is forced and harsh, his joints crack from writhing, his groans and bellows, bursts out into speech with scarcely intelligible words, strikes his hands together continually, and stamps the ground with his feet; his whole body is excited and "performs great angry threats"; it is an ugly and horrible picture of distorted and swollen frenzy—you cannot tell whether this vice is more execrable or more hideous. Other vices may be concealed and cherished in secret; anger shows itself openly and appears in the countenance, and the greater it is, the more visibly it boils forth (*De Ira* 1.1.3–4).

Seneca then references several animals as evidence of angry appearances, mirroring the methods of the physiognomists.

One can also point to examples in which physiognomic conventions are mocked or subverted. Consider the following passage from Lucian:

> Did you see them behaving also as I said just now I saw your master behaving, Hermotimus? I mean lending money and making bitter demands to be repaid, quarrelsome and most contentious in conversations and generally behaving themselves as they usually do? Or is this of little importance to you, so long as the dress is decent, the beard long, and the hair close-cropped? Then this is to be our strict rule and law for the future in these matters according to Hermotimus: we are to distinguish the best men by their appearance, their walk, and their hair, and whosoever has not

---

[45] Archilochus, *Elegy and Iambus II* 58 (LCL).

> these signs and does not look sulky and meditative is to be spurned and rejected! You're surely making fun of me, Hermotimus; you're trying to see if I can spot the catch (*Hermotimus* 18–19).

Likewise consider the following example drawn from Plato's *Republic* which mocks the use of physiognomic conventions, specifically the nose and skin color:

> That's not something one expected *you* to say, Glaucon! A devotee of sexual passion shouldn't forget that it's *all* young men of the right age who somehow bite and sting the passionate lover of boys, and seem to merit his attention and embraces. Isn't this how people like you behave towards your favorites? One boy, because he's snub-nosed, you'll praise with the description of "charming"; another's hooked nose you call "royal"; while the one in between you regard as just right. You call the dark-skinned "manly" to look at, and the fair-skinned "children of the gods."[46]

Although this passage is *attacking* the use of physiognomy, it is still useful to note insofar as it acknowledges that such conventions were certainly in practice. Examples such as these from Lucian and Plato are important to note for a couple of reasons. First, they demonstrate that not everyone in the ancient world was, as it were, a physiognomist. Not everyone believed the pseudo-science to be reliable or, as is demonstrated by the quote from Plato, consistently applied. The apparent charge from some would be that physiognomics could be manipulated in order to arrive at a desired conclusion.[47] Second, these examples demonstrate that even those who do not advocate the practice of physiognomics are nonetheless aware of these conventions. If even the opponents of physiognomics are aware that such conventions were present in the culture, then this is all the more reason for the reader of the biblical text to be aware of the possible implications of physical descriptions for the meaning of the text.

In Homeric Epics

The Homeric epics[48] are not only the oldest and greatest of the Greek writings, they also became the foundation for culture and education. In

---

[46] Plato, *Republic* 5.474D (trans. S. Halliwell; Warminster, Eng: Aris & Phillips; 1998), 111–12.

[47] Such a charge, of course, is not without base. Polemo was especially adept at using physiognomics manipulatively as a rhetorical tool in order to win his case and convince his audience.

[48] It is recognized that the Homeric epics may or may not have been composed

this study of physiognomy, the status enjoyed by the Homeric epics is important because it can be concluded that if the epics were already using physical descriptions to imply moral character, then such practice would quickly permeate the cultural and educational landscape. Such physical descriptions are very much present in these foundational epics.

Evans argues that the physiognomy used by Homer is not the iconistic or photographic kind where one describes stable physical feature; rather, Homer uses the transient features that express emotion.[49] While I dispute Evans's claim that Homer lacks iconistic descriptions and will give examples momentarily, that Homer uses transient features as a means of characterization is important as well. Here we shall cite a single example. In book 13 of *Iliad*, we find a conversation between Meriones and Idomeneus concerning bravery and prowess in combat. The conversation then turns to the visible differences between the coward and the brave. Idomeneus says,

> For if now all the best of us were being chosen beside the ships for an ambush, in which the valor of men is best discerned—there the coward comes to light and the man of valor; for the color of the coward changes ever to another hue, nor is the spirit in his breast checked so that he sits still, but he shifts from knee to knee and rests on either foot, and his heart beats loudly in his breast as he imagines death, and his teeth chatter; but the color of the brave man changes not, nor does he fear excessively when once he takes his place in the ambush of warriors, but he prays to mix immediately in woeful war. (*Il.* 13.275–86)

Here we find that the inner character of the soldier is revealed by his physical features—one whose complexion changes, whose body shifts, whose teeth chatter, or whose pulse races is not fit to be counted among the brave. It is the stoic, unswerving warrior who is brave, and this can be seen even in the body.

Yet the Homeric epics are not limited to this kind of physical description only. Indeed, the epics make extensive use of physical characteristics, often in the epithets attributed to characters. There are several dozen characters in Homer who receive an epithet of physical description,

---

by the same author, but we will frequently refer to the epics simply as "Homer" with that knowledge in mind. The case does not stand on the assumption that one man composed both epics; rather, the case is being made that physiognomics is being used at the earliest stages of Greek literature.

[49] Evans, "Literary Portraiture in Ancient Epic: A Study of the Descriptions of Physical Appearance in Classical Epic," *HSCP* 58 (1948): 290–91.

whether it be the eyes, the height, or the hair, and here we name only a few prominent and interesting examples. The reader frequently encounters the "long-haired Achaeans", a description that says something of the manliness and battle-ready character of the Greeks. Achilles is most often described as "swift-footed", as is the war god Ares. Aeneas bears the epithet "swift of foot" as well (*Il.* 13.482), and only a few lines later, Aeneas is called "peer of Ares" (*Il.* 13.500). Clearly, to be swift of foot is a physical marker that identifies a fearsome warrior, and the epithet appears next to several other such warriors throughout the epics. Aias (Ajax), the so-called "bulwark of the Achaeans", is simply "huge", as is Ares (*Il.* 7.211, 208 respectively). So fearsome in battle is Aias that he is actually said to come into battle smiling (*Il.* 211). "Hebe of the beautiful ankles" is the wife of Heracles (*Od.* 11.603). Helen is given little more in the way of a physical description than "fair-haired" (*Il.* 3.329, 7.355, 8.82, 9.349, and 11.369), fair-cheeked (*Od.* 15.123), and "of white arms" (*Od.* 22.227), but all of these are descriptions that are common to the goddesses.[50] One also finds handicapped deities, most notably Hephaestus "the god of the two lame legs" (*Il.* 1.608, 14.239) and Polyphemus, the famed Cyclops who is blinded by Odysseus. More will be said below about both, as they present good examples of the ways that disabilities can be used as physiognomic markers as well.

In book 10 one meets Dolon, who is described as "to be sure ill-favored to look on but swift of foot" (*Il.* 10.316). He volunteers for a spy mission ordered by Hector. A spy who can run is, to be sure, advantageous, but the fact that he is ugly would also imply a morally defective character, just the sort of person to send on a spy mission. When he is captured by Odysseus and Diomedes, his defective character is again highlighted when he becomes a terrified and cowardly prisoner, volunteering information in exchange for his own safety.

Furthermore, one also finds short descriptions used as insults. Consider for example Achilles when he insults Agamemnon in the opening pages of the *Iliad* by calling him "dogface" (*Il.* 1.159). The dog was commonly known as a scavenger, and it is Agamemnon's theft of Achilles's prize—the maiden Briseis—that triggers the wrath of Achilles. A few paragraphs later, Achilles accuses Agamemnon of cowardice using zoological descriptions: "You heavy with wine, with the face of a

[50] Note, for example, that Hera is "white-armed" on 23 occasions in Homer, Aphrodite is "fair" and "fair-crowned", and Athene is fair-haired on three occasions (*Il.* 6.92, 273, and 303).

dog but the heart of a deer, never have you dared to arm yourself for battle with your troops,... It is surely far better to take back the gifts of whoever through the wide camp of the Achaeans speaks in opposition to you, People-devouring king" (*Il.* 225–231). Here, Achilles makes his point using zoological insults, and the point is made quite clearly.

Homer, however, is by no means limited to short, one-word descriptions. Perhaps the most famous of the descriptions found in Homer is that of Thersites in book 2 of the *Iliad*:

> Now the others sat down and were restrained in their places, only there still kept chattering on Thersites of measureless speech, whose mind was full of a great store of disorderly words, with which to revile the kings, recklessly and in no due order, but whatever he thought would raise a laugh among the Argives. Ugly was he beyond all men who came to Ilios: he was bandy-legged and lame in one foot, and his shoulders were rounded, hunched together over his chest, and above them his head was pointed, and a scant stubble grew on it. Hateful was he to Achilles above all, and to Odysseus, for those two he was in the habit of reviling; but now with shrill cries he uttered abuse against noble Agamemnon. (*Il.* 211–222)

After a lengthy speech reviling Agamemnon—which, incidentally, is not incorrect about the king—he is rebuked by Odysseus and struck on the back with a staff (2.265). Thersites is clearly described as a rude and worthless individual—ugly, lame,[51] hunched over,[52] and balding with a pointy head.[53] Given the physical description, the reader might even come to expect some sort of ill fate to find Thersites, for certainly he will make no contribution to the battlefield dominated by brave, mighty, and heroic warriors, among whom he would certainly never be numbered.

Eurybates, a highly honored travel companion of Odysseus, is also given a physical description in book 19 of the *Odyssey*. Odysseus is talking to Penelope, but his identity to this point is not yet revealed, and she thinks him to be a friend of her husband. After describing the clothing of Odysseus, he adds the following: "Furthermore, a herald attended him, a little older than he, and I will tell you of him, too, what manner of man he was. He was round-shouldered, dark of skin,

---

[51] See Ps-Aristotle 810b where the strong leg indicates strong character, while the weak leg indicates one who is morally lax, and weak ankles indicates a weak character.

[52] See Ps-Aristotle 807b where the "shameless man" is described as hunched over.

[53] See Ps-Aristotle 812a where the pointy head indicates one who is impudent or boldly rude.

and curly-haired, and his name was Eurybates; and Odysseus honored him above his other comrades, because he was like-minded with himself" (*Od.* 19.244–48). Notice here that Odysseus says he will speak of "what manner of man he was," and then does so by giving a physical description. That is to say that the physical description is supposed to tell Penelope the kind of person Eurybates was. Eurybates is also said to be of a like mind to Odysseus, a characteristic that is also supposed to be apparent from the description as well.

Also noteworthy is the striking resemblance between Telemachus and his father in the early books of the *Odyssey*. The resemblance—though not spelled out in specific physical characteristics—is mentioned on at least three occasions. Although Telemachus has never himself seen his father, he knows of his father's heroic deeds and character and knows that he too is expected to behave in like manner. In many ways, he learns of his own character as those who knew his father describe the character of his father and remark about the *physical* similarities between the father and son. Such conversations take place at least three times: with Athene (*Od.* 1.206ff), with Menelaus (*Od.* 4.149ff), and with wise Nestor (*Od.* 3.124ff). Though a detailed physical description is largely lacking, these three individuals expect Telemachus to be of the same quality of character as his father, based largely on physical appearance alone.

From these examples it is clear that in the earliest of Greek literature the physical description of a person implied something about the moral character. Such a practice was not something invented by later Greek traditions, but is something that is rooted in the very beginnings of Greek antiquity. We now turn physiognomy as seen in the ancient biographies.

Biography

Of all of the places where one would expect to find physiognomics in practice, one would expect to find it in biography. That is to say that if the primary purpose of the ancient biography—the *bios*—as a genre is to demonstrate the essential character of the protagonist, then physiognomic descriptions become a powerful tool. A physical description, then, carries far more weight than a simple verbal description. More than that, the description is a means of painting the portrait of the *inner character* of the one being described. Let us consider several examples taken from Suetonius, Plutarch, and others.

Plutarch is an example of an author who states overtly that he is using physical descriptions in order to portray character. In *Cim.* 2.3 he writes that "a portrait which reveals character and disposition is far more beautiful than one which merely copies form and feature." That is to say that the purpose of each biography is not to offer a photograph of someone's likeness; rather, the purpose is to capture the person's character and disposition. In many cases, as we shall see below, Plutarch employs physical descriptions as a way of portraying someone's character.

No biographer, however, makes more extensive use of the conventions of physiognomy than does Suetonius. Evans draws the direct connection between Suetonius and the use of physiognomics in the physical descriptions, claiming that Suetonius knew the writings of Ps-Aristotle. Evans seeks to demonstrate the literary connection, and then continues further by noting that Suetonius and Polemo were known to be contemporaries and knew each other.[54] Evans also offers a helpful explanation of what Suetonius is doing with the physical description of each of the emperors. She concludes that Suetonius, "though not tampering in any way with the traditional portrait of an emperor, has nevertheless at times laid particular interest on certain aspects of the physique, which from the point of view of the physiognomists indicate either the virtuous or vicious nature of an emperor's character."[55] Suetonius, then, serves as the clearest example of a biographer who employs the conventions of physiognomy in order to capture the essence of his subjects. Let us now turn to some of the specific examples of physical descriptions of the emperors as found in Suetonius.

Let us begin with the description given to Augustus, a description that lauds Augustus and that is praiseworthy on nearly every point:

> He was unusually handsome and exceedingly graceful at all periods of his life, though he cared nothing for personal adornment. His expression, whether in conversation or when he was silent, was so calm and mild. He had clear, bright eyes, in which he liked to have it thought that there was a kind of divine power, and it greatly pleased him, whenever he looked

---

[54] Evans, "The Study of Physiognomy in the Second Century A.D.," *TAPA* 72 (1941): 96–108.

[55] Evans, "Roman Descriptions of Personal Appearance in History and Biography," *HSCP* 46 (1935): 63. In the later part of this article, Evans gives a nice running comparison of certain emperors with the characteristics of the animals in Ps-Aristotle, such as for example the ways that Caligula parallels the panther and goat.

> keenly at anyone, if he let his face fall as if before the radiance of the sun; but in his old age he could not see very well with his left eye. His teeth were wide apart, small, and ill-kept; his hair was slightly curly and inclined to golden; his eyebrows met. His ears were of moderate size, and his nose projected a little at the top and then bent slightly forward. His complexion was between dark and fair. He was short of stature (although Julius Marathus, his freedman and keeper of his records, says that he was five feet and nine inches in height), but this was concealed by the fine proportion and symmetry of his figure, and was noticeable only by comparison with some taller person standing beside him. (*Aug.* 79)

Noteworthy in this description is the way in which Augustus is portrayed as nearly divine. "Unusually handsome", "exceedingly graceful", and especially the bright and clear eyes that conveyed something of "a kind of divine power" all are descriptors that laud Augustus almost to the status of deity. Descriptors such as the eyebrows that meet are frequent descriptions of royalty as well as semi-divine figures such as Heracles. Descriptions that demonstrate Augustus's moderation are also significant, such as his ears and his complexion. To the physiognomists, extremes are rarely desirable; rather, moderation in all categories is usually the most perfect form. The only descriptor that would appear to be negative is his short stature, a characteristic that is typically a negative one, often implying traits such as greed, deceit, or even sexual depravity. Why include that negative descriptor? Presumably, as Evans has noted, most of the Roman world is already familiar with the actual appearance of the emperors, and Suetonius is not exactly free to alter their true-to-life appearance. If it is widely known that Augustus was short, then what Suetonius does here is significant in that he offers justification for why this particular attribute is misleading in this case. Suetonius does not attempt to hide the stature of Augustus, as the noted record keeper had done; instead, Suetonius notes that the stature was well-concealed by a well-proportioned and symmetrical body. What has happened is that Suetonius has taken a physical attribute that is known to be negative and has redeemed it in the case of Augustus by explaining the stature as a part of the moderation of the emperor's body style.

If the description of Augustus is overwhelmingly positive, the description of Caligula is demonic. Augustus, perhaps the greatest of the emperors, has a much better physical description that Caligula, who is perhaps the worst of the emperors. Known to be insane, neurotic, and a terror to the people, Caligula's description lives up to his character:

> He was very tall, and extremely pale, with a huge body, but very thick neck and legs. His eyes and temples were hollow, his forehead broad and grim, his hair thin and entirely gone on the top of his head, though his body was hairy. While his face was naturally forbidding and ugly, he purposely made it even more savage, practicing all kinds of terrible and fearsome expressions before a mirror. (*Cal.* 50)

In this description, one is struck by all of the extremes, especially in comparison to the moderate attributes of Augustus. Notice the extremes of Caligula's appearance—he is "very tall" and "extremely pale." To be tall is good—it implies courage, leadership, and strength. But at a certain point (never specifically defined by the physiognomists), to be *too* tall becomes negative. Ps-Aristotle even claims that to be too tall is bad because the blood reaches the extremities slowly, thus making one dim-witted.[56] Likewise, a moderate complexion like that of Augustus is to be desired, but Caligula is extremely pale. His hair is also extreme. Rather than having flowing, curly locks, Caligula has thin hair, he is bald on top, and is disproportionately hairy on the rest of his body. Clearly to be "handsome" is a good thing, but Caligula is so ugly that his face is described as "naturally forbidding" by Suetonius. The most striking aspect of the description is of course that Caligula practices in the mirror in order to make his face even more detestable and terrifying. In a world in which it is widely believed, in Ps-Aristotle's words, that "soul and body react on each other; when the character of the soul changes, it changes also the form of the body, and conversely, when the form of the body changes, it changes the character of the soul" (808b), it appears that Caligula not only has a terrifying and detestable soul, but that he is actively seeking to make it worse! It is also worth noting in the description of Caligula that most of these descriptors can also be found in Ps-Aristotle's descriptions of the panther and the goat. Since the panther is the prototypical animal for the female type, one notices that Caligula is also being described as effeminate, something that no man desires to be in the ancient world.[57]

---

[56] "Excessively small men are quick; for as the blood travels over a small area, impulses arrive very quickly at the seat of the intelligence [i.e., the heart]. But the excessively large are slow; for as the blood travels over a large area the impulses arrive slowly at the seat of the intelligence" (813b:8–12).

[57] Certainly Suetonius is not the only author in the ancient world to demonize Caligula. Compare Suetonius's description of Caligula to that found in Seneca: "He himself was a most fruitful source of ridicule, such was the ugliness of his pale face bespeaking his madness, such the wildness of his eyes lurking beneath the brow of an

Another notable description in Suetonius is that of the semi-crippled emperor Claudius. To be physically disabled, as we shall explore later in this chapter, is automatically assumed to be a negative reflection on one's character. The disabled were often disowned and disenfranchised as well, and descriptions of the disabled who overcome their handicap are indeed rare. With that in mind, Claudius fares reasonably well in the eyes of the physiognomists and in the eyes of his biographer:

> Claudius had a certain majesty and dignity of presence, which showed to best advantage when he happened to be standing or seated and especially when he was in repose. This was because, though tall, well-built, with a handsome face, a fine head of white hair and a firm neck, he stumbled as he walked owing to the weakness of his knees; and because, both in his lighter moments and at serious business, he had several disagreeable traits. Those included an uncontrolled laugh, a horrible habit, under the stress of anger, of slobbering at the mouth and running at the nose, a stammer, and a persistent nervous tic of the head, which was apparent at all times but especially when he exerted himself to the slightest extent. (*Claud.* 30)[58]

Certainly this description is a mixed bag for Claudius. A runny nose, a shaky voice, and a nervous tic would all likely indicate a certain lack of self-confidence and likely even cowardice. Such a characterization would also match his lameness, described here as "weakness of his knees". Yet Claudius is not ultimately doomed by these characteristics, since he was also tall, well-proportioned, handsome, and had good hair. These characteristics, as Suetonius notes, give the lame emperor an air of "majesty and dignity of presence." Certainly Claudius's description is rather ambiguous with a strong mix of both positive and negative characteristics. Not surprisingly, his reign as emperor is remembered by Suetonius in a commensurate way.

Claudius, ever aware of his own physical shortcomings, was also aware of the implications of physical appearance for the reign of his successor. Suetonius relays the story of Titus and Britannicus being examined by a physiognomist, the end result of which was the declaration that Titus was fit to be emperor:

---

old hag, such the hideousness of his bald head with its sprinkling of beggarly hairs. And he had, besides a neck overgrown with bristles, spindle shanks, and enormous feet" (*Constant.* 18.1, LCL). Clearly Seneca is using the ugly, negative physical description to point to the detestable character of Caligula as well.

[58] The translation is that of Robert Graves, *The Twelve Caesars* (New York: Penguin, 1957).

> [Titus] grew up at Court with Britannicus, sharing his teachers and following the same curriculum. The story goes that when one day Claudius's freedman Narcissus called in a physiognomist to examine Britannicus's features and prophesy his future, he was told most emphatically that Britannicus would never succeed his father, whereas Titus (who happened to be present) would achieve that distinction. (*Tit.* 2, translation Graves)

The choice, of course, was made based on the assumed character traits that accompanied the physical features of the two boys.

Claudius was not the only emperor that was said to be self-aware of the power of physiognomy. Augustus frequently sought to offer explanation for the less than ideal appearance of Tiberius. Suetonius writes,

> He was large and strong of frame, and of a stature above the average; broad of shoulders and chest; well proportioned and symmetrical from head to foot. His left hand was the more nimble and stronger, and its joints were so powerful that he could bore through a fresh sound apple with his finger, and break the head of a boy, or even a young man, with a flip. He was of fair complexion. His hair was rather long at the back, so much so as even to cover the nape of his neck; which was apparently a family trait. His face was handsome, but would break out on a sudden with many pimples. His eyes were unusually large and, strange to say, had the power of seeing even at night and in the dark, but only for a short time when first opened after sleep; presently they grew dim-sighted again. He strode along with his neck stiff and bent forward, usually with a stern countenance and for the most part in silence, never or very rarely conversing with his companions, and then speaking with great deliberation and with a kind of supple movement of his fingers. All these mannerisms of his, which were disagreeable and signs of arrogance, were remarked by Augustus, who often tried to excuse them to the senate and people, by declaring that they were natural failings and not intentional. (*Tib.* 68)

Here again we find a mixed physical description, neither wholly good nor wholly bad. What is striking in this case is that Suetonius directly explains what the description implies, namely that his mannerisms were "disagreeable and signs of arrogance." His unusually large eyes are another example of an extreme attribute rather than a moderate one; left-handedness most frequently implies a devious and deceptive character; and while pimples are not directly addressed in the handbooks, one might assume from this description that the sudden appearance of the pimples implies an inconsistency, unpredictability, and capriciousness to his character as seen in his now-handsome, now-pimpled face. It is striking that, according to Suetonius, the highly lauded emperor Augustus would both recognize the physiognomic implications as well as try to justify them as "natural failings" rather than devastating indices of the character of his soul.

Before leaving Suetonius, let us also make note of three other descriptions of emperors that are decisively negative. Domitian, known in Christian circles as an enemy of and persecutor of the church, does not fare well with Suetonius either:

> Domitian had a ruddy complexion; large, rather weak eyes; and a modest expression. He was tall and well-made, except for his feet which had hammer-toes. Later, he lost his hair and developed a paunch; and, as a result of protracted illness, his legs grew spindled. He took as a personal insult any reference, joking or otherwise, to bald men, being extremely sensitive about his own baldness. (*Dom.* 18, translation Graves)

Compare that description to the one given to the lesser-known emperor Otho:

> Otho, who did not look or behave like a very courageous man, was of medium height, bow-legged, and with splay feet; but almost as fastidious about appearances as a woman. His entire body had been depilated, and a toupee covered his practically bald head, so well made and fitted that no one suspected its existence. He shaved every day, and since boyhood had always used a poultice of moist bread to prevent the growth of his beard. (*Otho* 12, translation Graves)

In both cases, hair is a significant marker, and to lack hair is quite negative. In the case of Domitian, he is so aware of the negativity associated with baldness that he takes it as a personal insult, a reaction very much in keeping with the wrath often associated with his reign in general. In the case of Otho, he actually makes an effort to remove all hair from his body and to prevent the hair from growing, the sort of description that paints Otho as extremely effeminate. In a world where manliness is the goal, Otho seeks to go to the opposite extreme, while Domitian recognizes his shortcomings and seeks to compensate with anger and a show of strength.

Perhaps the most unusual description is that given to Nero. The description, which is not given in Suetonius until a few paragraphs prior to the narration of the death of Nero, is unusual particularly because of its restraint: "Height: average; body: pustular and malodorous; hair: light blond; features: pretty, rather than handsome; eyes: blue and rather weak; neck: squat; belly: protuberant; legs: spindled" (*Nero* 51, translation Graves). Undoubtedly the description is a negative one. It shares many negative descriptors already mentioned, such as weak eyes and spindled legs, and certainly a "pustular" and offensively-smelling body is quite negative as well. It is curious, however, that the description is not any more negative than it is. One might expect a description for the emperor who famously burned Rome to be as devastating as that given to Caligula, and certainly Nero had the reputation to match. Nevertheless, Suetonius leaves Nero with a quick, sparse description—though undoubtedly a negative one—and withholds it until the final paragraphs of the biography.

If in Suetonius we find textbook examples of physiognomic descriptions of the emperors, we find a quite different use of physiognomics in Plutarch. Plutarch is no less aware of the conventions of physiognomy, as his use of descriptions will demonstrate. What differs is that Plutarch does not prove to be the believer in the accuracy of physiognomic practice that Suetonius does.

Tatum, who has done a substantial amount of work on the physical descriptions in Plutarch, categorizes Plutarch's use of physical description into two categories. The first is the set description that comes at the beginning of a life, usually accompanying basic material like the person's place of origin, and which functions in an ornamental way as a means of introduction. The second kind of description is the kind that is worked into the story later in a way that more easily fits the narrative. Tatum claims that "in both cases... the physical description is integrated into the action, the themes and the lesson of the life."[59] Whereas Suetonius employed a physical description in nearly every case, Plutarch uses physical descriptions in less than half of his *Lives*. Such descriptions do, however, appear consistently in the case of a royal life.[60]

It is notable that while Plutarch is clearly aware of the prevalent worldview of the physiognomists, he more often than not appears to disagree with it. That is, he often employs the conventional descriptions but then topples them, demonstrating how a particular character either fell far short of his stately physical appearance or, in some cases, outperformed what would be expected based on the physique. This distrust of physiognomics would also account for why Plutarch is so sparing in his use of physical descriptions and why Plutarch does not

[59] W. Jeffrey Tatum, "The Regal Image in Plutarch's Lives," *JHS* 116 (1996): 139. He also includes an exhaustive list of both categories in n27. Notably, many of the descriptions are of momentary and transient facial expressions, the kind of physiognomics that all of the handbooks declare to be unreliable.

[60] Tatum ("Regal Image," 139n28) helpfully notes that the only exceptions seem to be *Numa*, *Cleomenes*, and *Artaxerxes*.

include them in the majority of the *Lives*.[61] The reader of Plutarch can frequently see that he is toppling the physiognomic conventions as insufficient and inaccurate. Tatum summarizes: "Externals may mirror inner reality, or they may not. But in every case they are hazardous guides to character."[62] Let us now examine some selections of Plutarch's use of physical descriptions.

Perhaps the best example of a character that falls far short of what his physical description implies is Demetrius. Plutarch describes Demetrius early as follows:

> Demetrius, the surviving son, has not the height of his father, though he was a tall man, but he has features of rare and astonishing beauty, so that no painter or sculptor ever achieved a likeness of him. They had at once grace and strength, dignity and beauty, and there was blended with their youthful eagerness a certain heroic look and a kingly majesty that were hard to imitate. And in like manner his disposition also was fitted to inspire in men both fear and favour. For while he was a most agreeable companion, and most dainty of princes in the leisure devoted to drinking and luxurious ways of living, on the other hand he had a most energetic and eager persistency and efficiency in action. Wherefore he used to make Dionysus his pattern, more than any other deity, since this god was most terrible in waging war, and on the other hand most skillful, when war was over, in making peace minister to joy and pleasure. (*Demetr.* 2.2–3)

To be described as tall and beautiful—so beautiful, in fact, that his likeness eluded the artists—should imply something of his courage and stately leadership. His very appearance, Plutarch tells us, inspired those who saw him. The question in this case, however, is whether this description is actually true to his character or whether it is merely pretentious. In *Demetr.* 41–42, Demetrius is criticized as he is compared to actors, accused of pretending to appear royal when in fact he is rather despicable in character, especially with his refusal to properly dispense justice. According to Plutarch, the behavior of Demetrius ultimately subverts his royal appearance. In fact, the statement that is ultimately damning of Demetrius is in 42.5: "And surely nothing so befits a king as the work of justice.... Thus a power devoid of wisdom advances evil to the place of good, and makes injustice co-dweller with fame."

---

[61] For a more detailed exploration of Plutarch's ambivalence toward the usefulness of physiognomics, see Tatum, "Regal Image," 135–151.

[62] Tatum, "Regal Image," 150.

Demetrius's reign was marked by injustice, and thus the king that *appears* to be a good king to the naked eye turns out to be an awful king. A similar phenomenon, as we will see in the next chapter, happens with King Saul in 1 Samuel.

While many of the physical descriptions are employed by Plutarch only to be subverted, it is certainly not the case with all. Romulus, the great and ideal king from the past and the founder of Rome, is not surprisingly portrayed quite positively. The initial description is brief, found at the birth of Remus and Romulus: "Delivered she [Ilia] was of two boys, and their size and beauty were more than human. Wherefore Amulius was all the more afraid, and ordered a servant to take the boys and cast them away" (*Rom.* 3.4–5). While "size and beauty" are not particularly specific—we are not told *how* tall or strong they are, nor are we told *in what way* they are beautiful—it is significant that it is the size and beauty of the boys that scares Amulius. Their appearance, even as infants, makes it clear that they are of royal and divine descent (sons of Mars after he seduces Ilia). Amulius has, in effect, "physiognomized" the boys and the conclusion threatens him, and rightly so. Later, Plutarch himself draws the conclusion based on their physical appearance: "the noble size and beauty of their bodies, even when they were infants, betokened their natural disposition" (*Rom.* 6.2). The subsequent behavior of the boys confirms the description as well: "and when they grew up, they were both of them courageous and manly, with spirits which courted apparent danger, and a daring which nothing could terrify. But Romulus seemed to exercise his judgment more, and to have political sagacity" (*Rom.* 6.2).[63] The legend that the twins were raised by wolves is also important here, especially since the boys are often portrayed in subsequent art as wolves. The wolf is a significant animal to the zoological method of physiognomy, described in Polemo as proud and wrathful beast that is vicious when on the attack.[64] Romulus certainly acts in accordance with his physical description.

Another great figure treated by Plutarch is Alexander, and Alexander's physical description is outstanding:

---

[63] Contra Tatum, "Regal Image," 144, who for some reason that is beyond my comprehension thinks that the behavior of the boys is contrary to what in implied is their physical appearance.

[64] Foerster 1.172.

> His physical features can be seen particularly clearly in the statues of Lysippus, who was, in fact, the only sculptor Alexander regarded as good enough to portray him. Lysippus has perfectly captured what many of Alexander's successors and friends tried to imitate, the way he held his neck cocked with a slight inclination to the left, and his melting gaze. Apelles' famous picture, 'The Wielder of the Thunderbolt,' has not accurately reproduced his complexion, but makes him too dark and swarthy. He had a pale complexion, they say, and his skin used to take on a ruddy tinge especially around the chest and face. Moreover, his skin used to emit a delightful odour and, as I have read in Aristoxenus' *Memoirs*, his mouth and whole body used to be bathed in a fragrance that filled his clothes. This was perhaps due to the unusually hot and fiery blend of humours in his body;...It was the heat of Alexander's body, presumably, which gave him his fondness for drink and also made him impatient. (*Alex*. 4.1)

Alexander, who is undoubtedly a great king, has physical features that his successors try to emulate. Clearly, they are emulated because they give the *appearance* of royalty and the swagger of a great leader. Notice though in Plutarch's description the explanation for the ruddy appearance of Alexander. "Ruddy" is a descriptor that appears numerous times in the physiognomic handbooks and which is often ambiguous. Perhaps the most notable trait, however, that is associated with ruddiness is a hot temper—red hair and a red face naturally imply a red hot temper as well. What is significant here is that Plutarch not only describes Alexander as ruddy (contrary to Apellus's portrait), but he also explains exactly why he appeared this way. Namely, it is the "hot and fiery blend of humours" that account for both his appearance and his temperamental behavior. In the case of the description of Alexander, Plutarch undoubtedly is aware of the conventions of physiognomy, and he makes use of them to describe the great conquering king.

One example within Plutarch's work of one who emulated Alexander is Pompey. Pompey is given a royal description as well, and one which in many ways intentionally parallels Alexander:

> At the outset, too, he had a countenance which helped him in no small degree to win the favour of the people, and which pleaded for him before he spoke. For even his boyish loveliness had a gentle dignity about it, and in the prime and flower of his youthful beauty there was at once manifest the majesty and kingliness of his nature. His hair was inclined to lift itself slightly from his forehead, and this, with a graceful contour of face about the eyes, produced a resemblance, more talked about than actually apparent, to the portrait statues of King Alexander. (*Pomp*. 2.1)

Pompey may or may not have actually resembled Alexander, but certainly he tried to mimic the great king and, according to Plutarch, the people talked about his appearance as if he resembled Alexander. The point, of course, is that if Pompey looks like Alexander, then he can be expected to behave and govern like Alexander as well, a conclusion that Pompey would no doubt like to elicit from his audience.

One further description from Plutarch needs to be mentioned, that of Antony. His description is notable because it has merged with the description of Heracles. Plutarch writes of Antony,

> He had also a noble dignity of form; and a shapely beard, a broad forehead, and an aquiline nose were thought to show the virile qualities peculiar to the portraits and statues of Heracles. Moreover, there was an ancient tradition that the Antonii were Heracleidae, being descendants of Anton, a son of Heracles. And this tradition Antony thought that he confirmed both by the shape of his body, as has been said, and by his attire. (*Ant.* 4.1–2)

Antony, according to Plutarch, tried to portray himself as Heracles, a billing no doubt difficult to live up to. Yet Plutarch's description of Antony's beard, forehead, and nose are often common attributes to Heracles, and it appears that Plutarch is employing those descriptions in order to introduce Antony.

Plutarch and Suetonius are by no means the only biographers to make use of physical descriptions. As we briefly explore a few examples from other biographers, the descriptions of Heracles are a good place to begin.

The description of Heracles by Philostratus is perhaps the best known description of the semi-divine hero:

> As to the being whom most men used to call the Heracles of Herodes, this was a youth in early manhood, as tall as a Celt, and in fact about eight feet high. Herodes describes him in one of his letters to Julian. He says that his hair grew evenly on his head, his eyebrows were bushy and they met as though they were but one, and his eyes gave out a brilliant gleam which betrayed his impulsive temperament; he was hook-nosed, and had a solidly built neck, which was due rather to work than to diet. His chest, too, was well formed and beautifully slim, and his legs were slightly bowed outwards, which made it easy for him to stand firmly planted. (*Vit. soph.* 552; LCL, *Philostratus and Eunapius*)

While a man who is eight feet tall with meeting, bushy eyebrows, a hooked nose, and bowed legs does not at first glance appear positive, these descriptors are high praise in the world of the physiognomists. Notice specifically in this description the bowed legs and the accompanying explanation of their significance. Not only does Philostratus offer a physiognomic description of Heracles, he even offers some exegetical work as to the meaning of that appearance.

Heracles is also described by Clement of Alexandria: "Hieronymus the philosopher sketches his bodily characteristics also,—small stature, bristling hair, great strength. Dicaearchus adds that he was slim, sinewy, dark, with hooked nose, bright gleaming eyes and long, straight hair."[65] Nearly everything in this description matches that of Philostratus with the notable exception that while Philostratus's Heracles is eight feet tall like a Celt, Clement's Heracles is short. In both cases, however, the description is given as an index to the character of Heracles.

Philostratus also describes a certain vinedresser by the name of Palamedes, and here he uses physical descriptors in comparison with famed Greek heroes of the past:

> In height he was the same as the greater Ajax; in beauty, Protesilaos says, he vied with Achilles, Antilokhos, Protesilaos himself, and with Trojan Euphorbus. His soft beard was springing up and with the promise of curls; his hair was cut close to his skin; his eyebrows were noble, straight, and came together above the nose, which was perfect as a square and stately. The resolve of his eyes appeared unshaken and fierce in battles, but when he was at rest their gaze was full of comradely affection and affable; he also is said to have possessed the most marvelous eyes among mortals.[66]

The physiognomic comparison is obvious: to be as tall as Ajax and a beautiful as Achilles is laudatory indeed. Many of his descriptors also parallel those of Heracles as well. Certainly Philostratus introduces this character in a way intent on drawing favor from the audience and raising expectations as to his outstanding ability and character.

One other significant writer who employs physical descriptions is Diogenes Laertius. Let us consider two of his descriptions of famous philosophers. Concerning Aristotle, he writes,

> Aristotle, son of Nicomachus and Phaestis, was a native of Stagira. Hermippus in his book *On Aristotle* relates that his father traced his ancestry to Nicomachus the son of Machaeon and grandson of Asclepius. Aristotle resided with Amyntas, the king of Macedon, as court physician and counselor. Aristotle was Plato's most gifted disciple. He spoke with a lisp, as we learn from Timotheus the Athenian in his book *On Lives*.

[65] Clement of Alexandria, "Exhortation to the Greeks," LCL, 63.

[66] Philostratus, *Heroikos* (SBL Writings from the Greco-Roman World 1; Atlanta: SBL, 1977), 111. *Heroikos* 33.39.

> Also, his legs were slender (so they say), his eyes small, and he was conspicuous for his dress, his rings, and the way he wore his hair (*Lives of the Philosophers* 5.1).[67]

Concerning Zeno, he writes,

> Timotheus of Athens in his book *On Lives* says that Zeno had a twisted neck. Apollonius of Tyre adds that he was slender, moderately tall, and dark-complexioned; for this reason, Chrysippus relates in the first book of his *Proverbs* that Zeno was called an Egyptian. He had heavy legs and was stout and sensitive. For this reason Persaeus in his *Convivial Reminiscences* claims that he refused many invitations to dine. Zeno liked to eat green figs and to lie in the sun. (*Lives of the Philosophers* 7.1, trans. Caponigri)[68]

Aristotle is described as speaking with a lisp, an indication of one who is effeminate.[69] He is also described as having slender legs and small eyes, both of which imply womanly characteristics or moral laxity.[70] Zeno does not fair much better, as his twisted neck would indicate cowardice and effeminacy,[71] as would his slender body type (Ps-Aristotle 810b), and his dark-complexion.[72] His heavy legs would indicate that he is foul-minded and shameless (Ps-Aristotle 810a). Clearly, then, these two philosophers are negatively portrayed in terms of their physical descriptions. Again, one might recall the helpful response that Socrates is said to have given Zopyrus (Cicero, *Tusc.* 4.37.80)—the assumptions about his natural character may indeed be true, but they can be overcome through the power of reason.

Ancient biography is by no means the only place where we find physiognomy in practice in ancient literature. As noted above, Elizabeth Evans has catalogued thousands of examples that span every major genre of literature, and the collective weight of those examples

---

67 The translation is that found in Diogenes Laertius, *Lives of the Philosophers* (trans. and ed. A. Robert Caponigri; Chicago: Henry Regnery Company, 1969).

68 Ibid.

69 A strong voice is properly manly. See especially Polemo's chapter 52 (Foerster 266–68) which is entirely devoted to the voice. Cf. Ps-Aristotle 813a where the high-pitched voice indicates one who is gentle and effeminate.

70 On the legs, see Ps-Aristotle 810a where thin legs denote one who is salacious. On the small eyes, note particularly Ps-Aristotle 810a where small eyes are typical of the panther, meaning feminine and cowardly.

71 Cf. Ps-Aristotle 811a where a long and thin neck indicates cowardice. See also Polemo chapter 61 (Foerster 276) on the androgen where a bent neck is one indicator.

72 See Ps-Aristotle 812a where the dark or "swarthy" complexion indicates cowardice, and the Egyptian is specifically names as the prime example of the cowardly person with a dark complexion.

is overwhelming. Without recounting dozens more examples, let it suffice to say that physiognomics is in practice in others genres in much the same way as in biography, including history,[73] satire,[74] comedy,[75] and even rhetoric.[76] Likewise, many of the Church Fathers are fond of physiognomics. They will be discussed in chapter five in the treatment of the New Testament and early Christian literature, but it is important to say at this point that the collective witness of the Church Fathers demonstrates that early Christians, just like the culture around them, thought in physiognomic terms.

---

[73] See, for example, the 4th-century historian Ammianus Marcellinus who writes, *Amm. Marc.* 15.8.16: "Gazing long and earnestly on his eyes, at once terrible and full of charm, and on his face attractive in its usual animation, they divined what manner of man he would be, as if they had perused those ancient books, the reading of which discloses from bodily signs the inward qualities of the soul" (*Amm. Marc.* 15.8.16). See also the description of Scipio Africanus in Livy 28.26, where the very sight of the great general inspires sufficient terror to squelch a revolt and melt the hearts of his enemies. See also Tacitus, *Ann.* 13.8 for a description of Domitius Corbulo. For a discussion of examples from the histories of Livy, Tacitus, Ammianus Marcellinus, and Pliny, see Evans, "Roman Descriptions," 43–84.

[74] See for example Juvenal *Sat.* 9.1–24. See also Petronius, *Satyricon* 126, in which a servant girl claims to able to diagnose character from the face and the walk, saying, "Look at me; I know nothing of omens, and I never attend to the astrologer's sky, but I read character in a man's face, and when I see him walk I know his thoughts." A few paragraphs later in a humorous scene, the slave girl receives a physical description, as the physiognomist becomes the physiognomized.

[75] Here one might think especially of Aristophanes. In *The Clouds*, Aristophanes indirectly satirizes Socrates and the so-called New Learning associated with him by mocking the students of Socrates. Often it is the physical appearance of the students that is being mocked. See, for example lines 103, 182, and 1497 where the descriptions include markers such as a deathly pale complexion, scrawny bodies, and ears like bats. Aristophanes also makes use of the racial method of physiognomy to mock various Greek peoples in *Lysistrata* (examples cited earlier in this chapter).

[76] As was mentioned above, Polemo makes extensive use of physiognomics as a tool for invective, less often for encomium. Dio Chrysostom even composes an "Encomium on Hair", found in Dio Chrysostom, *V: Discourses LXI–LXXX* (trans. H. Lamar Crosby, LCL; Cambridge: Harvard University Press, 1964), 332–343. For a discussion of physiognomy in rhetorical practice, see Barton, *Power and Knowledge*, chapter 2. A strong link can also be drawn between physiognomic descriptions and what the rhetorical handbooks call "ekphrasis of persons". See, for example, Theon, 118, where Homer's description of Thersites, which is certainly a physiognomic description as will be seen below, is used by Theon as the primary example of an ekphrasis of a person. Furthermore, delivery was one of the five major areas of study in rhetoric, and it was composed of two parts: voice and body language/gesture. These, too, are part of the study of physiognomy. On this point one might especially note Cicero, *De Or.* 3.216, 222, where he says that the countenance is the image of the mind, that is, the face/body reflect the soul. On this topic, see especially Gleason, *Making Men*, who deals extensively with voice and deportment.

Conclusion

This chapter has demonstrated that the practice of physiognomics was very much a part of the ancient cultural landscape. For many in antiquity, to see a person's body was to understand his character, and in such a world a physical description is often loaded with implied character traits. We find evidence of this practice as early as Homer, and such practice continues throughout Greco-Roman literature, spanning every era and every genre. Thus the reader of Greco-Roman materials, including the biblical material that grew up in that era, must be keenly aware of the implications that physical descriptions may have for the character of the one being described. Let us turn now to one specific character trait, the eyes.

CHAPTER THREE

EYES, SIGHT, AND BLINDNESS: LEARNING TO *SEE* WITH PHYSIOGNOMIC EYES

Thus far we have demonstrated the pervasiveness of what Evans terms the "physiognomic consciousness" in the Greco-Roman world, and we have examined numerous examples of the ancient practice of reading character in physical features. Far and away the most important of those characteristics is the eyes. Ps-Aristotle closes his work by underscoring the importance of the eyes, saying, "In all selection of signs some give a much clearer demonstration of the subject than others. Clearest of all are those that appear in the most favorable positions. The most favorable part for examination is the region round the eyes, forehead, head and face" (814b). Likewise, Polemo devotes the first third of his book to the examination of nothing but the eyes.

This chapter will be devoted to the examination of the eyes in the physiognomic worldview of the Greco-Roman milieu. Not only will we examine the eyes, but in order to understand the function of blindness in ancient literature we must also know something about the feeling toward disabilities in general. The final section, then, will examine the function of blindness in Greco-Roman literature, taking into account what the physiognomists say about the eyes and what the culture in general thinks of the disability of blindness.

In the world of the physiognomists, perfection is ideal and thus disability of whatever sort is almost entirely negative since it falls far short of perfection. Yet one finds a large number of blind characters in Greek literature, and understanding the implications of blindness on their character is essential. This book contends that an ancient audience would not only think of blindness on the literal level—lacking eyesight—but that an audience would also likely think in metaphorical terms, that is, lacking *spiritual* vision. The essential point is that in a world in which audiences are conditioned to think in terms of physiognomics, in which an audience naturally associates physical characteristics with moral character, it is essential that we as readers move beyond the physical blindness of a character and seek the implications for character that an ancient audience would quite naturally hear in the text. Hamm asserts that "the use of physical seeing as a metaphor for spiritual insight is a commonplace in the religious literature of the world,"[1] and I would argue that such a metaphorical usage of blindness is by no means limited to religious literature either. Before attending to the eyes and to blindness, let us first discuss the place of disabilities in the ancient world, particularly in a world in which such a physical deficiency would imply a corresponding moral deficiency.

Disability in the Greco-Roman World

While this chapter is not a study on disability per se, a rudimentary understanding of disability in the ancient world is necessary in order to understand what an ancient auditor might have thought of a blind character in literature. Many modern studies on disability are available,[2] and this work is not one them. Instead, this study is interested exclusively in the understanding of disability in the ancient world, and it leaves to other, more capable scholars the task of teasing out the implications for the modern reader.

Perfection in the Greek world is ideal; disabilities miss the mark of perfection. Therefore to be disabled, in the mind of a physiognomically-

[1] Dennis Hamm, "Sight to the Blind: Vision as Metaphor in Luke." *Bib* 67 (1986): 457. See also William Johnston, *The Inner Eye of Love: Mysticism and Religion* (San Francisco: Harper & Row, 1978).

[2] To name only a few, see especially the following: David T. Mitchell and Sharon L. Snyder, eds., *The Body and Physical Difference: Discourses of Disability* (Ann Arbor: University of Michigan Press, 1997), whose introductory chapter also contains extensive bibliography for those interested in pursuing disability studies; Garland, *Eye of the Beholder*; Donald J. Kirtley, *The Psychology of Blindness* (Chicago: Nelson-Hall, 1975); and for specifically Christian disability studies, see the following: Nancy L. Eiesland, and Don E. Saliers, eds., *Human Disability and the Service of God: Reassessing Religious Practice* (Nashville: Abingdon, 1998); Lynn Holden, *Forms of Deformity* (JSOTSup 131; Sheffield: JSOT Press, 1991); Felix N. W. Just, "From Tobit to Bartimaeus, from Qumran to Siloam: The Social Role of Blind People and Attitudes Toward the Blind in New Testament Times" (Ph.D. diss., Yale University, 1997); Nicole Kelley, "The Theological Significance of Physical Deformity in the Psuedo-Clementine *Homilies*," *PRSt* 34 (2007): 77–90; Kerry H. Wynn, "Johannine Healings and the Otherness of Disability," *PRSt* 34 (2007): 61–75. Particularly interesting is Eiesland, *The Disabled God: Toward a Liberation Theology of Disability* (Nashville: Abingdon, 1994), which is a kind of theological primer written from the perspective of disability studies. Drawing on a range of theological methods, including social scientific methods and liberation theology, she paints a picture of a God who is on the side of the disabled and pursues justice and liberation for the disabled. In fact, she even argues that we meet a disabled God in the Eucharistic meal itself, where we find as a central symbol of Christianity a God who brings redemption through the brokenness of his own body.

conscious world, is to fall far short of the desired mark, both physically and, by implication, morally/spiritually. Garland writes,

> By their own imperious reckoning, the Greeks and the Romans stood head and shoulders, culturally speaking, above all other races on earth in part because they alone exemplified the ideal human type. Any departure from that ideal type, however trivial, was therefore interpreted as a mark of the despised barbarian, whose attributed physiological defects were regarded as an expression of the latter's cultural limitations.[3]

Among the best examples in Greek literature is Polyphemus, the Cyclops found in the *Odyssey* 9. Even before he is blinded, Polyphemus is already a physical monstrosity whose physical characteristics are outlandishly deviant from the norm.[4] In fact, in a world in which it is believed that the further one gets from Greece or Rome, the more wild the deformity, Polyphemus' appearance alone would imply that Odysseus is nowhere near home. Polyphemus is enormous in size and has only one eye. To deviate from the norm so drastically physically would also imply to the reader that Polyphemus would likewise be deviant in terms of his moral character and social practice, and indeed he is. Rather than offer the requisite hospitality, the Cyclops eats his guests, an act that is as socially freakish as the appearance of the monster is physically freakish. To blind Polyphemus is to add disability to his deformity, and it is also a way of making his physical condition match his morally blind spiritual condition.

Sometimes the departure from the ideal is, in Garland's words, trivial—too tall, too short, an imperfect complexion, etc. At other times the departure from the ideal body is far from trivial—blindness, lameness, deafness, or any number of other disabilities that might befall a person. One of the more notable examples of such a disability and the resulting treatment of the disabled is Hephaestus. Hephaestus is the only crippled deity, and in fact he is the only Greek deity who manifests any sort of disability at all. Garland describes his plight, calling him "a solitary misfit among an unageing population of divinely perfect

---

[3] Garland, *Eye of the Beholder*, viii.

[4] One might think of Polyphemus in terms of the racial or ethnographical method of physiognomy and come to much the same conclusion. By that method, the further one gets from the Greek mainland the more deviant the appearance and the more deviant the character. The deviant appearance and character of Polyphemus, in such a worldview, are an indication that Odysseus is an unfathomable distance from home.

deities."[5] His Roman counterpart, Vulcan, is essentially written out of the mythology with no significant myths about him, perhaps because the Romans were uncertain what to do with a disabled member of the pantheon.[6] Strikingly, we do not know why Hephaestus is lame since there is no such explanation offered anywhere in the mythology.[7] Readers are introduced to the crippled metal worker in Homer. A particularly moving scene can be found in *Odyssey* 8, where Hephaestus laments his condition when his wife Aphrodite is continually unfaithful to him: "No one is responsible for the fact that I am defective except my own parents, and I wish they had never given birth to me" (*Od.* 8.311–12). Hephaestus's reaction is indicative of the general feeling toward disability—it is a pitiable condition that makes the person, to a greater or lesser degree, a social outcast. And the disability is often associated with blame, either of the victim, the victim's parents, or the gods.[8]

Unfortunately, to be disabled in the ancient world also meant that one was often mocked, the object of ridicule and humor, and Hephaestus provides a clear example of such treatment as well. While it is offensive to modern sensibilities, and one might imagine also offensive to many in the ancient world as well, the mockery of the disabled was an all-too-common practice in the Greco-Roman world. In Garland's words, "Laughter in antiquity knew no moral boundaries, and from Homer onwards the physical discomfort of others was a constant source of merriment."[9] Mockery is especially central to the symposium,[10] one example of which is the ridicule of Hephaestus at the end of book 1 of the *Iliad*. At the end of a drunken feast marked by a heated fight between Zeus and Hera, the mood is lightened: "The [Hephaestus] poured wine for all the other gods from left to right, drawing sweet nectar from the bowl. And unquenchable laughter arose among the

---

[5] Garland, *Eye of the Beholder*, 61.

[6] See Garland, *Eye of the Beholder*, 59, for a discussion of the Hephaestus/Vulcan myths.

[7] Garland suggests that he is lame for a simple reason—metal working is one of the few professions open to the lame. This is, of course, speculative, but it is nevertheless noteworthy that at least the lame were still able to pursue a trade, even if the number of fields open to the lame was greatly limited. See Garland, *Eye of the Beholder*, 62.

[8] In this vein, see Garland, *Eye of the Beholder*, 29.

[9] Garland, *Eye of the Beholder*, 76. See also chapter 5 of Garland's book, a chapter that is devoted entirely to the ridicule of the disabled in the ancient world.

[10] See Garland, *Eye of the Beholder*, 83–86 for a discussion of the symposium and the treatment of the disabled.

blessed gods, as they saw Hephaestus puffing through the palace" (*Il.* 1.597–600). The laughter, of course, is the exertion of the servant god who bears the epithet "the god of the two lame legs".

Generally speaking any time there is a symposium, one can expect to find plenty of alcohol, lots of lewd conversation, and quite often the mockery of the disabled. Evidence has survived such as crippled dancers painted on pottery. Domitian is even said to have set up battles between dwarf gladiators: "Then comes a bold array of dwarfs, whose term of growth abruptly ended has bound them once for all into a knotted lump. They give and suffer wounds, and threaten death—with fists how tiny!"[11] Plutarch tells us that a symposium might even feature rude requests such as "ordering stammerers to sing, or bald men to comb their hair, or the lame to dance on a greased wine-skin" (*Mor.* 621E). Plutarch, thankfully, does not approve of such ridicule. The story that follows illustrates his disdain for rude guests:

> Thus, by way of rudely mocking Agamestor the Academician, who had a weak and withered leg, his fellow banqueters proposed that each man of them all drain off his cup while standing on his right foot, or pay a penalty. But when it came the turn of Agamestor to give the order, he commanded them all to drink as they saw him drink. Then he had a narrow jar brought to him, put his defective foot inside it, and drained off his cup; but all the others, since it was manifestly impossible for them to do so, though they tried, paid the penalty. Thus Agamestor showed himself the urbane gentleman; and, following his example, one should make his ripostes good-natured and merry. (*Mor.* 621F–622A)

Thus we find that though at least some in the culture disapproved of the mocking of the disabled, it was very much a part of the culture. Unfortunately, it appears that the rejection and ridicule of the disabled is far more frequent than compassion.

It is also worth mentioning that in the Roman era the cognomen often labeled a disability held by the original bearer. Though subsequent generations kept the surname, there appears to be no evidence that there was a social penalty for having a handicapped name such as Cocles (one-eyed), Caecus (blind), or Balbus (Stutterer).[12] Thus we

---

[11] See Statius, *Silvae* 1.6.56–64. In this same text one also finds untrained women having sword fights.

[12] See Garland, *Eye of the Beholder*, 78–79 for a more complete list of cognomen describing physical features.

find that a particular disability not only affects the bearer of the disability, but it might also be remembered in the form of a family name for generations to follow.

The Eyes: Window to the Soul

When one looks to the literature it is clear that the eyes hold the place of prominence when it comes to diagnosing character. The idea that the eyes are the window to the soul is not a modern one, as the ancients knew well that one can learn much about an individual simply by observing the eyes. Theocritus writes an epitaph of a certain Eusthenes that said, "This is the grave of Eusthenes, a physiognomer skilled to discern the character from the eye."[13] It is important, then, to note the importance placed on the eyes in a physiognomically-conscious world. We look first to the position of honor given to the eyes as a marker in the physiognomic handbooks, and then we look to the larger body of Greek literature that likewise confirms the importance of the eyes.

In the first half of Ps-Aristotle's handbook, the author describes several *types* of people (the brave man, the coward, etc.). Nearly every type of person has a description of the eyes as a part of it. For example, the brave man has "a bright eye, neither too wide opened nor half closed" (807b), an indication that is comparable to the eyes of the lion described as "bright, deep-set eyes, neither very round nor very narrow" (809b). The coward has "eyes weak and blinking" (807b), and the author later tells us this is because "the first movement of flight starts with the eyes" (813a). The insensitive man has eyes that are "pale and dull" (807b), similar to the eyes of the panther which are "small eyes rather pale, hollow and somewhat flat" (810a). Ps-Aristotle also tells us that "weakness of the eye signifies two things, softness and effeminacy on the one hand, depression and lack of spirit on the other" (808a). For Ps-Aristotle, then, it is impossible to miss the emphasis placed on the eyes—truly the eyes are the best marker for discerning the character of the individual.

When opening the handbook of Polemo, one is immediately struck by the weight of material given to the study of the eyes, and it is the eyes that Polemo clearly believes to be the most nearly immutable and

[13] Theocritus, *Epigrams* 11. The translation is found in A. S. F. Gow, *Theocritus* (vol. 1; Cambridge: Cambridge University Press, 1950), 247.

thus most reliable physical marker. While the bulk of Polemo's chapters follow a bottom-to-top progression through the signs of the body, beginning at the toenails and feet and ascending the body from there, the eyes are not treated with the signs of the face where one might expect. Instead, Polemo fronts the discussion of the eyes, taking up the signs of the eyes in the very first chapter and devoting nearly one-third of the handbook to this topic. Both the placement of the discussion and the volume devoted to the eyes make it impossible to misunderstand Polemo's emphasis here. While Ps-Aristotle talked about the eyes as a part of nearly every character type, he comes nowhere near the level of importance given to the eyes by Polemo.

Most of Polemo's examples of the eyes seem to be drawn from people in his contemporary world, people he apparently knows. Generally, Polemo is using physiognomy as invective, and this is probably never more clear than we he discusses the eyes. Most examples of eyes found in Polemo reveal various negative traits on the part of their owners, with the exception of Hadrian (noted earlier). To have "much light in the eyes," as Hadrian did, was for the Greco-Roman culture like unto life itself. As we shall see in the discussion of blindness, to lack light in the eyes (i.e., to be blind) is like unto death, and in fact characters who *lack* light in their eyes often wish for death, thinking it a better fate. Hadrian, however, has the brightest of eyes and is thus most worthy of praise.

It is clear then that for the physiognomists the eyes are by far the most important marker. One might expect then that in a world in which physical markers are so important to understanding character, examples of eyes used in this way would abound in literature. Indeed this is the case, and we recount here a few examples to illustrate the point.

Recall the emphasis given to the eyes in the descriptions already given above by Suetonius and others. Augustus's eyes were "clear, bright eyes, in which he liked to have it thought that there was a kind of divine power, and it greatly pleased him, whenever he looked keenly at anyone, if he let his face fall as if before the radiance of the sun" (*Aug.* 79). Caligula's eyes were hollow (*Cal.* 50). Tiberius's eyes were "unusually large" and capable of seeing in the dark (*Tib.* 68). Domitian's eyes were described as large and rather weak (*Dom.* 18), and Nero's eyes were "blue and rather weak" (*Nero* 51). Also recall Plutarch's description of Alexander and his "melting gaze" (*Alex.* 4.1). Likewise, Philostratus said of Heracles that "his eyes gave out a brilliant gleam which betrayed his impulsive temperament" (*Vit. soph.* 552). Thus, as we have already seen on numerous occasions, eyes are a pivotal part of many physical descriptions.

The Homeric epics, too, are filled with descriptions of the eyes.[14] Many of the epithets involve the eyes. Athene, the goddess who in many ways drives the battle, has as her most frequent epithet "flashing-eyed Athene." The moniker is used of Athene more than eighty times, numbering it among the most commonly used epithets of any character in Homer. Other frequent epithets include the following: "bright-eyed," most often of the Achaeans; "grey-eyed," used of several characters; "dark-eyed," used to describe a few otherwise obscure characters; and "ox-eyed," often used of Hera but also of others. Not only are the eyes found in the epithets, but eyes are often used to describe the warriors on the battlefield. Hector's eyes are said to "blaze with fire" (*Il.* 12.466; 15.607) when he is in battle, a sign that in both cases indicates that none except the gods themselves can contend with him. Similarly, the eyes of Achilles are described as blazing as if they were flames (*Il.* 19.16; 19.366; 20.172). In each of these cases the eyes of Achilles indicate his fierce wrath.

Examples of descriptions of the eyes can be found in countless authors in the ancient world, and we need not recount every example here. Suffice it to say that in a culture that has learned to think in physiognomic terms, the eyes are the most important marker of character and are used frequently in this way. If the eyes are so important, it is not a far step to recognize the importance of the *lack* of eyesight and the largely negative conclusions that might be drawn from one whose eyes are as far from perfect as possible. It is to the study of blindness in Greco-Roman literature that we now turn.

Blindness in Greco-Roman Literature: Developing a Topos

Nothing is said in the physiognomic handbooks about blindness.[15] This omission, however, should not be alarming, since the handbooks are

---

[14] Homer uses a number of synonymous terms for the eyes, and a TLG search on these roots in the two epics returns hundreds of references. The sheer volume of references alone gives witness to the importance of the eyes for Homer and his world.

[15] It should be noted that Polemo provides a chapter on the color of the eyes, and it may well be that in the description of eye colors that he has the distinctive eyes of the blind in mind, though we cannot be certain. Among the eye colors he discusses are red, blueish-gray, white, black, olive, and pale. The blueish-gray eye (Latin: glaucus)

primarily interested in describing that which is ideal. Disabilities, then, are rarely if ever addressed in the handbooks because they so clearly fall short of the ideal body. While the handbooks talk about eyes and omit discussion of blindness, the larger body of Greco-Roman literature is inundated with examples of blindness. In a world where one is conditioned to think physiognomically, to encounter a blind character would inevitably cause the reader to make assumptions about the moral character of the blind person. Furthermore, since the trend in physiognomics is to conclude that the further one deviates from perfection the worse the corresponding character trait must be, to be blind then must inevitably lead the ancient hearer to think negatively about the blind person. While there are noteworthy exceptions, this logic of physiognomics holds true in the overwhelming majority of examples.

When discussing the understanding of blindness in the Greco-Roman world, one work stands out above the rest. Bernidaki-Aldous's *Blindness in a Culture of Light* has helpfully assembled a good number of the primary sources.[16] She is from the island of Crete and is herself blind, thus fostering much of her interest in the subject of blindness in the Greek tradition. Her first paragraph calls blindness and light a paradox:

> Everyone would agree that the study of extant Greek literature and everything we know of Greek culture leads us to this conclusion: the Greeks presented us with one of their greatest paradoxes in their attitudes toward blindness. Anyone who has ever read Greek literature will have sensed some kind of contradiction in Greek attitudes about blindness. The most striking paradox, for example, is the fact that in a culture where "to live" is synonymous with "to see the light" and "to die" equals "to go to Hades, i.e., Darkness," (to Hades where you neither see nor are seen), we find that the blind have a very special place of honor and power. The blind have been consistently assigned the ultimate religious, moral, social and political powers, especially in their roles as poets and seers.[17]

indicates the "disappearance of humanity and hardness of character," comparing such eyes to those of wild animals (chapter XXXIX, Foerster 246). Given the comparison with wild animals, however, it is unlikely that Polemo here has in mind the opaque eyes of the blind when he describes the blue-gray eye. On the surface the pale or fading eye seems like a fiting description of the blind eye, and it indicates fear and timidity. While the description "pale" could be an accurate description of a blind eye, the corresponding trait of fearfulness is not something that is readily attributed to blind characters in the literature and prevents us from concluding that Polemo has in mind the blind eyes here.

[16] Eleftheria A. Bernidaki-Aldous, *Blindness in a Culture of Light: Especially the Case of* Oedipus at Colonus *of Sophocles* (New York: Peter Lang, 1990).

[17] Bernidaki-Aldous, *Blindness in a Culture of Light*, 3.

We find in the Greek literature an uncomfortable ambivalence toward blindness. "Light" was coveted in that culture, and the word φώς was often used synonymously for "life." For example, Achilles, the greatest of Greek heroes, is willing to suffer death in order to gain τιμή (honor) in the *Iliad*, but in the subsequent volume, the *Odyssey*, when Odysseus speaks with Achilles in Hades, Achilles says he would give up the highest honors (τιμή) in Hades to see the *light* again.[18]

Similarly, light was so much coveted that we often find Greek heroes bidding farewell to the light in their speeches at the moment of death. While the hero will bid farewell to numerous things in a final speech, the one constant that is almost always present is the farewell to the light. For example, Alcestis bids farewell to the sun in Euripides, (*Alc.* 241–249); a speech from Polyxena in Euripides three times laments the loss of the light before Odysseus carries her away to her death (*Hec.* 367–437); and in Sophocles, Ajax bids farewell to "the shining light of this radiant day" and to "the Sun-god charioteer, for the last time and never more again" on his way to Hades (*Aj.* 854–59). Also Oedipus, who is himself already blind in *Oedipus Coloneus* having blinded himself in the previous play, nevertheless bids farewell to the light which he has not seen in years (*Oed. col.* 1549–52).[19] Such is the pattern for farewell speeches beginning in Homer and continuing through most of Greek literature.

Thus Bernidaki-Aldous is correct in saying that "In Greek culture it is not a figure of speech to say that life equals light and that death equals darkness. Life and light as well as death and darkness for the Greeks is an experience, a way of life, the understanding of the meaning of existence as human condition dictates."[20] So, for example, Hades is often referred to as "the darkness," "the place where one cannot see or be seen," or even in the biblical material, "outer darkness." In Euripides's *Phoenician Maidens*, Antigone tells Oedipus of the death of his family by saying "they will no longer see the light" (*Phoen.* 1547–48). He is told concerning their death that they have "left the light", which clearly means to die. Similarly, in Sophocles one finds an example where Clytemnestra has a dream about Agamemnon coming back to life, and she uses the description "returning to the light" (*El.* 417–19).

[18] This example, and others, can be found in Bernidaki-Aldous, *Blindness in a Culture of Light*, xiii.

[19] These and other examples of bidding farewell to the light are discussed in more detail in Bernidaki-Aldous, *Blindness in a Culture of Light*, 11–18.

[20] Bernidaki-Aldous, *Blindness in a Culture of Light*, 18.

It is clear, then, that in the Greek world "light" and "life" were frequent synonyms. Sight and light were greatly to be desired, and those who lacked either were most to be pitied—there is no more pitiable and nightmarish condition in the Greek worldview than to lack light, which is also to lack eyesight. In fact, most of the blind characters that we encounter in Greek literature are pitiable characters—usually old, either carrying a staff or led by a guide if not both, helpless, and among the most pathetic characters to appear on a Greek page or stage. Yet there is a haunting ambivalence about blindness—while it is terrifying, unsettling, and pitiable, it is also something which inspires awe because it occasionally means a link to a supernatural insight, a supreme form of supernatural vision that apparently compensates for a lack of physical vision. Greek literature, then, presents us with an ambivalence, indeed even a paradox, concerning blindness.

How, then, is one to understand the characterization of the blind in Greek literature? Bernidaki-Aldous calls blindness a *topos* in Greek literature,[21] a conclusion with which I agree, and the description of that *topos* can be found in the categories that follow. That is to say that when a blind character is introduced into a book or play, the character tends to follow a set character type, such that an ancient audience would have assumed certain things immediately on the sheer basis of blindness alone. The rhetoricians would know this kind of a character as a *topos*, and it is the sort of diagnosis of character that the physiognomists practiced regularly.

In the pages that follow, I wish to lead the reader through a series of examples of blindness in Greek literature. The categories below are essentially an adaptation of Bernidaki-Aldous's work.[22] I have supplemented her work with more examples in places.[23] More significantly, I prefer to talk about these groupings as "elements of the *topos*" rather

[21] Bernidaki-Aldous, *Blindness in a Culture of Light*, 4.

[22] Her categories, in order, are as follows: 1) Blindness especially combined with old age: a condition of utter helplessness, dependence, and misfortune; 2) Blindness as ignorance: Seeing as light, truth, moral goodness; 3) Blindness as punishment; 4) The blind prophet or seer.

[23] I have chosen to supplement her work because so much of her book focuses on the character of Oedipus only. A simple TLG search of just the nominative form of τύφλος yields several thousand occurrences, demonstrating the impossibility of an exhaustive survey. More importantly, however, it demonstrates the widespread fascination with blindness in the Greek world that has to this point been largely overlooked by New Testament scholars.

than as "categories", since nearly every blind character would fit multiple categories. These are not separate grouping, but rather they are multiple layers to the same *topos*, the *topos* of the blind. Also, as will be explained later, I have placed much less emphasis on her final category—the blind prophet. In the groupings that follow, elements 1, 2, and 3 are true of nearly every occurrence of blind characters, and thus it seems that the first three elements would be the basic assumed *topos*, the assumptions that a physiognomically-conscious world would immediately make when encountering a blind character. The groupings are as follows, and a series of examples[24] for each group will follow in the subsequent pages:

1) Blindness is viewed, perhaps without exception, as a negative condition—those who are blind are helpless, dependent upon others, and often have found disfavor with the gods. Blindness is considered the worst of misfortunes that can befall a person.
2) Blindness can be a punishment, inflicted by god or man, for crimes intentional or unintentional.
3) Blindness means ignorance, while seeing can mean a knowledge of truth and goodness. Thus a blind character is morally and spiritually ignorant as well. Blindness can also be used in a purely metaphorical way of those who have sight but who are morally blind.
4) Blindness can be used as the inverse of the previous category—the blind (often prophets) are on rare occasions the ones who truly see/understand, often as opposed to those with physical sight but who are spiritually blind. The blind are at rare times endowed with prophetic powers.

It is crucial to note that these groupings are not mutually exclusive but are different layers to the *topos*. It is to be expected that most often the same blind character may fit multiple categories. That is to say that even if one encounters one of those rare blind characters who are endowed

[24] The most extensive collection of examples of blindness in a single place that I am aware of is Albert Esser's *Das Antlitz Der Blindheit in der Antike: Dei Kulturellen und Medizinhistorischen Ausstrahlungen des Blindenproblems in den Antiken Quellen* (Leiden: E. J. Brill, 1961). This work is an excellent sourcebook that gives a collection of references to blindness in Greek literature. Esser not only studies examples of blindness in literature, which is the primary focus of this paper, but he also looks at prominent examples of blindness as depicted in the arts. See, for example, plates 3 and 4 and the subsequent discussion, in which the blinding of Polyphemus and of the Centaur are depicted.

with prophetic insight, it does not mean that the character is not at the same time helpless and/or punished by the gods. In fact, most blind characters fit multiple groupings. It is also important to note that the fourth group—the blind seer—is playing on the basic *topos*, extending it to more metaphorical meanings. It is, however, the first three elements that provide the metaphorical strength for the final usage, one which is found considerably less frequently in the literature. Let us examine some examples of blindness in each of these groupings.

Examples of Blindness in Greco-Roman Literature

In later literature Ovid (*Ib.* 259–74) looks back and lists many of the ancient Greek characters afflicted with blindness, including Homer, Phoenix, Oedipus, Teiresias, Phineus and his sons, Polymestor, Polyphemus, Demodocus, and Thamyris. Some of these famous blind characters are remembered quite fondly, especially Homer the (presumably) blind poet and Teiresias the quintessential blind prophet. And while blind characters are by no means limited to the Greco-Roman world,[25] there are far more examples of blind characters in Greek and Latin literature than simply those recounted by Ovid. Let us begin our study of blind characters with those that fit the first element of the *topos*, the blind who are pitiable and helpless.

---

[25] While our interest here is with blind characters in antiquity, the same beliefs about sight and blindness have very much persisted in subsequent cultures, right up to the present. For a good treatment of blind characters in folklore ancient and modern, see H. Von Schumann, *Traüme der Blinden* (Basel: S. Karger Co, 1959). This work is a study of blind characters in myth, fairy tales, legends, and even oral traditions across a number of cultures ancient and modern. Also, see Donald J. Kirtley, *The Psychology of Blindness* (Chicago: Nelson-Hall, 1975), esp. 60–80, 121–34. This work is a treatment of blindness in light of modern psychological principles, but the author lists a number of helpful examples of blindness (though, sadly, lacking exact references for most of the examples) both ancient and modern. One interesting example from the *Canterbury Tales* is worth mentioning just to illustrate the point. It comes from "The Merchant's Tale"—there is a blind old knight named January who has all the stereotypical characteristics of the blind. He is pitiful, helpless, etc. He occasionally helps his wife May into a tree where she carries on an affair with her lover Damian while January stands around unsuspecting. King Pluto magically restores the knight's sight, however, and he sees the whole sordid affair. Though his eyesight is healed, he is still, as it were, quite blind, for when he confronts his wife about the affair, she is able to convince him that what he has seen is not real but is the result of his excitement over his restored sight. She gets away with the affair, and the knight is portrayed as being stupid, pitiful, and blind—metaphorically speaking—even after his sight is restored.

Blindness as the Most Negative of Conditions

The first grouping represents the majority usage of blindness, and thus probably represents the majority feeling among Greek auditors. That blindness is the most negative condition that can befall a person, often even worse than death itself, is the basic assumption involved in the *topos* of blindness. That is, the standard or conventional opinion of blindness is that blindness makes a person handicapped, helpless, pitiable, and physically dependant upon others. Bernidaki-Aldous asserts that "the blind character, usually old as well, with a guide or a staff, is indeed the most pathetic character to appear before the Greek public."[26] Even those characters, such as Teiresias, who are positive blind characters are portrayed as dependent and pitiable nonetheless. Therefore, even among characters who are portrayed positively, the *blindness itself* is considered negative and the blind person is a figure much to be pitied. It is also this majority opinion that gives the other uses of blindness such literary power.

Nearly any example in Greco-Roman literature of a blind character will reflect this opinion of blindness as a pitiable condition that renders the blind person helpless and dependant upon others. We list here only a few representative examples to illustrate the point.

Teiresias is the most famous of blind characters in Greek literature, appearing numerous times in numerous works. Though a blind prophet who is wise, gifted, and almost altogether heroic in literature, he is nonetheless pitied by those around him and is dependant upon others. Take for example his own statement in *Antigone* that the blind always have a guide, and that one sees for two.[27] He himself is led around by a boy (*Ant.* 1087). Likewise in Euripides (*Phoen.* 834–48) Teiresias is led around by his daughter Manto. Later in that same play (line 1530–81), Oedipus appears, old and blind, being led by his daughter Antigone. The blind, even those like Teiresias who can see things in the spiritual world that are hidden from the sighted, are dependant upon the sight of others.

Not only are the blind dependant upon guides, but they are also pitied, viewed as pathetic in the eyes of most of the sighted world.

[26] Bernidaki-Aldous, *Blindness in a Culture of Light*, 36.

[27] Oedipus says, "Prince of Thebes, two wayfarers as one, having between us eyes for one, we are here. The blind man cannot move without a guide" (*Ant.* 988–90).

Sometimes this pity takes a tragic tone. Just before Oedipus blinds himself in *Oedipus Tyrannus*, the Chorus announces that "You would be better off dead than to live blind!" (*Oed. tyr.* 1367). Bernidaki-Aldous helpfully points out that both Oedipus and the Chorus begin their lament after his blinding, *not* after the discovery of incest and murder. It is the blinding that is cause for mourning more so than his sins.[28] Notice also that immediately after Oedipus's blinding, his helplessness and need for pity is announced (*Oed. tyr.* 1292–96): "he has no strength and no one to guide him, and his torture is more than man can suffer, as you yourselves will see. The palace doors are unbarred just now and you will soon see such a sight that even he who most abhorred him would now pity him nonetheless."

Sometimes the blind are pitied in a way that takes a satirical or mocking tone. Consider for example, Juvenal, who talks about Catullus Messalinus, who is a blind consul under Domitian and is his informer. He is incredibly pathetic in this scene, loving a woman he has never seen, and then giving a speech in which he gestures toward a beast on his left that is actually on his right.[29] Or consider Aristophanes's *Women of the Assembly* (known as *Ecclesiazusae*), where one finds the political assembly mocking a certain Neokleides who is blind, or at least severely visually impaired, as he stumbles towards the speaker's platform: "It's scandalous that *he* should dare to speak, when the subject is the city's preservation. He doesn't know how to preserve his own eyesight!" (*Eccl.* 400–02). Though he was allowed to participate in the political system, the fact that he was derided and that the people dreaded him taking the stand indicates that his disability severely hampered his credibility and rhetorical effectiveness. Furthermore, it certainly does not seem to imply to his hearers that he has some kind of special clairvoyance as a blind seer.

Perhaps the most pathetic and pitiable depiction of blindness in all of Greek literature is that of Polyphemus in Euripides's *Cyclops* (665ff). The blinded Polyphemus is just painful for the reader to experience, and presumably still worse yet for the viewer of the performance of the play. The impact of the scene is all the more heightened because of the juxtaposition of the blindness to the enormous and once powerful

[28] For further discussion of this point, see Bernidaki-Aldous, *Blindness in a Culture of Light*, 34.

[29] Juvenal, *Sat.* 4.113–21.

creature. Though the scene is a comedic one in the play, it is also a painful and pathetic one as well.

Finally, it should also be noted that this grouping should also include blindness associated with old age. It is very common to find characters whose eyesight is said to fade with age, and often the "dimming of the eyesight" is also a dimming of one's life. Such imagery is, as we will see in the next chapter, very common in the Old Testament in particular. Garland also lists several other potential causes for blindness that would have happened relatively frequently, including various plagues and diseases, malnutrition, environmental pollution, accidents, and war.[30] Whatever the cause of the blindness, though, the reaction and interpretation of that blindness is consistent from the audience—blindness is negative, pitiable, and pathetic.

Blindness as Punishment

The second element of the blind *topos* is often an assumption of punishment. That is, in Greco-Roman literature there are numerous examples of characters who have been blinded as a punishment for some sort of crime. Sometimes the blinding is inflicted by other humans, sometimes the blinding is inflicted by the gods. Sometimes the blindness is a punishment for crimes committed intentionally, and sometimes it is a punishment for crimes committed by complete accident. There are several types of violations that most frequently lead to blinding. Most often, it involves some sort of infringement upon the divine world—either the person is revealing forbidden knowledge of the divine world, or the person has somehow transgressed the boundaries of the divine world. Blindness is also often used as a punishment for crimes of a sexual nature, sometimes against humans but regularly against deities.[31] Blindness is also used for punishments for egregious violations of human institutions like the hospitality system. Let us point to some representative examples of blinding as a punishment, recognizing that

[30] Garland, *Eye of the Beholder*, 20. On war, it is interesting that Julius Caesar mentions that four of the six centurions in one cohort were blinded in a single battle (*Bell. civ.* 3.53), and Garland (*Eye of the Beholder*, 23) seems to think this is not unusual in war.

[31] G. Devereux, "The Self-Blinding of Oidipous in Sophokles: *Oidipous Tyrannos*," *JHS* 93 (1973): 36–49. See especially pages 40–42 for a longer list of examples of blindness as punishment for sexual crimes. He even goes so far as to argue that castration and blinding are equivalent (pg. 44). Devereux argues that blinding is an appropriate punishment for sexual crimes and sees this as a consistent pattern in ancient literature.

such punishment happens so frequently that a Greco-Roman audience would be conditioned to think that when encountering a blind person, the blindness is itself evidence of a crime or sin committed by that person.

Most frequently, blinding is the result of some sort of transgression against the divine world. Sometimes the transgression is a sexual violation, but more often it is an issue of the human venturing too far into the divine world and overstepping his natural boundaries. Teiresias is a good place to begin. He was commonly believed to have been blinded as punishment for accidentally glimpsing Athena as she bathed, according to Apollodorus (*Bibliotheca* 3.6.7). He "saw the goddess stark naked, and she covered his eyes with her hands, and so rendered him sightless."[32] Though his crime was accidental, it still had to be punished. But because his crime was accidental, the gods compensated him with the gift of prophecy and by granting him honor and a long life. Another common story of Teiresias's blinding is ascribed to Hesiod but paraphrased as follows by Apollodorus:

> Hesiod says that he beheld snakes copulating on Cyllene, and that having wounded them he was turned from a man into a woman, but that on observing the same snakes copulating again, he became a man. Hence, when Hera and Zeus disputed whether the pleasures of love are felt more by women or by men, they referred to him for a decision. He said that if the pleasures of love be reckoned at ten, men enjoy one and women nine. Wherefore Hera blinded him, but Zeus bestowed on him the art of soothsaying. The saying of Teiresias to Zeus and Hera was "Of ten parts a man enjoys one only; But a woman enjoys the full ten parts in her heart." (*Bibl.* 3.6.7)

Though the legends for how Teiresias became blind are inconsistent, both legends contain the central element of divine punishment.

Homer himself also provides an interesting case study While the traditional belief that Homer was blind is not without its critics, his blindness is widely accepted. Yet very little in ancient literature is said about Homer's blindness. One place where it is addressed is in Plato's *Phaedrus* (243 a–b), where Socrates claims that Homer is blind because

[32] Similarly, Erymanthos, a child of Apollo, saw Aphrodite bathing and was blinded as a result. Aphrodite was bathing following her affair with Adonis (Photius, *Bibliotheca*, 190). One might also note the case of Philip of Macedonia who was famously blind in one eye. Though the injury took place in battle, it may well have had divine motivation. It was, after all, the very eye he used to spy on his wife Olympias when she was sleeping with the god Ammon who was in the form of a serpent (Plut. *Alex.* 3).

he told his story about Helen. Since Helen is considered divine or semi-divine by many, and the story does not paint her in a positive and pure way sexually, Homer is punished and blinded. Homer's case is juxtaposed to a certain Stesichorus, a famed lyric poet of the sixth century B.C.E., who is blinded for the same reason. However, Stesichorus has the good sense to compose a retraction, thus receiving forgiveness and restoring his eyesight.[33]

To anger a deity is certainly risky. Lycurgus is blinded by Zeus for his treatment of Dionysus in book 6 of the *Iliad*. Eventually Zeus issues punishment: "Then at Lycurgus did the gods who live at their ease grow angry, and the son of Cronos made him blind; and he lived not for long, since he was hated by all the immortal gods" (*Il.* 6.138–41).

Yet sometimes the infringement can even be an indirect one. Sometimes seeing a forbidden statue rather than the actual deity, or worse yet stealing it, could case blindness. Such is the case with the Palladium, the famed statue that had fallen directly from the heavens. Ilus took it from Athena's shrine in Ilium (Troy) when the city was burning, and he was subsequently blinded because "the Palladium might not be looked upon by a man."[34] He later repented and was given his sight back. Likewise, Antylus was blinded when he took the Palladium from the burning temple of Vesta in Rome. He, too, later appeased the goddess and was given his sight back.[35] Likewise soldiers of Alexander the Great were blinded for entering the temple of Demeter at Miletos. Intent on plundering the temple, they were blinded upon entering.[36] Also, a certain Aipytos entered a temple of Poseidon at Mantineia, a temple which no human had ever entered. He was blinded and then died.[37] It was not just the gods of the Greeks who used blindness as a punishment—so also the Egyptian king Pheros was blinded after he threw his spear at the Nile, angry because it was flooding.[38]

Arrogantly over-stepping one's bounds as a human was also not tolerated. Consider the example of Thamyris, who was punished for challenging the Muses to a singing contest.[39] In this version of the story,

[33] Stesichorus can also be found in Hesiod, *Catalogue of Women and Eoeae* 67, in Hesiod's *Homeric Hymns and Homerica* (LCL).

[34] Plutarch, *Mor.* 309F., contained in the work *Parallel of Greece and Rome.*

[35] Plutarch, *Mor.* 310A.

[36] Valerius Maximus, *Memorable Deeds and Sayings*, 1.1 *ext.* 5.

[37] Pausanias, *Descr.* 8.5.4–5, 10.3.

[38] See Herodotus, *Hist.* 2.3.

[39] Apollodorus *Bibliotheca* 1.3.3 is just one place this story may be found. The contest is also mentioned in *Iliad* 2.594–600, though without mention of blindness.

not only does he declare that he will win, but he demands as a prize that he will have sex with each of the Muses ("he would approach all of them"). He of course lost, and thus lost both his eyes and his ability to sing as a result. Consider also Phineus in Apollonius of Rhodes's *Argonautica* (2.183–85). Here Phineus is punished by Zeus for over-prophesying.[40] He is punished with a combination of blindness, old age, and starvation.

One may also over-step one's bounds as a human by failing to offer proper worship and thanks to a deity. For example, Asclepius, who is usually known for healing people, is once said to heal a blind man and then re-blind him for not properly giving thanks: "Hermon of Thesus. His blindness was cured by Asclepius. But, since afterwards he did not bring the thank-offerings, the god made him blind again. When he came back and slept again in the Temple, he made him well."[41]

Not all cases of blindness were as a result of a violation against the divine world itself. Sometimes the blinding was inflicted by humans, usually for violations of some sort of human institution. Most famous here are the stories of Polyphemus and Polymestor. Polyphemus (found most notably in *Odyssey* 9), the famed Cyclops and son of Poseidon, is blinded by Odysseus as punishment for his savage behavior. Polyphemus, who physiognomically speaking is monstrous and despicable, grossly violates the hospitality system by eating his guests. Polyphemus's story is also told in Euripides's *Cyclops*. Here, Odysseus proclaims that the blinding was the punishment for Polyphemus's "unholy banquet" (*Cycl.* 690–700). Polyphemus egregiously violates the hospitality system and he is blinded as recompense.

Polymestor is also blinded as punishment.[42] Polymestor, like Polyphemus, is guilty of violating the hospitality system by killing his guests. Every character in the play agrees that the blinding is understood as punishment for his violation. The Chorus says so in lines 1085–87: "Wretch! Wreaked on you are ills intolerable: foul deeds you did, and awful penalty a God has laid on you with heavy hand." So also

[40] Notably, Phineus had the gift of prophecy *before* he was blinded. He was blinded as punishment for disclosing the will of the gods accurately and often. He is, then, *not* an example of a blind prophet—one who is given prophetic power to compensate for the loss of eyesight—but is instead a prophet who is later blinded as punishment for his prophetic activity.

[41] *Inscriptiones Graecae* 4.1.121–22, Stela 2.22. The translation is that of Wendy Cotter, *Miracles in Greco-Roman Antiquity: A Sourcebook* (New York: Routledge, 1999), 18.

[42] Euripides, *Hec.* 1034ff. Polymestor's blinding is also mentioned in Ovid *Metam.* 13.404–575.

Agamemnon (1240–51) and even Polymestor himself (1252–53) agree. In this story, Hecuba is said to dig out his eyeballs with her fingernails, and then she turns her wrath on the now empty eye socket. A similar story can also be found in another work by Euripides, where Alcmene, an enraged mother, exacts revenge by blinding the already severed head of Eurystheus.[43]

Often the human institution that is violated is of a sexual nature. One might think of the example of Phoenix, who is blinded because of incest with his step-mother—although the crime may well have only been an accusation.[44] A similar case is found in Apollodorus (*Bibliotheca* 3.15.2–3), where the sons of Phineus are blinded as punishment for raping their step-mother, although it appears that this was an untrue accusation. Yet the alleged crime was punished nonetheless. The Argonauts in turn punished Phineus, presumably by blinding him also. He meets the same fate in Sophocles's play *Phineus*.

Certainly the blinding inflicted from human to human is not always just, and the injustice will occasionally provoke a response from the gods as was the case with Phineus. Another case would be that of Euenius. Euenius is blinded by the Apollonians because he fell asleep when he was supposed to be guarding the sheep, allowing wolves to eat the flock.[45] In this story, though, a god determines that the blinding is too harsh of a punishment and orders that the people compensate him. They cheat him by not telling him about the oracle, so the gods compensate the man further with the gift of insight.

As these examples are sufficient to demonstrate, there are myriad cases of blinding as punishment,[46] and there is little doubt that an auditor in the first century might suspect that a blind character is being punished for something. Given the pervasiveness of blindness as punishment, such an assumption would certainly be a part of the *topos* of the blind character assumed by an auditor in a physiognomically-conscious world.

[43] Euripides, *Heracl.* 843ff. The story is also told in Apollodorus, *Bibliotheca* 2.8.1.

[44] This story is found in Euripides, *Phoenician Women*.

[45] Herodotus, *Hist.* 9.93ff.

[46] Many more examples can be found listed in Bernidaki-Aldous, *Blindness in a Culture of Light*, 57–78.

Blindness as Ignorance

The third major component of the blind *topos* is blindness as ignorance. A physiognomic view of the world would quite naturally lead one to ascribe to the physically blind all manner of blindness—moral blindness, spiritual blindness, and mental blindness/ignorance. It is, of course, this widespread belief of metaphorical blindness connected to physical blindness that makes the rare appearances of the so-called "blind seer" so powerful.

To point to only a couple of examples of physical blindness as the equivalent of ignorance, consider Ajax and Patroclus. In Sophocles's *Ajax* (69–96), Athena confuses Ajax, makes him ignorant, and impairs his judgment by simply confusing his *sight*. She literally, "puts madness" on his eyes. Here, temporary blindness leads to temporary ignorance and mental impairment. One might also point to the *Iliad* and the death of Patroclus. After Patroclus has decimated the battlefield and fights like the mighty Achilles, Apollo and Athene join the fight. Apollo slips behind Patroclus and strikes him so hard that it dazes him. The terminology used for the stunned state in which Patroclus finds himself is that "blindness seized his mind" (*Il.* 16.805).

While a reader would likely immediately assume some sort of metaphorical blindness when meeting a blind character, it is also very much the case that "blindness" became a widespread metaphor for moral ignorance. That is, "blindness" can be ascribed to someone who has two perfectly good eyes in order to say that their sight—metaphorically speaking—is impaired in some way. In fact, the Greek words for "sight" and "knowledge" are even semantically linked—one might think especially of εἰδώς, the participle of οἶδα meaning "to know", and εἶδον, the aorist form of ὁράω, meaning "to see". Blindness, then, as a metaphor for ignorance is quite widespread.

Plato was one of many who were fond of this usage. One might think especially of his famous allegory of the cave in which there is a play between sight/knowledge and blindness/ignorance throughout.[47] The prisoner *thinks* he understands reality because he can *see* shadows on the wall. However, the shadows are not reality; they are merely a poor reflection of reality, dimly lit in the darkness of the cave. Socrates repeatedly declares that for the prisoner to understand the true reality

[47] The allegory of the cave is found in Plato, *Rep.* 7.514aff.

rather than simply the shadows, the prison must "look towards the light" (515c), and his eyes must "become steady" (517a), and truth is represented by the light and by the sun.[48] In the case of the prison, the literal eyes must make an adjustment to the light. The allegorical meaning for the reader, of course, is that the eyes of the mind—metaphorical use—must be opened. Socrates even declares that the process of seeing the light is a painful one. He says, "And if he is compelled to look straight at the light, will he not have a pain in his eyes which will make him turn away and to take in the objects of vision which he can see, and which he will conceive to be in reality clearer than the things which are now being shown to him?" (515e). Or again, "Suppose someone dragged him away from there by force along the rough, steep, upward way and didn't let him go before he had dragged him out into the light of the sun...when he came to the light, wouldn't he have his eyes full of its beam and be unable to see even one of the things now said to be true?" (515e–516a).

Plato then spells out the metaphor even more thoroughly. Consider the following paragraph on the lips of Socrates:

> If a man is intelligent he will remember that the bewilderments of the eyes are of two kinds, arising from two causes—from coming out of the light into the darkness or from going from the darkness to the light. This is as true of the mind's eye as it is of the bodily eye. And if he held that these same things happen to a soul too, whenever he saw one that is confused and unable to make anything out, he wouldn't laugh without first asking whether that soul of man has come out of the brighter light, and is unable to see because unaccustomed to the dark, or having turned from darkness to the day is dazzled by the greater brilliance. And then he would deem the first soul happy for its condition and its life, while he would pity the second. (518a–b)

Socrates then questions the claim of certain teachers who profess that they "put into the soul knowledge that isn't in it, as though they were putting sight into blind eyes" (518b–c). Playfully, Socrates even paints the picture of the cave for Glaucon early on and repeatedly asks him

---

[48] Cf. *Rep.* 6.508d–e, where there is a discussion of the idea of the good, and ignorance is compared to darkness while intelligence is compared to light. See also *Rep.* 6.506c, where he writes, "Haven't you noticed that all opinions without knowledge are ugly? The best of them are blind. Or do men who opine something true without intelligence seem to you any different from blind men who happen to travel the right road?" See also Plato, *Gorg.* 479b, where "to be blind" and "to be ignorant" are synonyms. Here it is not just ignorance that is described as blindness, but also moral deficiency.

if he sees the scene, to which Glaucon consistently replies "I see". Though Glaucon affirms that he sees—i.e., he can picture in his mind the scene being painted—it is clear that he does not *see*—i.e., the deeper meaning of the scene eludes him. Plato's *Republic* is a significant and foundational text, and to find within it such a strong use of the blindness-as-ignorance metaphor is weighty and indicative of the power of the metaphor in Greco-Roman culture.

This metaphorical usage of blindness if by no means limited to Plato. Philo also uses blindness in this way frequently, and the following example is typical of Philo's usage: "They have shown the godliness of heart which above all leads up to friendship and affinity, and we must rejoice with them, as if, though blind at the first they had recovered their sight [ἀναβλέπω] and had come from the deepest darkness to behold the most radiant light" (*Virt.* 179).[49]

Seneca even composes a letter on blindness in which he draws the comparison at the outset between a clown who does not realize she is blind and each of us who are spiritually or metaphorically blind, hardened by sin and vice. He writes,

> You know Harpasté, my wife's female clown; she has remained in my house, a burden incurred from a legacy. I particularly disapprove of these freaks; whenever I wish to enjoy the quips of a clown, I am not compelled to hunt far; I can laugh at myself. Now this clown suddenly became blind. The story sounds incredible, but I assure you that it is true: she does not know that she is blind. She keeps asking her attendant to change her quarters; she says that her apartments are too dark. You can see clearly that that which makes us smile in the case of Harpasté happens to all the rest of us; nobody understands that he is himself greedy, or that he is covetous.... The evil that afflicts us is not external, it is within us, situated in our very vitals; for that reason we attain soundness with all the more difficulty, because we do not know that we are diseased. (*Ep.* 50.2–4)

As these examples demonstrate, to be physically blind is also to be metaphorically blind, whether the blindness is spiritual, moral, or mental. The expectation, then, in a physiognomically-conscious world is that a person who lacks eyesight is also deficient with respect to his metaphorical sight as well. It is this assumption that makes the final group—however rarely it occurs in the literature—so powerful and effective.

---

[49] See also *Fug.* 144.2, often translated "blind in understanding," a common concept that appears dozens of times in Philo.

The Blind Who See Clearly[50]

The final grouping above—the physically blind as ones who can see / understand the spiritual world clearly—is a rare category indeed. It is important that the reader understands that the blind prophet or the blind seer is *not* a frequent character in ancient literature. Nonetheless, it is present often enough and prominently enough in the ancient world to warrant our attention. It is also a category that draws a great deal of attention because it is a fascinating use of blindness as it shatters the conventional *topos* of the blind man. While many of the above elements of the blind *topos* still hold true for the blind-who-sees-clearly—the person is still pitiable, helpless, and often the object of punishment—the typical assumption of spiritual blindness is toppled. That is, in a few rare cases, the blind person is *not* spiritually blind as expected, but is to the contrary the one character who truly has insight into the spiritual world.

Lucian is typical of many in the ancient world who thought that the blind were able to judge clearly because they were unbiased by physical appearance (see Lucian, *Hermot.* 18–19). Likewise Aristotle says, "The blind have a better memory in that, being released from the contemplation of observable phenomena, their faculty of recollection is more powerful" (*Eth. eud.* 1248b.1–3). Similar to modern culture, the ancients believed that a loss of one of the senses was often compensated for by the other senses. Philo, for example, reflects this idea: "for they though deprived of one sense have the others more abundantly" (*Cher.* 58.6). It is not a far leap, then, for the Greeks on rare occasions to have attached spiritual insight or prophetic powers to the blind—though, again, even these characters were considered unfortunate and pitiable.

There are very few examples of what could be called a blind seer. Most famously, one recalls Teiresias. Though there are not many like him, Teiresias appears so often and prominently in Greek literature that it is often assumed that his blindness is typical of *all* prophets, even when there are so few examples other than him. We first meet Teiresias, the blind prophet from Thebes, in the *Odyssey* (*Od.* 11) when Odysseus goes to the underworld in order to seek his counsel. Teiresias foretells

[50] I prefer the terminology of the "blind-who-sees-clearly" to the conventional terminology of the "blind prophet" or "blind seer" because the category encompasses more than simply the prophet, and because there just are not many blind prophets in ancient literature in order to warrant the terminology.

Odysseus's journey home in vivid detail. In subsequent literature, Teiresias becomes the quintessential prophet, appearing in numerous works of literature, including a conversation with Oedipus in *Oedipus Tyrannus*, a work which we will examine in more detail below.[51]

After Teiresias, the examples of blind seers are rare and often obscure. The most prominent example after Teiresias is Phineus who, though blind, guides Jason and the Argonauts in the *Argonautica*. A lesser-known seer is Phormio. He is a fisherman from Erythrae who lost his eyesight but received a vision in a prophetic dream (Pausanias, *Descr.* 7.5.7). When his vision was heeded by some, it is reported that he regained his eyesight. Another lesser-known seer is Ophioneus. He is a Messenian seer who was blind at birth, and is said to practice his "divination", as it were, by "learning the facts relevant to each case, both private and public" and then divining the future from there.[52] We even find a strange story of Democritus, who sets out to blind himself in order to gain better spiritual insight: "A man worthy of reverence beyond all others and of the highest authority, of his own accord deprived himself of eyesight, because he believed that the thoughts and meditations of his mind in examining nature's laws would be more vivid and exact, if he should free them from the allurements of sight and the distractions offered by the eyes."[53]

Beyond these few examples, examples of blind prophets are almost non-existent. Nevertheless, Bernidaki-Aldous is typical of many classicists when she asserts that "Blindness... has been considered one of the most horrible punishments imposed by gods and mortals alike.... Whether the trespass... is voluntary or accidental, blindness is often the penalty. When the trespass is unintentional, however, the victim of so horrible a fate is often granted compensation in the form of prophetic or poetic insight."[54] Examples to support such a claim are indeed rare. Teiresias probably fits this category, since he is, according to one story, blinded for seeing a goddess naked. Since the incident was accidental on the part of Teiresias, Zeus grants him prophetic insight in order to compensate.

---

[51] For a thorough exegetical treatment of Teiresias in his many appearances in literature, see especially Bernidaki-Aldous, *Blindness in a Culture of Light*, 72ff, as well as R. G. A. Buxton, "Blindness and Limits: Sophokles and the Logic of Myth," *JHS* 100 (1980): 23ff.

[52] Pausanias, *Descr.* 4.10.6. He later regained his sight with a sharp pain in his head (4.12.10) before losing it a second time and returning to his birth condition (4.13.3).

[53] Aulus Gellius, *Noct. att.* 10.17.

[54] Bernidaki-Aldous, *Blindness in a Culture of Light*, 57.

One might also here think of the example of Euenius mentioned above. Blinded by the Apollonians for failing at his shepherding duties, the gods eventually grant him spiritual insight. Yet even these examples are rare and are easily the exception to the blind *topos*.

Worse yet, it is critical orthodoxy among scholars of Greek literature that Apollo employs blind oracles, particularly at Delphi. Bernidaki-Aldous is one of many scholars who make such a connection between blind oracles and blindness-as-insight; however, there is very little literary evidence that such an assumption is warranted. Bernidaki-Aldous, like so many authors, simply asserts the connection between the god of light and prophecy and the blind prophets who work for him without giving examples to warrant such a conclusion.[55]

The same trend holds true with the cousin of the blind seer, the blind poet. Here again, one finds a widely held assumption that poets are blind, yet very few examples can be found to substantiate the claim. As Teiresias is the prime examples of the blind seer, so Homer is the quintessential blind poet. Yet his blindness is as much legend as fact. Dio Chrysostom thinks that blindness is a prerequisite for all poets and is not unique to Homer: "Moreover, all the poets are blind, and they do not believe it possible for anyone to become a poet otherwise" (*Or.* 36.10.10), and Dio claims that all blind bards have contracted this blindness from Homer himself. Garland notes that blindness was a prerequisite for the bard, "at least in the popular imagination."[56] However, according to Garland's claim, we have record of only one other blind poet, a certain Xenokritos of Lokria, who is rather insignificant.[57]

Homer's blindness is beyond our ability to prove or disprove; it is simply the stuff of legend. The fact is that there are almost no cases of a real life blind poet in the Greek world that can be substantiated. Nevertheless, one does find a few *fictional* blind poets that reflect some of the popular imagination. For example, in *Od.* 8.63ff, one finds Demodokos in the court of the Phaeacians. He is described as the one "whom the Muse loved exceedingly, yet gave him both good and evil: she deprived him of eyesight, but bestowed upon him the gift of sweet song" (*Od.* 8.63–64). He is revered and given a separate table and a silver throne. Garland also infers that Phemios, the bard in the

[55] Bernidaki-Aldous, *Blindness in a Culture of Light*, 57.
[56] Garland, *Eye of the Beholder*, 33.
[57] See Garland, *Eye of the Beholder*, 33.

palace of Odysseus, is blind based on the fact that someone brings the lyre to him and places it his hands, though he is never actually directly said to be blind.[58] Finally, Sophocles is known to have written a play—*Thamyras*—that is no longer extant in which he has a blind poet, but since the play is lost, we can say very little about it except that this is one more example. Examples of the blind bard are as few as the examples of the blind seer.

It is interesting that Bernidaki-Aldous, who has done the most extensive work on the blind seer/poet, does not seem to be able to list many examples of blind poets or blind seers. In fact, her argument for the enduring nature of the *topos* of the blind poet or blind seer is that "the average Greek had surely consulted some blind seer or at least had known someone who had" and that "the average Greek must somewhere have seen some blind poet reciting Homer by heart."[59] These sorts of statements are hardly to be considered evidence though, and they clearly reflect both the assumptions on the part of the particular author as well as the assumed critical orthodoxy of much of scholarship without offering adequate support. It is clear that the blind seer or blind poet is a occasionally recurring character, but so few examples have survived in the literature that far too much is made of this category. In fact, the category is so rare that it is noteworthy that it occurs at all, and it is significant particularly insofar as it breaks the mold of the expected *topos* of the blind character. In a world that thinks physiognomically, the blind-who-sees-clearly would be an anomaly, not the expected norm. Let us look now at one example—the case of Oedipus in Sophocles's *Oedipus Tyrannus*—where the *topos* of the blind is used effectively by contrasting those who have or do not have literal and metaphorical sight.[60]

By far the most memorable use of the blindness imagery comes to us in Sophocles's famous *Oedipus* plays, and in particular *Oedipus Tyrannus*. It is in this play that Oedipus blinds himself. Early in the play, before Oedipus learns of the twisted and sordid tale that is about to unfold, he seeks the counsel of the blind prophet Teiresias in order to

---

[58] *Od.* 1.153ff. See Garland, *Eye of the Beholder*, 33–34 where Garland makes this case.

[59] Bernidaki-Aldous, *Blindness in a Culture of Light*, 6. In fact, many of her examples are blind poets from subsequent history, such as John Milton who wrote *Paradise Lost* and other works while blind. While an interesting example, Milton does nothing for building the case for the blind poet in ancient Greece.

[60] The best treatment of the blindness and sight imagery in this play is the second half of Bernidaki-Aldous's *Blindness in a Culture of Light*.

understand a Delphic oracle. Oedipus is a great riddle-solver—having bested the Sphinx—and is supposed to be the wise man that sees and understands everything clearly. Yet he cannot see the twisted details of his own life that will soon be his downfall. His vision, metaphorically, is quite impaired. The one whose vision is 20/20, however, is blind Teiresias. Teiresias is reluctant to tell the king what he sees, but both the audience and Oedipus know that the blind Teiresias is the one who "sees" clearly. In one instance, Teiresias says, "And I say, since you have reproached me with my blindness, that you have sight, but cannot see what trouble you are in..." (*Oed. tyr.* 412–13). Here we have a blind prophet who truly sees being contrasted with one who has physical sight but who understands nothing.

Eventually Oedipus learns of the meaning of the oracle, knowledge that crushes him and brings about his tragic downfall. Before he blinds himself, interestingly, he bids farewell to the light: "Oh, oh! All is now clear! O light, may I now look on you for the last time, I who am revealed as cursed in my birth, cursed in my marriage, cursed in my killing!" (*Oed. tyr.* 1182–85). The Chorus,[61] however, thinks death is better than blindness: "I do not know how I can say that you were well advised; for you would have been better dead than living blind" (*Oed. tyr.* 1367–68). The Chorus also expresses horror at the sight of Oedipus: "O grief terrible for men to see, O grief most terrible of any I have yet encountered! What madness has come upon you, unhappy one? Who is the god that with a leap longer than the longest has sprung upon your miserable fate? Ah, ah, unhappy one, I cannot even bear to look on you, though I wish to ask you many questions and to learn many answers and perceive many things; such is the horror you inspire in me" (*Oed. tyr.* 1297–1306).[62] In the case of Oedipus, blindness is to be understood as a tragic result and as a terrifying spectacle.

[61] Significantly for our purposes, according to Bernidaki-Aldous (*Blindness in a Culture of Light*, 96), the Chorus "represents the average, common, well-meaning citizen." If correct, we have here a valuable insight into the way the average ancient auditor would have thought of blindness—pitiable and gruesome are the characteristics found here.

[62] The Chorus is horrified, it would seem, not only at his circumstances but also at his grotesque appearance. The Chorus wishes to ask him questions, but is unable to do so because they cannot look at him—a condition that may point to the offensiveness of his circumstances but which certainly points to the grotesque appearance of the self-blinded king.

In the person of Oedipus, then, we find the most developed example of the blindness motif in which the physically blind have the best spiritual vision while the physically sighted are spiritually blind. We find a marked contrast between Teiresias and Oedipus—Teiresias is physically blind but spiritually sighted, while Oedipus is physically sighted but spiritual blind, though he certainly *thinks* he is spiritually sighted. Additionally, we also have the tragic self-blinding that is a result, at least in part, of Oedipus's inability to see truly. Interestingly, it is only *after* Oedipus blinds himself that he begins to see truly what is going on in his world. He makes his physical condition match his spiritual condition—blindness. Subsequently, his spiritual sight begins to heal. Sophocles here has employed the *topos* of blindness but has masterfully toppled the expected character types, and it is this toppling of the expectations of the audience that makes the play so powerful and compelling.

Conclusion

As we have seen in this chapter, the eyes are the most important physiognomic marker. It is the eye that most clearly indicates the character of the individual, and it is difficult to disguise the true nature of the eye. In that same vein, blindness would indicate to a physiognomically-conscious audience that not only is the physical eyesight absent, but also the moral and spiritual sight as well. To be blind would indicate to many that the person is pitiable beyond measure, under the oppression of a deity, and is morally deficient. Very occasionally a blind character may possess prophetic insight, but such a case is a small minority and an exception that proves the rule. Given this *topos* of blindness in the Greco-Roman world, we now turn attention to the biblical text where blindness and eyesight are used in very similar ways.

CHAPTER FOUR

PHYSIOGNOMY AND BLINDNESS IN THE OLD TESTAMENT AND SECOND TEMPLE JUDAISM

The previous two chapters explored physiognomics, especially concerning the eyes, as an established practice in the Greco-Roman world. The early Christians were very much a part of that culture, and the New Testament grew up in conversation with that world. Likewise, the early Christians were deeply steeped in the Old Testament and Jewish culture, and the New Testament grows up in conversation with that tradition as well. For that reason, it is significant to this project that we examine what presence physiognomics had in the Jewish milieu, especially concerning blindness. That is the goal of this chapter.

The first and most obvious question is that if physiognomy as a pseudo-science is the invention of the Greeks as was asserted in chapter two, can one properly read the Jewish texts in light of the those practices? This chapter begins by addressing that concern. Next, having established the legitimacy of reading the Old Testament with an eye toward physical markers, this chapter will explore several examples of physiognomy in practice. This chapter will treat two examples in detail and then offer suggestions for how other examples might be read. Finally, this chapter will especially concern itself with eyes and blindness specifically. Several prominent examples of blindness emerge, whether as a result of old age, punishment, or an accident. This chapter contends that such examples of blindness imply a second, figurative layer of meaning that adds depth that is often missed by biblical interpreters.

Linking Physiognomy to the Old Testament

Can we rightly read the Old Testament in light of physiognomic conventions, or would such a reading be anachronistic? It is the contention of this chapter that the use of the physical body to indicate one's character is very much practiced in the Hebrew Bible. While the Greeks likely invented physiognomics as an organized, scientific discipline, the practice of reading the body was widespread throughout the cultures of Mesopotamia as well. The evidence, though sparsely preserved, is sufficient.

The reader will recall that Cicero (*Tusc.* 4.37.80) names Zopyrus, a Syrian magician, as the first to practice physiognomy in Athens by physiognomizing Socrates. If Cicero is to be believed, then we know that the study of the signs of the body was in practice at least among Israel's nearest northern neighbor. Barton likewise notes that the Greeks were not the first people to engage in physiognomics. In fact, claims Barton, the practice can be found throughout Mesopotamia from the second millennium B.C.E. forward, though it is usually used not to read one's character but to predict one's future in ways similar to astrology.[1] Nevertheless, it is significant for understanding the Old Testament that the Mesopotamian cultures were already accustomed to thinking in terms of bodily markers.

A couple of sources place some form of physiognomics in Babylon as well, the most plausible place for the Israelites to gain direct exposure.[2] Take for example the work of Kraus,[3] who indexes works from Babylon and in Akkadian that in most cases long predate the earliest handbooks we have in the Greek world. Kraus indexes texts ranging from Nineveh to Assur to Ur to Babylon, an indication that this practice was widespread across the Fertile Crescent. Unlike Ps-Aristotle, these Babylonian texts on physiognomy are not full-scale handbooks that have survived antiquity, but enough has survived to definitively demonstrate that the cultures of the Ancient Near East were no strangers to the practice of reading the signs of the body.

A final source worth noting is a Syriac document on physiognomics translated by Furlani.[4] This tractate gives us one more indication of the presence of the study of physiognomics in the cultures surrounding Palestine. Furlani notes that this treatise does not bear any resemblance

---

[1] Tamsyn S. Barton, *Power and Knowledge: Astrology, Physiognomics, and Medicine Under the Roman Empire* (Ann Arbor: University of Michigan Press, 1994), 100. See also A. MacC. Armstrong, "The Methods of the Greek Physiognomists," *GR* 5 (1958): 52, who makes essentially the same claim. While Barton lists several examples of Mesopotamian physiognomy, the best source is a collection of these fragments found in J. Bottéro, "Symptômes, signes, écritures," in *Divination et rationalité* (ed. J.-P. Vernant; Paris: Éditions du Seuil, 1974), 70–199.

[2] For such an assertion among biblical scholarship, see Mikeal C. Parsons, *Body and Character in Luke and Acts: The Subversion of Physiognomy in Early Christianity* (Grand Rapids: Baker Academic Press, 2006), 39.

[3] Fritz Rudolf Kraus, *Die Physiognomischen Omina Der Babylonier* (Leipzig: J. C. Hinrichs Buchhandlung, 1935). See also Kraus, *Texte zur babylonischen Physiognomatik* (Berlin: E. F. Weidner, 1939), where he reproduces images of the Babylonian texts.

[4] Giuseppe Furlani, "A Short Physiognomic Treatise in the Syriac Language," *JAOS* 39 (1919): 289–294.

to the four extant Greek handbooks. It does bear slight resemblance to a fragmentary text falsely attributed to Polemo. Furlani proposes that the Syraic tract predates this Ps-Polemo fragment, although it is impossible to say by how long. Thus while we cannot use this Syriac manuscript to say that physiognomics was definitely in practice during the period of the Old Testament, it does give us an indication of yet another non-Greek occurrence of the practice of physiognomics in the Mediterranean world.

Given the number of places in the regions surrounding Israel in which we can now place the practice of physiognomics, we can safely conclude that such practice is likely to be found in the culture and writings of ancient Israel and Judah as well. The study of the body for the purpose of understanding character is a study that is ancient indeed. One need not propose any sort of direct influence; it is sufficient to conclude that if other Mesopotamian cultures believed that character was perceivable through the body, ancient Israel may well have thought in similar terms and can be expected to reflect many of the same thought patterns and assumptions about the world. Israel does not exist in a vacuum, and it in many ways partakes in and shares the worldview of the surrounding cultures.

Examples of Physiognomy in the Old Testament and Second Temple Judaism

Examples of possible physiognomy scenes in the Old Testament are numerous, and references to various parts of the body are littered throughout the Hebrew Bible in nearly every genre. Such scenes are especially common in, though by no means limited to, the Deuteronomistic History. While an exhaustive exegesis of each potential scene is not possible, we will explore a few. Specifically, we will look in detail at two scenes in which an awareness of physiognomics enhances the reading of the text. First, we will look at the story of Ehud, the left-handed judge. Second, we will examine Israel's first king, the tall and handsome Saul. In the case of Ehud, the expected physiognomics hold true perfectly. In the case of Saul, the physical description is something of a red herring, a way of leading the reader to expect one thing only to find exactly the opposite. After exploring these two examples in some detail as test cases, we will then offer some brief suggestions as to how a physiognomic reading might enhance our interpretation of several other passages. Let us begin with Ehud.

Ehud, the Left-Handed Benjaminite

The story of Ehud (Judg 3:12–30) is the first narrated story of the judges, following the brief mention of Othniel.[5] As the story begins, God has raised up Eglon of Moab as oppressor of Israel because Israel has "done what is evil in the sight of the LORD" (3:12). When the people repented, God raised up a deliver, introduced as "Ehud son of Gera, the Benjaminite, a left-handed man" (3:15). He will deliver tribute to Eglon, but first he makes a short sword or dagger and conceals it under his clothing by attaching it to his right thigh. As he journeys to pay the tribute, the narrator tells us that "Eglon was a very fat man" (3:17). After paying the tribute, Ehud sends away those who traveled with him and returns to the king with a message: "I have a secret thing for you, O King" (3:19). The King, eager to hear a secret word, orders Ehud to be silent, dismisses his guards, and grants Ehud a private meeting. During this meeting, Ehud reveals the secret—the dagger—and thrusts it into the belly of the king until the fat swallows the weapon to its hilt. Locking the doors, Ehud makes a stealthy escape. The murdered king lies undiscovered for some time as his guards assume that he is using the bathroom. By the time they discover the king, Ehud has escaped and mustered an army. The Israelites are delivered and Moab is defeated.

The Ehud story is certainly among the most entertaining of biblical stories as it is a story filled with humor, irony, and mockery of enemies. The story is so entertaining to the modern reader that it has prompted one biblical scholar to draw parallels between the Ehud story and a modern wild west shootout movie![6] A straightforward reading of the text, even without a knowledge of physiognomics, does make sense

[5] For commentaries on Judges, see especially the following: Robert G. Boling, *Judges* (AB 6A; Garden City, NY: Doubleday, 1975); Victor H. Matthews, *Judges and Ruth* (New Cambridge Bible Commentary; Cambridge: Cambridge University Press, 2004); Barnabas, Lindars, *Judges 1–5: A New Translation and Commentary* (Edinburgh, Scotland: T&T Clark, 1995); A. D. H. Mayes, *Judges* (OTG; Sheffield: JSOT Press, 1985); George Foote Moore, *A Critical and Exegetical Commentary on Judges* (ICC; New York: Schribner's Sons, 1903); Robert Polzin, *Moses and the Deuteronomist: A Literary Study of the Deuteronomic History* (New York: Seabury Press, 1980); Tammi J. Schneider, *Judges* (Berit Olam: Studies in Hebrew Narrative and Poetry; Collegeville, Minn: Liturgical Press, 1985); J. Alberto Soggin, *Judges: A Commentary* (OTL; Philadelphia: Westminster Press, 1981); Barry G. Webb, *The Book of Judges: An Integrated Reading* (JSOTSup 46; Sheffield: JSOT Press, 1987.

[6] Eric S. Christenson, "A Fistful of Shekels: Scrutinizing Ehud's Entertaining Violence (Judges 3:12–30)," *BibInt* 11 (2003): 53–78.

of the story—Ehud is left-handed, thus he can smuggle a dagger on his right thigh; Eglon is fat, thus his fat folds can swallow the hilt of the dagger. The physiognomic overtones, however, offer a deeper level of understanding, a level of understanding that is rarely noticed by those who read this text. It is those overtones that we wish to tease out here—what would an ancient auditor steeped in a physiognomic worldview have heard in this text's descriptions of the two main characters in addition to the straightforward reading?

Ehud is introduced as a left-handed Benjaminite.[7] "Left-handed" in this text is literally "restricted in the right hand."[8] Some commentators take that reference to mean that Ehud had a physical handicap in his right hand,[9] but to do so is to make non-sense of the story since a crippled right hand would give away his dominant left hand that will draw a hidden weapon from his right thigh. If he is handicapped, the secret weapon would be compromised and obvious. It is better to take the reference as a roundabout way of saying merely "left-handed." In addition, "Benjaminite" literally means "son of the right hand."[10] There is definite irony involved in having a left-handed son of the right hand or literally a "son of the right hand who is restricted in the right hand." The pun is a feature of the text that nearly every commentator notices.[11]

Yet the description would imply far more than an ironic twist to the ancient audience. To a physiognomically-conscious hearer, his character would be immediately clear from the description. Most commentators on this passage make note that to be left-handed indicates that Ehud will be underhanded, deceitful, cunning, and crafty.[12] Sternberg, for

[7] It may well be the case that "Benjaminite" is a kind of ethnographical physiognomy that is peculiar to the Old Testament. Certainly the Benjaminites will develop a seedy reputation, a reputation that spoils Saul in many ways as we shall see in the next section. At this point in Judges though, the Benjaminites have not behaved all that offensively, thus we must be cautious in invoking the stereotype. It is notable though that in 20:16, Benjamin has 700 left-handed soldiers experienced with the sling that are virtually unbeatable.

[8] Hebrew: אִטֵּר יַד־יְמִינוֹ.

[9] See for example Moore, *Judges*, 93; Schneider, *Judges*, 49; and Soggin, *Judges*, 50.

[10] Hebrew: בֶּן־הַיְמִינִי.

[11] For example, see Boling, *Judges*, 86; Schneider, *Judges*, 49; Soggin, *Judges*, 50; however, see also Lindars, *Judges 1–5*, 141, who argues that such a reading is "over-interpretation."

[12] For example, see Boling, *Judges*, 88; Lindars, *Judges 1–5*, 139; Matthews, *Judges and Ruth*, 60; Mayes, *Judges*, 20; Schneider, *Judges*, 50; and Webb, *The Book of Judges*, 131.

example, notes that there are "cultural associations of right vs. left" and that to have a left-handed judge is a contradiction, since one does not expect a "sinister deliverer."[13] Polzin calls Ehud "repugnant, deceitful, and cruel."[14] Yet neither commentator explains where those associations come from and why it is that to be left-handed implies that one is sinister.

While physiognomic handbooks do not specifically address being left-handed, there are widespread cultural assumptions about right and left as representing male and female, respectively.[15] Greek sources attest to a very old belief that the right side of the male is more developed and the left side of the female is more developed. Aristotle gives witness to these traditions that long predate him when he explores various theories on how gender is determined (*Gen. An.* 763b). According to one theory, gender is determined based on whether the sperm comes from the right testicle to create male offspring or the left to create female. Furthermore, a male child is carried on the right side of the womb while a female child is carried on the left side.[16] Aristotle attributes this theory to a certain Anaxagoras and other "physiologers." Later, he even recounts the theory of a certain Leophanes who believed one could select the gender of his offspring by "tying off" the undesired testicle, though Aristotle rejects this possibility (*Gen. An.* 765a). While Aristotle makes a different case for how gender is determined, the fact that he spends so much time addressing the notions of right and left gives witness to the popularity of such theories in the ancient culture.

The left side, then, is associated with the female. It would then follow that the powerful male should be right-handed. Yahweh, in fact, shows great strength and power in his right hand, and it is said that Yahweh destroys things with his mighty right hand.[17] Yet Ehud is left-handed. In a physiognomically-conscious world, to be left-handed is to be associated with feminine characteristics, and one of the most prominent feminine characteristics among the physiognomists is that females are cunning,

---

[13] Meir Sternberg, *The Poetics of Biblical Narrative: Ideological Literature and the Drama of Reading* (Bloomington, Ind: Indiana University Press, 1985), 332.

[14] Robert Polzin, *Moses and the Deuteronomist: A Literary Study of the Deuteronomic History* (New York: Seabury Press, 1980), 160.

[15] For a good discussion of right and left as male and female, see Geneva Misener, "Loxus, Physician and Physiognomist," *CP* 18 (1923): 15–20.

[16] Cf. Galen in Oribasius *Incerta* 22.3.18, where Galen is reported to have said that a male child gestates on the right side of the womb.

[17] See, for example, Exod 15:6 and 12, as well as Ps 20:6 and 89:13.

deceptive, and manipulative. Ps-Aristotle (810a) describes the panther in this way, which is the animal most typical of the female type. The panther's primary character trait, and thus the woman's primary trait, is "petty, thieving, and, generally speaking, deceitful." He also later characterizes the female sex as "scoundrels." The male is powerful, preferring a straightforward attack; but the female is wily.

Ehud certainly behaves in keeping with his deceitful characterization. He makes a number of left-handed moves, far more than the obvious drawing of a blade from the right thigh. Ehud concocts a left-handed scheme and executes it flawlessly. He not only crafts a blade, but he is crafty enough to smuggle it into the king's presence undetected. He is then clever enough to arrange a private meeting, and he does so with a cunning wordplay. He tells Eglon "I have a secret *thing* for you" (3:19), and the word translated "thing" is ambiguous. It could mean "thing" or it could mean "word" or "message." Eglon certainly expects a secret *message*, but Ehud has in mind a very different secret. Ehud then shifts the phrase in private, calling it "a thing from God for you" (3:20). With his left hand Ehud draws his "secret thing" from his right thigh, and the left-handed plot is executed. Ehud then makes a clever cover-up and escape, also a left-handed maneuver, as he somehow makes a stealthy escape out the back. Certainly Ehud's story is left-handed from beginning to end.[18]

Yet Ehud is not the only one given a physical description in this text. King Eglon is twice called fat in the text (3:17, 22), once when the tribute is delivered and once when the dagger is delivered. Notice that his troops are also fat, and they are going to meet the same fate at their fat king.[19] Many commentators also take note of Eglon's name, which is likely a derivative of the Hebrew "*egel*" (עֵגֶל) meaning calf, and it may be a diminutive form meaning "little calf."[20] Lindars, like many commentators, suggests that the name could be symbolic, implying that Eglon is the calf to be slaughtered as a sacrifice.

---

[18] One might also helpfully compare Ehud's his shrewd behavior with that of Judith, a woman who also plays an underhanded trick on an enemy in order to set up an assassination (see especially Judith 12–13). Judith, as a woman, behaves as the cunning and wily woman should; Ehud, being male, carries the same character traits by being labeled left-handed.

[19] 3:29—the term שָׁמֵן has a double meaning, both as "fat" or as "strong, robust."

[20] One scholar who makes this case is Barnabas Lindars, *Judges 1–5: A New Translation and Commentary* (Edinburgh, Scotland: T&T Clark, 1995), 137, though some attention to Eglon's name is present in nearly every standard commentary on Judges.

While the description of Eglon as fat is necessary for the plot of the story—his fat has to swallow the dagger and plenty of "dirt" must pour out—and while his name may carry sacrificial overtones, there is also a physiognomic layer to this story. In this case, to be fat is an indication of greed.[21] The conclusion is reasonable enough—one becomes fat, it is presumed, by overindulgence, and overindulgence is a luxury not afforded to the poor. It is the rich man who is fat, and the rich are greedy, so the logic goes. Thus the reader is not surprised by the hefty belly of the Moabite king, and the greed of Eglon actually permits the scheme to succeed. Not only is the king meeting an emissary carrying tribute, Eglon is also easily intrigued by the promise of a secret. Thus when Ehud says, "I have a secret thing for you," it is Eglon's greed that raises his curiosity. He is greedy for a secret message, greedy for some word from the divine. He immediately cries out "Silence!" to Ehud until Eglon can dismiss the guards and keep the secret all to himself. Thus, Eglon's greed, characterized by his fatness, falls victim to Ehud's underhanded trick, characterized by his left-handedness.

It could also be the case that the "filth" or "dirt"[22] that comes out of his body also has physiognomic overtones. Eglon is stabbed and the "dirt" that pours forth has an odor that causes the guards to think he is going to the bathroom and causes them to wait, as the text says, "until they were embarrassed" (3:25). Physiognomically speaking, now his true inner self has been exposed in a very literal way, and it is simply described as "dirt." To recognize that the innards of Eglon are filthy and smelly would, to a physiognomically-conscious audience, also indicate that his moral character is rotten as well.

Thus we have in the story of left-handed Ehud and fat Eglon an example of physiognomics very much at work in the characterization of the hero and villain, adding an often missed layer of meaning to the story. Ehud and Eglon live up to the physiognomic expectations perfectly. We now turn to a story that does the opposite.

---

[21] Barry G. Webb, *The Book of Judges: An Integrated Reading* (JSOTSup 46; Sheffield: JSOT Press, 1987), 129 is one scholar who notices that the fatness symbolizes Eglon's greed, though he offers no support for that assertion.

[22] Much has been made of the strange term here translated as "dirt." For a good exploration of the meaning of this term, see Michael L. Barré, "The Meaning of *pršdn* in Judges 3:22," *VT* 41 (1991): 1–11.

Saul, Head and Shoulders Above All Others

> There was a man of Benjamin whose name was Kish son of Abiel son of Zeror son of Becorath son of Aphiah, a Benjaminite, a man of wealth. He had a son whose name was Saul, a handsome young man. There was not a man among the people of Israel more handsome than he; he stood head and shoulders above everyone else. (1 Sam 9:1–2)

> When he took his stand among the people, he was head and shoulders taller than any of them. (1 Sam 10:23)

Perhaps the most common way of understanding the kingship of Saul in the history of interpretation is to understand him as something of a tragic figure, not unlike the tragic heroes of Greek dramas or even of Shakespeare. The overwhelming mass of scholarly opinion mirrors that of David Gunn, who writes, "Saul is a model of human failure; he is also a figure of tragedy, a figure who prompts sorrow."[23] That is to say, Saul is typically viewed as a potentially good king who has every chance to succeed, but because of a series of egregious mistakes the kingdom is torn from him and given to David. To the contrary, we will suggest that a physiognomic consciousness would lead an audience to different conclusions. Namely, Saul's physical appearance would lead the reader to expect Saul to be a great king, a brave warrior, and a successful leader. Instead, Saul turns out to be exactly the opposite in every way, and he is a poor choice to be king from the very beginning.[24] In

[23] David Gunn, *The Fate of King Saul* (Sheffield: JSOT Press, 1984), 27. See also P. Kyle McCarter, *I Samuel* (AB 8; Garden City, NY: Doubleday, 1980), 172; Mary J. Evans, *1 and 2 Samuel* (NIBCOT; Peabody, Mass.: Hendrickson, 2000), 45–46; and Walter Brueggemann, *First and Second Samuel* (IBC; Louisville: John Knox, 1990), 70.

[24] That Saul is a false start for the monarchy is obvious. That Saul is a bad king from the very beginning, however, and perhaps even set up by Yahweh and/or Samuel to fail, is a more narrowly held position. For others who hold that position as I do, and for those who treat the downfall of Saul, see the following: Kenneth Cohen, "King Saul: A Bungler from the Beginning," *BRev* 10 (1994): 34–39, 56–57; Howard Cooper, "'Too Tall by Half'—King Saul and Tragedy in the Hebrew Bible," *JPJ* 9 (November 1997): 5–22; Sam Dragga, "In the Shadow of the Judges: The Failure of Saul," *JSOT* 38 (June 1987): 39–46; Kyle Eslinger, *Kingship of God in Crisis* (Sheffield: Almond, 1985); Amos Frisch, "'For I Feared the People and I Yielded to Them'—Is Saul's Guilt Attenuated or Intensified?" *ZAW* 108 (1996): 98–104; Daniel Hawk, "Saul as Sacrifice: The Tragedy of Israel's First Monarch," *BRev* 2 (December 1996): 20–25, 56; Philips Long, *The Reign and Rejection of King Saul: A Case for Literary and Theological Coherence* (Atlanta: Scholars Press, 1989); and Robert Polzin, *Samuel and the Deuteronomist* (Bloomington: Indiana University Press, 1989). See also Robert D. Bergen, *1, 2 Samuel* (NAC 7; Nashville: Broadman and Holman Publishers, 1996), 121, who says that Saul's height is a unique descriptor among Israelites, but it is common among Israel's enemies, thus making this descriptor a subtle indictment of Saul from the very beginning.

this way, the narrator uses what I will call "literary misdirection"—the reader is led to think one thing about Saul only to find out exactly the opposite is true.

In the ancient world, a great king, a valiant warrior, or a noble leader is often characterized by noteworthy height and beauty. The Greek ideal king, who is expected to have among other things a physically superior body, is an ideal that dates back at least as early at the 4th century B.C.E.[25] One might assume that other Mediterranean cultures shared similar expectations of the king as well. One might recall Plutarch's description of Demetrius quoted in the second chapter, in which Demetrius is described as "a tall man, but he has features of rare and astonishing beauty, so that no painter or sculptor ever achieved a likeness of him" (*Demetr.* 2.2). It was also argued in the second chapter that Demetrius, like Saul, is given a description to which he fails to live up.

Concerning warriors and leaders, one might think of the *Iliad*. Aias (Ajax) is described as "huge Aias, the bulwark of the Achaeans" (*Il.* 7.211), only a sentence after Ares, god of war, is described as huge also. Aias is also said to "walk with long strides of his feet beneath him" (*Il.* 7.212). The sheer size of Aias strikes fear into the hearts of his enemies and implies that he is a mighty warrior. In a similar way, Achilles is tall and beautiful. When Priam, a noble king himself, comes to Achilles to beg for the body of Hector, the two men share a meal. During that meal, Priam takes note of the appearance of Achilles, and Homer says that Priam "did marvel at Achilles, how tall and how fair; for he was like the gods to look upon" (*Il.* 24.631–32). Achilles' character was diagnosed by a good and noble king, and the height and beauty of Achilles—the greatest of the Greek warriors by far—were the attributes most notable.

When the reader of 1 Samuel first meets Saul, his imposing physical presence is supposed to have the same effect as the descriptions of Aias or Achilles—Saul's height and beauty proclaim to anyone with eyes to see that he is the ideal king and the solution to the problems of the Israelites.[26] Those implications, of course, could not be more mistaken.

---

[25] See W. Jeffrey Tatum, "The Regal Image in Plutarch's Lives," *JHS* 116 (1996): 140.

[26] Among the commentary tradition, see especially the following: McCarter, *I Samuel*, 172 who writes that the beauty of Saul "is to be interpreted as a physical symptom of special divine favor;" Ralph Klein, *1 Samuel* (WBC 10; Waco: Word, 1983), 86; and David Jobling, *1 Samuel* (Berit Olam; Collegville, Minn.: Liturgical Press, 1998), 67.

Saul is clearly unfit to be king even from the very beginning, and once he becomes king he proves to be inept in almost every conceivable way. There is far more at work here than the often noted tension in the Deuteronomistic History between pro-monarchy and anti-monarchy. There is a clear anti-Saul polemic, and it begins with his seemingly positive description. Throughout Saul's narrative—and especially noteworthy, *prior to* his major sins that prompt the rebuking judgment from Samuel—he proves to be a pathetic king, a terrible leader, and utterly inept on the battlefield. Saul is indecisive and seemingly incapable of sound judgment. His one notable weapon—his spear—is mentioned on numerous occasions, always in a failure to hit the desired target (1 Sam 18:10–11; 19:9–10; 20:33) or laying idly by his head while he sleeps (1 Sam 26:7). He is unable to hold favorable military positions such as hilltops. In short, Saul is inept as king and a poor excuse for a warrior, exactly the opposite of what his description implies. Let us explore the narrative of 1 Samuel and highlight places where this is particularly clear.

We begin with Saul's seemingly positive introduction. 1 Samuel 8 narrates the demand for a king and Yahweh's acquiescence to that demand, noting especially that "they have not rejected you, but they have rejected me from being king over them" (8:7). Chapter 8 ends with Yahweh's order to Samuel to select a king, and 9:1 begins by introducing Saul. At first glance, this introduction seems innocent enough. We find a genealogical list of otherwise unknown forefathers, and we find a man who is taller and better looking that the rest of the people. This *seems* like the makings of any good hero story. Yet the astute reader of the Hebrew Bible knows that there is probably more at work than meets the eye.

First and most notably, even before Saul's physical description is given, his introduction is marred by his tribal heritage—Saul is a Benjaminite! Subtly missed in Saul's description, his tribal status serves as a kind of ethnographical physiognomy as the Benjaminites have a purely negative reputation. Any reader familiar with the chaos that ends the book of Judges only a few pages prior in the Deuteronomistic History cannot help but recoil uncomfortably at this introduction. The tribe of Benjamin is the tribe that was nearly erased from the map as punishment for their atrocious sins narrated in Judg 19. A traveling Levite stops off in the land of Benjamin to rest for the night, rather than seeking hospital[illegible]ng foreigners (Judg 19:15). During the night the perverse Benjam[illegible] demand that he be sent outside so that they could rape him—the Benjaminites have degenerated to the days of Sodom. The visitor sends out his concubine in his place. She is raped to the point of death and left at the doorstep. The Levite cuts up her body and sends the pieces to the corners of the kingdom, demanding that Benjamin be punished. The tribe is consequently routed, and if not for the theft of virgins from other cities, Benjamin would have been exterminated forever. The reader will also take note that the location of these atrocities was the city of Gibeah, the ancestral home of Saul. Could there be a poorer choice for king than to choose one from among the degenerate Sodom-like tribe that caused a civil war? Surely a Benjaminite cannot be expected to *unite* the people, nor can a Benjaminite be a suitable embodiment of the best Israel has to offer. His ethnographical heritage provides a key to understanding his physical description.

A simple country boy in search of some lost donkeys, Saul unwittingly stumbles upon a kingdom that he receives only reluctantly. The first action and first words of a character in biblical narrative are crucial to characterization. Thus it is noteworthy that Saul's initial quest of locating runaway animals is a wholesale failure. Saul's first act in the narrative is his inability to accomplish a simple task, a trait that will define his kingship. Alter points out that Saul's first line is telling—"Come, let us turn back..." (9:5). Saul's doubt is highlighted here, and the fact that his servant must advise him repeatedly is an indication of Saul's *lack* of leadership, in direct contrast to what his physical features might imply.[27] Thus in the first story of Saul's anointing as king, he is characterized as a failure, uncertain, and easily directed by others—certainly not the expected traits of the tall and handsome warlord king.

Following the story of Saul's private anointing to which only he and Samuel are privy, one reads the story of the public coronation. Saul's cowardly character is underscored vividly in this scene. For the public selection of the king, Samuel assembles the people at Mitzpah. It must not escape notice that Mitzpah is the site where the nation was first mustered against Benjamin in Judg 20. The first trip to Mitzpah was for the purpose of annihilating a despicable tribe from their midst; this most recent assembly was for the purpose of recognizing a king from

[27] Robert Alter, *The David Story: A Translation with Commentary of 1 and 2 Samuel* (New York: W. W. Norton & Company, 1999), 47. Alter (46) also makes the following helpful observation: "Saul's looming size, together with his good looks, seems to be an outward token of his capacity for leadership, but as the story unfolds with David displacing Saul, his physical stature becomes associated with a basic human misperception of what constitutes fitness to command."

the same unrepentant tribe. Numerous scholars have noticed the unusual method of choosing the king by lot.[28] Such a method of choosing occurs only two other times—the identification of Achan in Joshua 7 and the identification of Jonathan as the unauthorized warrior who attacks the Philistines (1 Sam 14:38–44). The other occurrences of this method, then, are in order to isolate a sinner who will be put to death; this occurrence is in order to isolate the unfortunate soul who must succeed Yahweh as Israel's king. Thus we have Yahweh usurping the method for identifying criminals in order to choose a king, a lottery that no one would want to win. Once the lot has fallen, all that remains is to locate the lucky winner, Saul of Gibeah. After extensive searching, however, Saul could not be found. Yahweh himself must intervene in order to find the chosen one. Saul is hiding among the baggage. After he is dragged out of hiding and into the public forum, it is again noted that Saul "was head and shoulder taller than any of them" (10:23), a line that is perhaps best read tongue-in-cheek. Clearly, the new king is reluctant at best and almost certainly cowardly as demonstrated by his behavior, yet once again the narrative asserts his physical presence as if to subvert the implied character traits one more time.

As 1 Sam 10 ends, we are left uncertain as to the future of either Saul or the kingship. Saul is unproven, especially as the military king for which the people cry out. He does not do what a king should do, such as establish a capital or gather an army; rather, he goes home and returns to the field as if nothing has happened. Chapter 11 provides the occasion for Saul to prove his legitimacy as king and as military champion. Generally, most readers understand the battle against the Ammonites as Saul's one shining moment, his one true success prior to his fall and rejection by Yahweh.[29] Yet the city which he rescues is Jabesh-Gilead, and this is not the first time the city has appeared in the narrative. She is the city in the end of Judges that fails to support the destruction of Benjamin. Consequently, Jabesh-Gilead was destroyed herself, except for a few hundred maidens who were used to repopulate Benjamin. As the calendar turns, the events at the end of Judges are

[28] See especially such different commentators as Alter, *The David Story*, 58, Polzin, *Samuel and the Deuteronomist*, 103–04, and McCarter, *I Samuel*, 196.

[29] One example of this standard opinion is Klein, *1 Samuel*, 109, who writes, "This pericope presents one of the oldest and most positive pictures of Saul. In a time of emergency he acted like one of the savior-judges of the confederacy and rallied all Israel to deliver Jabesh-Gilead. Gifted with the spirit, he met the crisis of the moment; surely God was with him.... He was a king in the best sense of the word."

not all that far removed from the events of Saul. In fact, the proximity of these two events has led at least one scholar to speculate about the possibility that Saul is a son or grandson of a stolen Jabesh-Gileadite maiden.[30] No hard literary evidence exists to prove such a claim, but given Saul's connection to Judges already (and the additional feature in this text that he summons the troops by cutting up an oxen reminiscent of the Levite's summons in Judges), such a reading seems plausible. If so, it would cast a shadow over the only clear military success of Saul's kingship, as the battle would appear to be fought out of familial ties rather than by command of Yahweh.

To complete the picture of Saul as an inept leader and as a military failure, a brief recounting of Saul's military blunders is in order. 1 Sam 13 contrasts the military prowess of Jonathan, who attacks a Philistine garrison in a one-man raid, with the ineptitude of Saul. Saul's relatively small force flees the hill country (a position that is high ground and readily defensible) and proceeds to hide in caves, holes in the rocks, tombs, and cisterns (13:6). Saul's leadership fails to hold the forces together. While Jonathan is boldly attacking the enemy, Saul is indecisively agonizing over what to do, conducting a divine inquiry that he does not even finish (14:19).

In 1 Sam 15, Saul defeats the Amalekites, but fails to devote everything to destruction, a move that results in his final rejection as king. By 1 Sam 17, David has been chosen as Saul's replacement and Saul is a lame duck. The Goliath story, though certainly a hero story for David, serves also to accentuate further Saul's military failures. Saul the handsome king who stands head and shoulders above the rest should be Israel's giant, the champion of Israel that faces the mighty Goliath, yet Saul is fearful like the rest of the soldiers (17:11). In an ironic turn, the Benjaminites are said to be notoriously accurate with a sling (see Judg 20:16). Thus, Saul the tall forgoes battle with the giant, letting David go in his place, and David gains the victory using the very weapon with which Saul should allegedly have proficiency. Once again, Saul's military ability is called into question.

Saul's lack of skill with the spear does not escape the notice of even the casual reader of the text. Twice Saul attempts to spear David, both times missing. In 18:10–11, Saul tries to impale David, and on this occasion Saul misses *twice*. In 19:8–10, Saul attempts again, and this

---

[30] Cohen, "Bungler," 37.

time manages to impale only the wall while David escapes. In 20:33 Saul attempts to spear his own son. This time there is no account of the target needing to elude the spear. It seems to be a foregone conclusion that Saul will miss. He always misses. In fact, we have no account of Saul ever making a kill, not even in battle. The only other appearance of Saul's spear is in 26:7. Here Saul is pursuing David but has fallen asleep. David and Abishai instead find Saul, asleep and with his spear stuck in the ground beside his head. At this moment, Saul could have been killed by the very weapon with which he sought to kill David on multiple occasions. Instead, David steals the spear peacefully.

When reading the life of Saul, then, the clear conclusion is that he is exactly the opposite of what his physical description implies. While he *should* be a valiant warrior, a successful king, and a brave military champion, he turns out to be a coward, an indecisive follower rather than a leader, and a poor choice for a king. The narrative has employed a king of literary misdirection—using the physical description to imply one thing about Saul, only to topple those expectations with the narrative.[31]

Other Examples

There are a number of other examples in which the ancient reader may have heard physiognomic overtones that enhanced the meaning of the text. Here we will list many of those examples and offer some brief suggestions as to what an ancient auditor might have heard in those descriptions. For simplicity's sake the examples are arranged in canonical order, with non-canonical Jewish texts appearing last.

Esau. Esau is given two physical descriptors. At his birth, Esau is described as "red, all his body like a hairy mantle" (Gen 25:25). To be ruddy can indicate a number of things (David is one of several in the OT who also carries this description), perhaps most importantly indicating a fierce temperament. According the Ps-Aristotle, the "passionate man" or angry/hot-tempered man (θυμώδους) is characterized as "sanguine and ruddy" (808a). Likewise, it is said that "the growth of the hair is considerable and starts low down" (808a). Later in the

[31] Notably, the narrative makes this point clear again with the choosing of David when Samuel is told by God, "Do not look on his appearance or on the height of his stature, because I have rejected him; for the LORD does not see as mortals see; they look on the outward appearance, but the LORD looks on the heart" (1 Sam 16:7).

handbook, Ps-Aristotle states that "those who have a ruddy colour about the breast are prone to ill temper: this is appropriate to that affection, for when men are enraged the parts about the chest burn" (812a). A hot temper, then, is linked to hot blood which manifests itself in a ruddy complexion.[32] Hairiness, as indicated above by Ps-Aristotle, may also indicate the same thing, but hairiness also bears additional meaning in Jewish tradition. Rabbinic sources note that his hairiness means that he is demonic.[33] Likewise, his hairiness is thought to denote his bestial nature, a feature that he appropriately shares with Cain in Jewish tradition.[34]

Esau, of course, is contrasted with his twin brother Jacob. Though Jacob lacks a physical description, he is certainly characterized as womanly, which establishes his character as cunning and deceptive. By implication, he is presumed to be far less hairy than Esau and has a different, likely higher-pitched voice, since these are the things that arouse the suspicion of his father, but they are not stated directly in the narrative. He is the favorite son of his mother, stays inside, cooks, and is "quiet, living in tents" (Gen 25:27). His behavior in the story is consistent with the expected behavior of a woman also, as he is deceptive and uses his wiles to accomplish his purposes. The two brothers are consistent with their outward appearance—Esau is a man's man who follows his appetites, while Jacob is perhaps the most shrewd and cunning character in the entire OT with nearly every piece of his narrative marked by some sort of trick, whether by him or against him.

Levitical Law. The Levitical Law is a somewhat different case since its genre is law and not narrative. Nevertheless, it is possible to read the law in light of physiognomics, and it is altogether likely that many of the restrictions found in the law reflect the same sort of assumptions about a person's character. While there are many noteworthy examples, let us point out two in particular. First, Lev 22:17–25 demands unblemished sacrifices. Second, Lev 21:16–18 requires only unblemished priests as servants in Yahweh's presence. While these sorts of laws reflect purity

---

[32] One might also think of the example of Alexander in Plutarch (*Alex.* 4.1), where he is described as ruddy and it is connected to his impatience and temperament.

[33] *Gen. Rab.* 65:15. See also *Gen. Rab.* 63:6, 8 where Esau is understood to represent Rome, the enemy of Israel. Here Esau is also demonized.

[34] Alter, *Art of Biblical Narrative*, 43 notes that Esau, and by extension Edom, are "linked with animality and gross appetite." See also Lynn Holden, *Forms of Deformity* (JSOTSup 131; Sheffield: JSOT Press, 1991), 17, who also takes note of the link between hairiness and Esau's bestial nature.

concerns, they may also reflect physiognomic concerns. Parsons notes that the physical blemishes are reflections of the presumed "moral blemishes" that would disqualify a priest, and the fact that there is no list of moral blemishes likely reflects the cultural assumption concerning the link between the outward physical appearance and the inward moral character.[35]

Samson. More will be said about Samson in the next section when his blindness is addressed, but Samson has an outstanding physical feature as well—his hair. His hair, the last remaining part of the nazirite vow that remains intact, is noted as the secret to his great strength. Hair in the ancient world was a sign of manliness and courage. A long, flowing mane is associated with the lion (see Ps-Aristotle 809b) and stiff hair like a lion is also a sign of great courage (807b). Samson, in keeping with the portrait of the lion, is portrayed as a fierce and courageous warrior and the manliest of men.[36] Certainly Samson lives up to that billing as he fights off the armies of the Philistines single-handedly.

David. David's introduction includes a physical description, and his introduction in general seems to be set up in stark contrast to Saul's. After Samuel is dispatched to Jesse's home to anoint a king and after he lays eyes on the first son, God gives the prophet a simple instruction: "Do not look on his appearance or on the height of his stature, because I have rejected him; for the LORD does not see as mortals see; they look on the outward appearance, but the LORD looks on the heart" (1 Sam 16:7). It is as if to say that the outward appearance has proven to be misleading: witness Saul. It appears that God rejects physiognomics as an acceptable barometer of character. Nevertheless, the physical description of David is not a negative one: "Now he was ruddy, and had beautiful eyes, and was handsome" (16:12). "Handsome" is a descriptor he shares with Saul and implies his inner beauty and fitness to rule. "Beautiful eyes" is certainly positive, and Alter notes that his

[35] Parsons, *Body and Character*, 30–31. Parsons offers a good treatment of the Levitical Law read physiognomically, including the interpretation of those laws in Qumran and in later Jewish traditions. For a good treatment of the function of disability in the Jewish law, see Tzvi C. Marx, *Disability in Jewish Law* (New York: Routledge, 2002).

[36] Note also that Samson is said to have killed a lion, and killing a lion would mark his superiority to the beast. For a good treatment of lion imagery in the Old Testament, see Brent A. Strawn, *What is Stronger Than a Lion? Leonine Image and Metaphor in the Hebrew Bible and the Ancient Near East* (OBO 212; Göttingen: Vandenhoeck & Ruprecht, 2005).

"good looks will play a crucial role in the magnetic effect he is to have on women and men."[37] As we saw with Esau, "ruddy" is a description that is not usually positive though. It indicates a fiery temperament and impulsiveness, but it is a descriptor he also shares with no less a figure that Alexander the Great.[38] While David is certainly shrewd and calculating in the political sphere, he has his fair share of impulsive and temperamental moments as well, perhaps foreshadowed by his ruddy complexion. Also notable is that David is *never* called "short," contrary to the widespread popular belief. He is certainly not as tall as Goliath, whose sheer height is an indication of his unstoppable military might, but David is not called short. Nor is David called short when he refuses the armor of tall Saul (who *should* be fighting Goliath as Israel's giant), only saying that "I am not used to them" (1 Sam 16:39). So while God warns Samuel against choosing a second king based solely on physical appearance, David's physical appearance is, in the eyes of the physiognomists, more than adequate.

Mephibosheth. After the transition of power from the house of Saul to the house of David is completed, a child of Jonathan is introduced to the story. In 2 Sam 4:4, Mephibosheth is introduced as crippled in his feet or lame, the result of a childhood accident. He reappears in 2 Sam 9 as the lone Saulide heir to whom David will show mercy on account of his friendship with Jonathan, and commentators rightly recognize that Mephibosheth is no political threat to David because of his handicap and thus a perfect candidate for David's mercy. To a physiognomically-conscious audience, such a conclusion is all the more clear. Ps-Aristotle says that "Those who have strong and well-jointed ankles are brave in character; witness the male sex. Those that have fleshy and ill-jointed ankles are weak in character; witness the female sex" (810a). His crippled ankles would indicate a weak character, and thus he is no threat to David and is an object of pity, constantly in need of the patronage of the king.

Absalom. The rebel son of the king does not get a physical description until several scenes into his story. After the rape of his sister Tamar by Amnon, Absalom's assassination of Amnon, and Absalom's return to Jerusalem, a laudatory and royal description is given:

---

[37] Alter, *The David Story*, 97.
[38] Plutarch, *Alex.* 4.1.

> Now in all Israel there was no one to be praised so much for his beauty as Absalom; from the sole of his foot to the crown of his head there was no blemish in him. When he cut the hair of his head (for at the end of every year he used to cut it; when it was heavy on him, he cut it), he weighed the hair of his head, two hundred shekels by the king's weight. (2 Sam 14:25–26)

Not only is his outward beauty remarkable, his outstanding feature is his lustrous hair, and indication of his manliness (see Ps-Aristotle 809b, where a lion-like mane is the epitome of the male type). It is a feature he shares with Israel's most fierce warrior, the mighty Samson, and for both Absalom and Samson the hair proves to be their undoing. With Absalom's rebellion and usurpation of the throne, in many ways ancient Israel is back where it started—with a king that *looks* like a king rather than God's anointed on the throne. Consider Absalom's kingly exploits: he assembles an army (15:1); he hears legal cases at the gate and dispensed justice, a king's activity (15:2–6); he makes his home in the capital in David's palace; and he even takes David's concubines, symbolic of supplanting the king (16:22). Absalom's character is certainly consistent with his hefty mane as he steals the hearts of the people.

Post-Biblical Sources. Certainly the practice of physiognomics is not confined to the canon, nor is it confined to narrative materials only. In fact, one finds physiognomics frequently employed in a number of non-canonical Jewish sources and traditions. Two are particularly noteworthy here. First, the apocalyptic traditions offered a physical description of the antichrist that was influenced by physiognomics such that the character of the evil one is clear from his body. One such example comes from the *Apocalypse of Ezra*: "The appearance of his face is as of a wild man. His right eye is like a star rising at dawn and the other is unmoving. His mouth is one cubit, his teeth are a span long, his fingers like scythes, the soles of his feet two span, and on his forehead an inscription 'Antichrist'" (*Apoc. Ezra* 4:29–32). Similar descriptions can also be found in *Apocalypse of Daniel* 9:11–26, *Apocalypse of Elijah* 3:15–17 and 5:20, and some 14 other Hebrew sources.[39] To describe the character of the antichrist by describing his physical appearance was a very common occurrence.

---

[39] For an excellent treatment of all of the examples of description of the antichrist read in light of physiognomics, see J. Massyngbaerde Ford, "The Physical Features of the Antichrist," *JSP* 14 (1996): 24–41.

Second, the texts at Qumran contain a number of texts that reflect awareness of physiognomics. Consider the following text:

> [The righteous person is one] whose eyes are neither dark nor light, whose beard is sparse and medium curly, whose voice resonates, whose teeth are fine and regular, who is neither tall nor short but is well built, whose fingers are thin and long, whose thighs are hairless, the soles of whose feet and whose toes are as they should be: he possesses a spirit eight parts from the House of Light and one in the House of Darkness. This is the birth sign under which such a person shall be born. (4Q186, Frag. 2 Col. 1.1–8; see also 4QCryptic 3:4; 4QMess ar. 1:2)[40]

These two streams of tradition, drawing ever nearer chronologically to the era of the New Testament, indicate that at least some streams of Jewish tradition were familiar with physiognomics and made use of those conventions in their writings. Let us now turn our attention specifically to eyesight and blindness as a specific subset of physiognomics in the Old Testament and Hebrew literature.

Blindness in the Jewish Writings

When reading the OT, the reader frequently encounters characters that have some sort of impaired vision—some characters are blind completely, some are said to have "dim" or "fading" eyesight, and sometimes characters have their eyes plucked out by enemies. In every case in the OT, the cause of the visual impairment is obvious, be it punishment, old age, or whatever else. Perhaps because there is an easy, surface explanation for the blindness in the text, few scholars look beyond the surface to notice the potential metaphorical implications of blindness. It is the contention of this study that these texts can also be understood on a metaphorical level; that is, though a character may be blind as a result of punishment or because of old age, also present in the text may be an implication of spiritual blindness of some sort.

---

[40] For a treatment of some of the Qumran texts in light of physiognomics, see the recent work by Parsons, *Body and Character*, 32–34, and in the subsequent pages Parsons also explores some other non-canonical Jewish sources not mentioned here. Also on Qumran, see Philip S. Alexander, "Physiognomy, Initiation, and Rank in the Qumran Community," in *Geschichte—Tradition—Reflexion* (ed. H. Cancik, et al.; Tubingen: JCB Mohr, 1996): 385–94.

That the Hebrew traditions would think of sight and blindness in metaphorical terms is beyond dispute. On the negative side, prophets such as Isaiah frequently refer to the people as being "blind" to the things of God. On the positive side, one might point to the office of "prophet" since in its earliest OT roots such a person is known as a "seer" (i.e. Samuel in 1 Sam 9:9 or Gad, David's seer, in 2 Sam 24:11). These are important simply because calling the prophet a seer is to invoke sight in a metaphorical sense—one who can "see" what is going on in the spiritual realm or even in the future.

Nevertheless, strictly speaking, there are *not* a large number of blind characters in the Hebrew writings, and notably *never* a blind prophet like one finds on occasion in the Greek literature. In fact, Felix Just[41] correctly points out that only one named character in the entire Hebrew Bible is said in the text to be "blind," and that is Zedekiah who is blinded by the Babylonians.[42] He points out that many of the characters in the OT, and thus most of the characters that will be described in this current chapter, are suffering from fading or dimming eyesight, which is, lexically speaking, a different condition.[43] Just is correct in the technical sense—there is a difference between the gouged out eyes of Zedekiah and the fading old eyes of Isaac, and Hebrew (as well as Greek and Latin) have nuanced vocabulary for each. However, all of these cases are significant to an understanding of eyesight and blindness in a physiognomically-conscious world nonetheless. This is the case because while we might make a technical distinction in the kinds of disorders of the eyes—whether congenital or old age or the result of an accident—an ancient auditor who thinks in physiognomic terms may see any and all such optical impairments as an indication of the character of the person. It is important here to remember Ps-Aristotle's rule that when the character of the person changes so does

[41] Felix N. W. Just, "From Tobit to Bartimaeus, from Qumran to Siloam: The Social Role of Blind People and Attitudes Toward the Blind in New Testament Times" (Ph.D. diss.; Yale University, 1997).

[42] Just's parameters, of course, would not include Tobit since he falls outside the Hebrew Bible, nor would he include Samson because though his eyes are gouged out, he is not actually labeled as "blind" in the text. He also does not include dimming eyesight in old age as blindness, even though someone like Isaac would easily fit the modern definition of blind. His parameters are lexical only.

[43] Just ("From Tobit to Bartimaeus," 24) distinguishes between three kinds of blindness: congenital blindness (blindness from birth, or sometimes even early childhood), adventitious blindness (blindness as the result of an injury or accident, perhaps even a disease), and blindness in old age.

the body, and vice versa. Thus, while Just is technically correct, it poses no problem for this current study because a physiognomically-conscious auditor would not likely draw such lexical distinctions.[44]

Here it is helpful to recall the basic *topos* of the blind character as sketched in the previous chapter, which may consist of any combination of the following elements: blindness is viewed as a pitiable negative condition marked by helplessness and dependence upon others; blindness can be punishment from the gods or from other people; and blindness can mean ignorance and/or spiritual blindness. When considering texts from the Hebrew Bible, those cases in which blindness or fading eyesight comes with old age fit into the first element of the *topos*, a pitiable condition marked by helplessness. It merits mention that not all parts of the *topos* are necessarily present in every case, and when we read the biblical writings, we must think of the *topos* as a guide rather than something to be rigidly applied. Thus while it is clear that Samson and Zedekiah are being punished by their enemies, for example, it might not necessarily be the case that those who suffer from dimming eyesight in old age are thought of as being divinely punished in some way. In other words, some elements of the *topos* may not be present in every case. What this chapter wishes to call attention to is the final element of the *topos*—blindness as ignorance or spiritual blindness—because it is an element of the narrative that is typically overlooked. An ancient auditor would instinctively conclude that a character with failing physical eyesight might also have a mirroring spiritual condition, and the modern reader of the Jewish writings needs to be attuned to such a reading.

This section will proceed much like the first half of this chapter. We will first examine in some detail three significant scenes in which physical blindness clearly indicates spiritual blindness. We will use the examples of Samson who lives his whole life blind only to ultimately be blinded by the Philistines, Eli whose eyesight fades and is unable to see the work of God, and Tobit who loses his physical eyesight and with it his spiritual sight as well. Following these three examples, we will mention in short a number of other examples in which eye impairments are present and offer some suggestions as to how the text might be read. Examples will follow in canonical order.

---

[44] See Just, "From Tobit to Bartimaeus," esp. 30–43 for his excellent treatment of the Hebrew lexical terms and their nuanced meanings. He does the same thing with Greek terms as well.

Samson

At first glance, the story of Samson does not appear to be a story about blindness. Samson is not blinded until the final verses of the four chapters devoted to his story, and his case would seem to be different. Yet a closer look at Samson's story illustrates that perhaps no character in the biblical narrative could be said to be more blind, figuratively speaking, than was Samson. Let us examine his narrative.[45]

The book of Judges is marked by a well known pattern of apostasy on the part of the Israelites, followed by God-ordained foreign oppression, repentance from the Israelites, and the raising up of a judge for deliverance. By the time the book of Judges has come to this final named judge, it is clear that the cycle is getting worse and no good end is in sight. In fact, with Samson the cycle has become so bad that there is no hint of repentance from Israel. The people have turned from Yahweh, represented at the outset of the narrative by the inability of Manoah and his wife to recognize the divine messenger (Judg 13:16). In addition, the people are being oppressed by the Philistines (Judg 13:1). Yet no repentance is to be found. God raises up a judge nonetheless—for what he is worth. The so-called judge, however, is blind to the work of Yahweh, he never commands the armies of Israel against the enemy, and he instead fights as a lone vigilante who opposes his enemies for his own personal reasons. Even at the end of the narrative, there is no real deliverance, and the people remain oppressed because they have not repented. It is only appropriate that the final judge in this case is one who is ultimately blind. Samson's story is by no means a hero story, but is instead the tragic story of a life blinded to Yahweh, paradigmatic of the plight of the people in general.

Although Samson is not actually physically blinded until the end of the story, his story is a story of blindness from start to finish. In the words of Polzin, "Samson is *par excellence* the unknowing judge. Although he prays at times to Yahweh, he appears never to have had any concern for the interests of Israel, nor any knowledge of the role predicted for him."[46] The Samson story begins with Samson's parents—the messenger

[45] In addition to the standard commentaries on Judges listed in footnote 5 above, a couple of excellent monographs are devoted entirely to the Samson narrative. See especially Jichan Kim, *The Structure of the Samson Cycle* (Kampen, Netherlands: Kok Pharos Publishing House, 1993), the first half of which is devoted to a survey of more than thirty major commentaries and works on the Samson narrative. Also see James L. Crenshaw, *Samson: A Secret Betrayed, a Vow Ignored* (Atlanta: John Knox Press, 1978).

[46] Polzin, *Moses and the Deuteronomist*, 181.

from God appears to the unnamed wife of Manoah and announces a pregnancy and the nazirite vow.[47] Note that the vow is *not* the choice of Samson, Manoah, or Manoah's wife; no human chooses that vow, and it should not be surprising that no human cares to uphold the vow throughout the narrative. Manoah does not believe his wife, so he petitions God that the messenger will appear to him too (13:8)—Manoah is in a sense blind to the spiritual experience that his wife has just had. When the request is granted, Manoah has no idea that the messenger is from God and is something more than human, despite the fact that he has just petitioned God for the messenger to reappear—he is blind to the spiritual world (13:16: "For Manoah did not know that he was the angel of the LORD"). It is not until the messenger ascends in the flames of the offering (13:20) that Manoah's eyes recognize what has just happened. Manoah has failed to see the work of God in his world, a problem his son will likewise share.

Samson first appears in 14:1, where he is immediately fascinated with a foreign woman. His first words in the narrative are when he declares that she is, literally, "right to my eyes" (14:3), a statement that introduces the eye imagery to his narrative. This eye imagery will in many ways define this narrative—Samson's eyes work just fine when it comes to picking out foreign women, but when it comes to seeing the work of God his eyes are in total darkness. His first statement is also hauntingly similar to the final verse of Judges that summarizes the hopeless plight of the Israelites: "in those days there was no king in Israel, and the people did what was right in their own eyes" (21:25). The eye imagery also serves to immediately call attention to Samson's spiritual blindness because he has no regard for the law of Yahweh that forbids him to have a foreign woman, a violation that becomes the defining pattern of his life.

Throughout the Samson narrative the spirit of Yahweh comes upon Samson and empowers him, but *never* at Samson's request. Samson, as far as the reader can tell, is entirely oblivious to the work of Yahweh, and Yahweh seems to use Samson *in spite of* Samson. Samson hardly speaks to Yahweh the entire length of his life, leaving the reader to conclude that Samson either does not know Yahweh or does not care.

[47] Polzin, *Moses and the Deuteronomist*, 181–83, believes that this calling scene is driven by the play between knowledge and lack of knowledge, ideas that are closely related to sight and blindness.

In fact, he only communicates with Yahweh in a single instance other than the moment before his death. The one exception is 15:18, following the slaughter of the Philistines with a jawbone. Here, he cries out to God only in order to complain about being thirsty.

The event that directly leads up to Samson's blinding is his relationship with Delilah. Delilah is bribed to discover the secret to his great strength, which is famously his long hair. The hair does not contain magical properties; it is merely the last part of the nazirite vow that Samson has not yet broken.[48] Once the hair is cut, however, the spirit of Yahweh leaves him as he has fully and utterly abandoned Yahweh in favor of his own human lusts. He awakes with his locks cut off, and the narrative states clearly that Samson "did not recognize that God has left him" (16:20)—he is spiritually blind, and it is at this point in the narrative that the Philistines pluck out his eyes (16:21).[49] It is here that Samson's outward physical condition is made to match his inward spiritual condition. His eyes for women have blinded him to Yahweh since his first action in chapter 14, and it is clear to the reader that Samson is utterly blind to Yahweh throughout his entire sighted life. It is only appropriate, perhaps even expected, that he should be physically blind to match his character.

The final scene of Samson's life is an ambiguous one, puzzling many readers as to whether or not Samson's final act is a redemptive act, a selfish act, or some combination of the two. With his eyes removed, Samson is the laughing stock of his enemies. In 16:28, Samson finally

---

[48] There is some debate over whether Samson has fully broken the vow. Clearly, in 14:5 when he kills a lion and then later eats honey scooped from the carcass, he has violated the prohibition against touching or eating that which is unclean. While the narrative never states that he consumed alcohol, most commentators assume it as part of his wedding party. Given Samson's behavior that rivals that of the modern college fraternity brother, the assumption seems safe enough; yet the narrative does not state it and the vow seems to be less significant to the narrator than most commentators seem to make it. Whatever is made of the vow, however, the point remains that the cutting of his hair is the final disregarding of Yahweh that seals his fate. Boling notes that "The plot revolves not so much around a broken vow, as it does around a vow that had never been taken seriously," and this seems an adequate summary. See Robert G. Boling, *Judges* (AB 6A; Garden City, NY: Doubleday, 1975), 250.

[49] On a literal level, Samson's blinding is as punishment. The Philistines blind Samson both as punishment for the havoc that Samson has wreaked in the past as well as a preemptive strike to prevent future mayhem and destruction. It may, however, also be possible to think of Samson's punishment as a punishment for sexual trespasses, of which he had many. On this line of thought, compare Bernidaki-Aldous, *Blindness in a Culture of Light*, 59–60, where she discusses blindness as punishment for sexual trespasses in the Greek world.

cries out to Yahweh in order to petition Yahweh for strength. It is the first time in the entirety of the narrative that Samson has acknowledged that his strength comes from Yahweh, and the first time Samson requests that Yahweh empower him. At first glance, there appears to be a shocking twist on the sight-blindness imagery, for it would seem that after Samson becomes physically blind that he has his first moment of spiritual insight. A closer look, however, confirms that Samson is still every bit as spiritually blind as he has been in the entire narrative. Notice the content of his prayer: "Lord God, remember me and strengthen me only this once, O God, so that with this one act of revenge I may pay back the Philistines for my two eyes" (16:28). His prayer is not a redemptive one. He does not pray that God will deliver Israel, but that God will grant him strength to avenge his two eyes. His is a prayer of revenge, and, as Polzin points out, his prayer displays "the same egocentric obliviousness to the affairs of Yahweh and the welfare of Israel that had characterized him throughout the story."[50] Though his actions ultimately kill many Philistines, he has no better spiritual insight at the end of his life than he did throughout the rest of it.

In summary, Samson's story is a story of blindness. In the end of the story, his physical condition is made to match his lifelong spiritual condition. Samson, like the Israelites he is supposed to deliver, is oblivious to Yahweh and has eyes that see only what is right in *his* eyes. The point of the story is plain enough to see—he who does what is right in his own eyes is utterly blind, while he who does what is right in the eyes of Yahweh can truly see. Ironically, Samson is the perfect picture of one who does what is right in his own eyes, the very things Judges is condemning (Judg 21:25).

Eli

Eli, the priest under whom Samuel is trained, is one of the best examples of blindness used both literally and metaphorically. On a literal level, Eli suffers from dimming eyesight in his senior years (1 Sam 3:2; 4:15), and many commentators limit the meaning only to this literal level.[51] A reader who is attuned to the metaphorical implications of physical descriptions, however, would hear a second layer of meaning. Namely,

---

[50] Polzin, *Moses and the Deuteronomist*, 194.

[51] See for example, Evans, *1 and 2 Samuel*, 28; Klein, *1 Samuel*, 32; and McCarter, *1 Samuel*, 98.

an ancient audience would have heard in Eli's blindness a judgment on his spiritual condition of blindness. Let us explore Eli's story and take note of how the blindness serves to characterize Eli.

Eli is first introduced in 1 Sam 1 when Hannah prays for a child. As is the case with biblical narrative, the first words of a character are essential to characterization, and Eli's first utterance paints a disturbing picture of the high priest of Yahweh. Seeing Hannah praying and noticing that only her lips moved without her audible voice, he assumes she is drunk (1 Sam 1:13). Even in the modern world, any priest worth his or her salt does not begin with the assumption that a distressed parishioner is drunk; a good priest should first assume there is a spiritual need that has brought the petitioner to the sanctuary. Eli's assumption already paints him as a poor minister, and what is worse, a minister who is *blind* to the spiritual condition of one who is praying in the sanctuary. Without being called blind, Eli's spiritual obtuseness is already apparent. Then he speaks for the first time: "How long will you make a drunken spectacle of yourself? Put away your wine" (1:14). Not only does Eli blindly misjudge the situation, he addresses Hannah with complete insensitivity. His spiritual insight is poor and his skills as a minister of the Lord are altogether lacking, and this is all apparent in the first chapter.

Eli's eyesight is not described until 1 Sam 3, which begins,

> Now the boy Samuel was ministering to the LORD under Eli. The word of the LORD was rare in those days; visions were not widespread. At that time Eli, whose eyesight had begun to grow dim so that he could not see, was lying down in his room; the lamp of God had not yet gone out, and Samuel was lying down in the temple of the LORD, where the ark of God was. (1 Sam 3:1–3)

The literal meaning of the text is clear. Eli is blind from old age, and visions from God were infrequent. But reading with sensitivity to physiognomics gives greater metaphorical significance to the text. We are first told that "The word of the Lord was rare in those days, *visions were not widespread*" or, as Miscall translates it, "no vision broke through."[52] Two primary explanations for the silence of God are possible—either God is not appearing to the people, or God is trying but the people and their spiritual leaders and not receptive. The narrator clarifies which is the case with the next sentence, a statement about Eli's blindness:

[52] Miscall, *1 Samuel*, 24.

"At that time Eli, whose eyesight had begun to grow dim so that he could not see, was lying down in his room; the lamp of God had not yet gone out." On a literal level, Eli was old, his eyesight was fading, and the lamp in the sanctuary still had oil burning. On a metaphorical level, however, much more is at work here. God is not communicating frequently with the people because God's priest has old blind eyes. Yet hope is not lost—though visions were infrequent, the "lamp" had not yet gone out completely. Samuel's calling would change all of that.

The standard scholarly reading of 1 Sam 3:1–2 is best captured by Kyle McCarter. He argues that "the point of the present passage is that visions were restricted in number" and that we should not conclude that Samuel and/or Eli were "unusually obtuse."[53] When in 3:2 the narrative states that Eli's eyesight is failing, McCarter calls the information "extraneous."[54] Yet McCarter, and likewise most of the standard commentators, has missed the symbolic significance of Eli's blindness which is the very point of the text. Alter sees the point: "there is an intimation here of some sort of breakdown in the professional performance of the house of Eli."[55] So also Eslinger who writes,

> The preciousness of Yahweh's word and the sparsity of vision could indicate either that Yahweh has nothing to say to Israel, or that the official receptors of the vision, the Elides, were unfit to mediate any revelations. Given that Eli is no longer called 'priest,' it is more likely that there is no suitable recipient for the revelations of Yahweh. In fact, this is exactly the point, for when Samuel has come to know Yahweh through the revelation of his word, Yahweh reappears at Shiloh.[56]

Polzin offers yet a third view, positing that it is Samuel who is portrayed as spiritually blind because he is unable to recognize Yahweh when he calls to Samuel.[57] I am suggesting, based on Eli's description as that of fading eyes, that Eli is the problem rather than Samuel. That is to say that Samuel does not recognize Yahweh because Eli is blind to

---

[53] McCarter, *I Samuel*, 97. I use McCarter as the standard here because his Anchor volume is an excellent work of historical-critical scholarship, and he is followed very closely by nearly all such commentaries subsequent to his.

[54] McCarter, *I Samuel*, 98.

[55] Alter, *The David Story*, 16. While Alter is in my mind the most helpful of the literary critics, his book offers no more than a couple of tantalizing sentences of commentary on each verse.

[56] Eslinger, *Kingship of God in Crisis*, 146.

[57] Polzin, *Samuel and the Deuteronomist*, 49–50.

Yahweh and thus unable to teach Samuel how to recognize Yahweh. The judgment falls on Eli who is directly called blind, not on the boy Samuel. Any harsh judgment upon Samuel by the narrator will wait until later in the narrative.

The implication, then, is clear enough; visions are infrequent because the conduit for the visions is "dim," and the lack of spiritual vision is far more important than Eli's physical eyesight. At this point the reader might recall what has been learned of Eli in the first two chapters of 1 Samuel. Not only was Eli's encounter with Hannah a reflection of his spiritual blindness, the reader has also learned that he is blind to the behavior of his unrighteous children. Notice that Eli has only *heard* (2:22) of what the sons are doing, and he gives them little more than a mild rebuke that is promptly ignored. God has already rejected Eli as priest (2:27–36) and will do so again when he calls Samuel. To this point in the narrative, very little has been seen of Eli that would indicate any kind of spiritual insight that one expects from the priest of the Lord.

Yet the language of sight and light does not end with Eli's old, dim eyes. 1 Sam 3:3 states that "the lamp of God had not yet gone out." Alter correctly understands that Eli "is immersed in permanent darkness while the lad Samuel has God's lamp burning by his bedside."[58] The mention of the lamp of God is taken by nearly all major commentaries as a time stamp that locates the calling of Samuel just before dawn.[59] While this is probably the case, we must not miss the symbolic richness here either. Even though under Eli's ministry visions from the Lord have become rare, the lamp is not yet extinguished; God is still at work and the boy Samuel will be the one to whom the Lord and his visions will soon come—and frequently at that.[60] To summarize, we find old, blind, and rejected Eli contrasted with young Samuel who is located in the temple of the Lord where Yahweh's lamp is, however dimly, still burning.

The scene that unfolds is the calling of Samuel. When God calls Samuel, the blindness of Eli is once again underscored. Samuel hears

---

[58] Alter, *The David Story*, 16. See also Bergen, *1, 2 Samuel*, 86.

[59] See especially McCarter, *I Samuel*, 98. Nearly every commentary that postdates McCarter's defers to him on this point. See especially Klein, *1 Samuel*, 32. Even the literary commentaries such as Miscall, Polzin, Alter, and Eslinger reference McCarter here, though they think the lamp is more than just a time stamp.

[60] See Alter, *The David Story*, 16 for a similar read.

God twice but mistakes the voice for that of Eli, because "Samuel did not yet know the Lord" (3:7). McCarter is typical here, taking the phrase as referring to nothing more than "the special relationship with Yahweh that Samuel was to enjoy."[61] But this statement is also a further judgment on Eli, a point which most modern commentators overlook. That Samuel could serve for years in the sanctuary under the tutelage of Eli and *not* know the Lord is a jarring statement, reflecting poorly on Eli, and further underscoring his spiritual blindness. Even if he failed at everything else, the priest of the Lord should have taught the acolyte how to discern the voice of Yahweh. Eli is *not* spiritually sighted; he has only enough spiritual vision to discern that it is in fact God who is calling Samuel—but this *only after* three visits from the boy! Twice Samuel mistakes Yahweh's voice for Eli, and twice Eli is oblivious to the appearance of God that is taking place. On the third calling, Eli with his dim eyesight finally perceives what is going on and Samuel is able to receive God's vision. Thus with the calling of Samuel, blind Eli is replaced.

As if only to further emphasize the point, the blindness of Eli is again mentioned in 4:15 just before Eli's death, the capture of the Ark, and the destruction of Israel's army. This time, his eyesight is worse that dim, it is gone completely: "Now Eli was ninety-eight years old and his eyes were set, so that he could not see." When word of the capture of the ark reaches Eli, he falls backwards from his seat and breaks his neck because "he was an old man and heavy" (4:18). This descriptor adds one more negative note to the characterization of Eli. As mentioned in the first half of this chapter, to be overweight indicates laziness and greed (perhaps eating too well from the offering of the people as his sons had done in 4:12–17), two characteristics that are unbecoming of the priest of God.

When reading the Eli narrative, then, the physiognomically-conscious reader would readily notice that the blindness of Eli is best understood not only as a physical blindness that comes with old age, but also as a spiritual blindness that obfuscates his vision of God.

[61] McCarter, *1 Samuel*, 98.

Tobit

The notion of physical blindness as an indicator of spiritual blindness is very much present outside of the Hebrew canon. Perhaps the most memorable story of blindness in the Hebrew tradition is the story of Tobit.[62] Tobit is the ideal Diaspora Jew, living a life of righteousness, justice, and mercy in a foreign land. After leaving a festival meal in order to bury a fellow Jew in accordance with the law, Tobit stops to rest. Falling asleep, bird droppings fall onto his eyes and eventually cost him his eyesight. The unfortunate accident sets in motion a chain of events that have all the makings a good adventure story, but this is not what interests us in the story. What is pertinent here is Tobit's spiritual vision. Before Tobit looses his eyesight, he is clearly a spiritually-sighted follower of the law. When he looses his sight, however, he also looses his faith in many ways—he becomes spiritually blind when he becomes physically blind. When his eyesight is restored at the end of the story, his spiritual vision returns as well. Let us examine his story.

The blindness of Tobit presents an interesting case because Tobit is the most fully developed narrative of a blind character in Hebrew literature. Whereas previous Hebrew characters had only a few verses or even a chapter involving their blindness, the blindness of Tobit is the central element of the narrative. Surprisingly, however, *none* of the standard commentaries on Tobit talk about blindness as characterization or as a metaphor in the narrative.[63] The standard commentaries

---

[62] There are numerous examples of blindness that occur in Jewish literature outside of the OT. Lamech of Genesis has a number of legends surrounding him, for example, and the builders of the Tower of Babel are said to be struck blind in 2 Bar 3:8. For a thorough catalogue of references to blindness in Jewish sources, see Holden, *Forms of Deformity*, 132ff. One of the most interesting examples is found in the *Apocryphon of Ezekiel*, where one finds a parable in which a king throws a party and invites everyone except a lame man and a blind man. Upset by their exclusion, the two execute a plot whereby the lame man rides upon the back of the blind man, the blind man providing the legs and the lame man providing the eyes. The two proceed to do damage to the property of the king, for which they are later convicted and flogged. The moral to the story is summed up in the final verses: "In the same way the body is connected to the soul and the soul to the body, to convict (them) of (their) common deeds. And the judgment becomes final for both body and soul, for the works they have done whether good or evil" (taken from Charlesworth's *Pseudepigrapha*). What is also important to this story is that the lame man apparently represents the body and the blind man apparently represents the soul. Here we find that blindness as a metaphor is standing in the place of the spirit.

[63] There are a number of good commentaries on Tobit that collectively comprise what I am terming the "standard commentaries." The most recent, and in many ways best, commentaries are Carey A. Moore, *Tobit: A New Translation with Introduction*

talk in terms of causation, biology, ancient medicine, and especially in terms of unjust suffering; but they *never* talk about blindness as a character trait that would in any way correspond to spiritual blindness.[64] A physiognomically-conscious audience, however, would have found a metaphorical element to Tobit's blindness, an element that is clear in the story.

The first two chapters of Tobit recount the litany of righteous deeds done by the title character. Written in first-person narration, Tobit introduces himself as follows: "I, Tobit, walked in the ways of truth and righteousness all the days of my life. I performed many acts of charity for my kindred and my people who had gone with me in exile to Nineveh" (1:3). In addition to this introduction, the first chapter tells the reader of a number of other righteous deeds of Tobit: he alone of all of his tribe worshipped in Jerusalem properly prior to exile (1:4, 6); he observed the festivals (1:6); he gave tithes as well as generous offerings to the orphans and widows (1:8); he married properly within the family (1:9); he refrained from the food of the Gentiles when all others did not (1:11); he gave food to the hungry and clothing to the naked (1:16); and he buried the dead, even when it was in disobedience to the Assyrian king (1:16). Additionally, there is a complete lack of any record of unrighteous deeds. The collective impact of this introduction is to show that Tobit's blinding was *not* punishment for some sin since he is as spiritually-sighted as one can hope to be. In fact, Tobit of all people should have been rewarded by God for his righteous deeds (cf. 1:13). Tobit is a character reminiscent of Job—faithful to Yahweh, righteous,

---

and Commentary (AB 40A; New York: Doubleday, 1996) and Joseph A. Fitzmyer, *Tobit* (Commentaries on Early Jewish Literature; New York: Walter de Gruyter, 2003). Frank Zimmermann (*The Book of Tobit: An English Translation with Introduction and Commentary* [New York: Harper and Brothers, 1958]) began much of the modern discussion on Tobit with his insistence that Tobit draws on a number of ancient folktales. Two thorough German commentaries have since dealt adequately with the form critical problems; see P. Deselaers, *Das Buch Tobit: Studien zu seiner Entstehung, Komposition und Theologie* (OBO 43; Guttenburg: University Press, 1982) and Merten Rabenau, *Studien zum Buch Tobit* (BZAW 220; Berlin: Walter de Gruyter, 1994). Also worthy of mention is an interpretive history of Tobit, Johann Gamberoni, *Die Auslegung Des Buches Tobias: in der griechisch-lateinischen Kirche der Antike und der Christenheit des Westens bis 1600* (SANT 21; Munich: Kösel-Verlag, 1969).

[64] Some of the more interesting reads are those that deal with the pharmacological and medicinal aspects of the story. See Moore, *Tobit*, 201–2 and Bernd Kollmann, "Göttliche Offenbarung magisch-pharmakologischer Heilkunst im Buch Tobit," *ZAW* 106 (1994): 289–99 for a pharmacological discussion of the healing of Tobit. While both of these studies provide important information concerning ancient medical practices, they miss the point in that they say nothing of how blindness functions in the narrative.

and undeserving of divine punishment in any way, yet Tobit, like Job, is afflicted with suffering that is difficult to explain.

In 2:4 Tobit leaves the dinner table to bury one of his countrymen in defiance of the Assyrian king. Obedience to Yahweh trumps obedience to the foreign government, and any reader would agree that Tobit has acted correctly—his spiritual sight is working perfectly. Once Tobit's eyes are blinded by bird dung, however, Tobit immediately becomes a different person. Like Samson losing his strength when his hair is cut, Tobit loses his spiritual vision when his eyesight is lost. Physical vision and spiritual vision go hand-in-hand here. The paragraph immediately following his blinding illustrates the point. Tobit's wife has taken up "women's work" (2:11) in order to sustain the family. When she brings home a goat as a gift from her employer, Tobit blindly refuses to believe his wife and forces her to return it, erroneously assuming that she has stolen it.[65] Anna even notes the absence of charitable acts that once defined Tobit (2:14). Here it is helpful to recall that Ps-Aristotle argued that when the form of the body changes, so does the moral character, and Anna seems to indicate that such a metamorphosis is true of Tobit as well. His blindness has immediately resulted in paranoia, mistrust of the people closest to him, and angry outbursts, all of these things in the immediate narration following his blinding.

The next chapter relays a strange prayer from Tobit. Though it begins with the acknowledgment that God is righteous, just, and sovereign over the affairs of earth, the reader is unconvinced of Tobit's sincerity because the praise is not the point of his prayer. After the initial praise, Tobit erroneously concludes that God is punishing him for his sins (which are non-existent so far as the narrative is concerned) and for the sins of his ancestors. Tobit's lack of spiritual vision has caused him to misread the situation, for there is certainly no indication that he is being punished by God for any reason. The point of his prayer, ultimately, is to ask for death:

> So now deal with me as you will: command my spirit to be taken from me, so that I may be released from the face of the earth and become dust. For it is better for me to die than to live, because I have had to listen to undeserved insults, and great is the sorrow within me. Command,

[65] Zimmermann, *Tobit*, 59 adds an interesting potential layer of meaning. He compares this text with Gen 38, claiming that Tobit would understand the gift goat as an implication of her unfaithfulness. If Zimmermann is correct, then we have one more example of Tobit's metaphorical blindness.

> O Lord, that I be released from this distress; release me to go to the eternal home, and do not, O Lord, turn your face away from me. For it is better for me to die than to see so much distress in my life and to listen to insults. (3:6)

Death, according to Tobit, is preferable to living life blind. Tobit's prayer makes it clear that it is not just his physical vision that has been lost.

One more example of his spiritual blindness that is noteworthy is his inability to recognize the angel Raphael who accompanies Tobias on his journey. While it is certainly not uncommon for humans to fail to recognize divine messengers in human form,[66] one would almost expect righteous Tobit to see what is going on, especially since he fully expects that "a good angel will accompany [Tobias]" (5:22). Yet to the contrary, when greeted by Raphael Tobit's spiritual blindness is again apparent when he replies, "What joy is left for me anymore? I am a man without eyesight; I cannot see the light of heaven, but I lie in darkness like the dead who no longer see the light. Although still alive, I am among the dead. I hear people but I cannot see them" (5:10). For Tobit to say, "I am a man without eyesight; I cannot see the light of heaven" is a crucial statement—not only can he not see the literal light of heaven (read: sun, moon, stars), he is also incapable of seeing the true light of heaven (read: the workings of God in the world). Tobit has become completely blind to the spiritual world that he once saw so clearly.

Tobit remains in both physical and spiritual darkness until the very end of the narrative when Tobias and Raphael return from their journey and heal Tobit's eyes. As soon as Tobit's physical eyesight is restored, his spiritual sight is restored as well. Immediately after his healing, Tobit sings a beatitude of praise (11:14–15). On a literal level, Tobit is certainly grateful for the healing and a hymn of praise to God is undoubtedly a proper response. On another level, Tobit's vision (both physically and spiritually) has now been restored such that he is again able to sing a hymn of praise. The book ultimately closes with a lengthy testament delivered by an aging Tobit to his son, a testament that indicates that the spiritual vision of the righteous hero of the opening chapters has been restored.[67]

---

[66] In fairness to Tobit, we should note that the identity of angels in human form is commonly mistaken by human characters in the OT, even the righteous ones; see for example Gen 18 when three "men" spend the day with Abraham on their way to Sodom.

[67] It is noteworthy that chapter 13 is *not* the first farewell address given by Tobit

Tobit's story is a story read on two levels. On one level, it is a story of a righteous man who inexplicably is blinded, loses his faith and his will to live, but ultimately finds God's mercy and is healed. On another level, it is a story of a spiritual visionary who goes spiritually blind, but who receives a healing touch that restores his spiritual sight as well. A physiognomically-conscious audience would no doubt see both levels of the story as physical sight and spiritual sight function in tandem.

Other Examples

There are a number of other examples of blindness in Jewish literature. As in the first half of the chapter, we will simply list many of the examples here and offer only brief comments about them. The examples are arranged in canonical order.

Sodom. In Genesis 19, the lust-filled citizens of Sodom have surrounded the home of Lot and are demanding that his two visitors be sent outside in order to be raped. As the situation reaches its most desperate moment, the two heavenly visitors shut the door and strike the men of Sodom blind so that they are unable to find the door to Lot's house (Gen 19:11). The mob, which is already clearly spiritually blind given their behavior, receives a commensurate physical condition. The spiritual and moral decadence of the city brings about its destruction, but when the messengers warn Lot of the impending judgment, he and his family are reluctant to leave. It is almost as if the sinful condition has become contagious, and Lot and his family have become spiritually blind as well. Whatever the case, we have in this story a clear example of blindness as a divine punishment and blindness as an indicator of the spiritual condition.

to Tobias; he gives an earlier one in chapter 4 that shares many parallels with Jesus' Sermon on the Mount. Chapter 4 at first seems to be an oddity, since it is a treasury of wisdom that is not expected from *blind* Tobit; it is the one speech of Tobit that seems incongruent with his blindness. Nothing seems to be wrong with the speech in chapter 4 (at least not in the sense of content—he does not pray for death or give bad wisdom as one might expect from a spiritually blind character), except that it is out of place. He gives a farewell speech at a moment when it is unnecessary since neither he nor his son is about to die. Chapter 13, then, seems to be a redo of the farewell address, this time properly timed. It is almost as if to say that the second testament given by a sighted Tobit is the replacement for the first testament given by blind Tobit. Read in this way, having two farewell speeches is not an alarming form critical problem; instead, it is one more way of underscoring Tobit's now-healed spiritual blindness.

Isaac. In Gen 27:1, the reader is told that Isaac is nearing his death and his eyes are dim and unable to see because of his old age. The story that follows is a story that preys upon the blindness—both physically and metaphorically—of Isaac. While some may seek explanation in a medical diagnosis of Isaac's blindness,[68] a second and more valuable layer of meaning would have been apparent to an ancient reader. A physiognomically-conscious reader would recognize in Isaac's blind condition a corresponding spiritual blindness. Indeed, it is not the physical blindness that enables Jacob to trick his father and steal the blessing meant for Esau; surely a good father could distinguish between two sons who are so radically different by more than a simple test of hairiness. It is Isaac's metaphorical blindness that drives the story.

Jacob. Jacob benefited from a mistaken blessing at his father's bedside, and at the end of his own life a scene unfolds that looks quite similar. Jacob is old and his eyesight is dim (Gen 48:10), and he lies in his bed when Joseph brings his two sons Manasseh and Ephraim to Jacob to be blessed. It appears at first that Jacob is functionally blind, "Now the eyes of Israel were dim with age, and he could not see well" (48:10). The next verse, however, informs the reader that he is not yet fully blind, as Jacob says, "I did not expect to see your face; and here God has let me see your children also" (48:11). Yet Joseph behaves as if dim-sighted Jacob is utterly blind, bringing them as close to Jacob as possible and positioning them correctly with the older son at the right hand and the younger son at the left. In a strange move, however, Jacob crosses his hands and gives the greater blessing to the younger Ephraim, much to the displeasure of Joseph. Joseph assumes what the reader might assume, that old Jacob has made a mistake because of his blindness, and that not only has Jacob's physical blindness caused him to cross his arms wrongly, but that his corresponding spiritual blindness has caused him to make a spiritual mistake by blessing the wrong son. But the astute reader notices that Jacob is not as blind as Joseph thinks—Jacob declares that he can see the faces of his grandchildren in 48:11, and in 48:19 he demonstrates that his spiritual vision is still functioning as well by declaring that he has knowingly blessed the correct sons. In Jacob's case, the apparent blindness is misleading, both to

[68] See, for example, S. Levin, "Isaac's Blindness: A Medical Diagnosis," *Judaism* 37 (1988): 81–83, who argues that Isaac's blindness is due to diabetes.

Joseph and the reader, causing both parties to reevaluate the eyesight (and, consequently, the spiritual condition) of dim-sighted Jacob.[69]

Blindness in the Torah. The Torah treats blindness in a way that is quite consistent with the later Greco-Roman world. The Torah seems to indicate that blindness is a pitiable and shameful condition, and the Torah generally treats blindness as a mark of uncleanness and thus probably also as spiritual impurity. Lev 21:18 bans any priest with a physical defect from offering bread in the sanctuary, and blindness is listed as the first of those disqualifying defects. Likewise, according to Lev 22:22 (cf. Deut 15:21 and Mal 1:8), no one is to offer as a sacrifice a defective animal, and once again blindness is the first disqualifying defect listed. These two laws regulate the priests and acts of worship, and blindness makes a priest or a sacrifice impure. There is also the much debated case of 2 Sam 5:8, which ends with the maxim "the blind and the lame shall not enter the house *of the lord*" (italics mine, indicating a textual variant). If "of the lord" is the proper reading, then it may be the case that the blind and the lame were banned from the Temple; if not, then the most likely reading is that they are banned from the house of David.[70] In either case, the blind (and the lame) are pitied characters who are socially, and perhaps religiously, outcast.

---

[69] On the eyesight of Jacob, see especially the following commentaries: Hermann Gunkel, *Genesis* (trans. Mark E. Biddle; Macon, GA: Mercer University Press, 1997), 448; Kenneth A. Mathews, *Genesis 11:27–50:26* (NAC 1B; Nashville: Broadman and Holman Publishers, 2005), 880; and Gordon J. Wenham, *Genesis 16–50* (WBC 2; Dallas: Word Books, 1994), 464–65.

[70] The debate over this text is indeed extensive, and I note here three brief studies that highlight the spectrum of opinion. Shmuel Vargon ("The Blind and the Lame," *VT* 46 [1996]: 499–500) argues that the "house" referred to in the well-known maxim "the blind and the lame shall not enter the house" is *not* a reference to the Temple; instead, it is a reference to *David's* house, which, interestingly, finds lame Mephibosheth entering it later in the narrative. For an example of a scholar who argues that "house" is a sanctuary of some sort, if not the Temple proper, see Saul M. Olyan, "'Anyone Blind or Lame Shall Not Enter the House': On the Interpretation of 2 Samuel 5:8b," *CBQ* 60 (1998): 218–27. He spends most of the article exploring what the ban would mean, if either the ban was against priests only (as in Lev and Deut) or against worshippers in general. A third view is forwarded by Anthony R. Ceresko ("The Identity of 'the blind and the lame' in 2 Samuel 5:8b," *CBQ* 63 [2001]: 23–30). He argues that the "house" in question is the royal family, and the "lame" and "blind" serve to foreshadow the illegitimacy of the rule of either Mephibosheth (and thus the house of Saul) and of Zedekiah (and thus of the Davidic monarchy in general). That is, the saying foreshadows the failure of both dynasties (Ceresko, 23–24).

Also like the Greeks, the Torah understands that blindness is often associated with divine punishment. Blindness is listed in Deut 28:28–29 as a specific curse for those that fail to follow the Law ("The LORD will afflict you with madness, blindness, and confusion of mind; you shall grope about at noon as blind people grope in darkness, but you shall be unable to find your way"). Here, the curse carries both literal and metaphorical meanings, and "madness, blindness, and confusion of mind" are all taken to mean very much the same thing. Perhaps literal blindness awaits the law-breaker, where blindness is a divine punishment for disobedience. Perhaps also there is a metaphorical meaning, where the one who tries to live life without the guidance of the Law will fair no better than the blind man who gropes around in the dark lost. The Law, then, is the necessary light and guide for the people of God, and to ignore that light and guide is to in essence blind oneself.

Yet also like the Greeks, there seems to be some element of mercy extended to the blind in the Torah. In the Torah one finds two statements preventing the taunting or mistreatment of the blind. Lev 19:14 forbids the placing of a stumbling block before the blind, and Deut 27:18 curses anyone who misleads a blind person on the road. The Torah's understanding of blindness, then, is very consistent with what one finds in the Greek-speaking world later.

Moses. Moses, of course, is not blind and is never said to be blind, and his presence in this list at first seems out of place. He is appropriately included here because of a seemingly throwaway line at the end of his life. In Deut 34:7 as Moses' death nears, it is surprising and odd that Moses is specifically said to *not* have had eyes that dimmed with old age: "Although Moses was one hundred and twenty years old when he died, his eye was not dim, nor his vigor abated." Why would the narrator bother to mention that his old eyes still worked well? An audience that thought in physiognomic terms would understand. Moses' spiritual vision had not faded with age, marked by his still-bright eyes. Not only was Moses not blind like so many of the patriarchs before him, he was exactly the opposite—his eyes, and thus his spiritual vision, were vibrant.

Ahijah. Ahijah is a prophet in the time of Jeroboam when the king's son falls sick. Jeroboam sends his wife to visit the prophet in order to know what will happen to the child. Ahijah suffers from dimming vision in his senior years and is blind: "Now Ahijah could not see, for his eyes were dim because of his age" (1 Kgs 14:4). In the case of Ahijah, his blindness is the vehicle whereby Jeroboam attempts to trick the prophet by sending his wife in disguise. Ahijah is blind,[71] and had he not been forewarned by God, the trick would have worked. Here, the one who is physically blind is expected to be spiritually blind as well—Jeroboam expects it, as does the physiognomically-conscious reader. Ahijah would be blind to the trick from the king, but Yahweh grants him insight that trumps his condition.

Elisha. In 2 Kgs 6:8–23 one finds an interesting play on sight and blindness. The armies of Aram are harassing Israel, but Aram is unsuccessful because of Elisha's mystical warnings to his countrymen. Eventually, the Arameans lay siege to the city of Dothan where Elisha is dwelling. Panicking, Elisha's servant comes to him to beg his counsel. Elisha's response juxtaposes his own spiritual sight with the spiritual blindness of his servant and the eventual physical blindness of the enemy:

> Elisha replied, "Do not be afraid, for there are more with us than there are with them." Then Elisha prayed: 'O LORD, please open his eyes that he may see.' So the LORD opened the eyes of the servant, and he saw; the mountain was full of horses and chariots of fire all around Elisha. When the Arameans came down against him, Elisha prayed to the LORD, and said, 'Strike this people, please, with blindness.' So he struck them with blindness as Elisha had asked. (2 Kgs 6:16–18)

The prophet has perfect spiritual vision, enabling him to see the heavenly host that protects him. The Arameans, of course, cannot see this invisible force, for if they could see it they would not have attacked. When Elisha prays that they be blinded, their physical condition is made to match the spiritual condition that the reader is already well aware of. The entire episode plays on imagery of sight and blindness.

Zedekiah. In 2 Kgs 25:7 (cf. Jer 39:7 and 52:11), Judah's final king Zedekiah is blinded by the Babylonians. This is an act of punishment from the perspective of the Babylonians, blinding a rebellious enemy.

---

[71] Technically, Ahijah *is* a blind prophet, but he is altogether different than the blind prophet tradition in the Greco-Roman literature. His blindness is not the vehicle for his spiritual vision, as is the case with the blind prophets of the Greeks. Ahijah is specifically said to be blind because of age, and it is not his blindness that enables him to deliver oracles from God because he had delivered oracles many times while younger and better sighted.

Likewise, from the perspective of the Deuteronomist, the blinding is punishment, but for different reasons. In the eyes of the Deuteronomist, the blinding of the king is also symbolic to the entire nation, punishment for the nation's failure to uphold the covenant. On an individual level, Zedekiah has demonstrated his own spiritual blindness sufficiently with his behavior leading up to the sacking of Jerusalem. His blindness is particular apparent in his refusal to heed the words of Jeremiah (see Jer 38; 52:2–3; 2 Kgs 24:18–20). Zedekiah is blinded by the Babylonians, but in many ways his blinding is merely representative of both his own spiritual blindness and perhaps even of the nation's spiritual blindness that led them to this destructive point.

Isaiah and Blindness. While this chapter focuses primarily upon narrative examples of blindness as a means of characterization, the use of blindness as a metaphor in Isaiah must also be included. The reader finds in Isaiah the concept of blindness used as a metaphor that captures the spiritual condition of Israel. Because the New Testament will pick up on many of these passages in order to make sense of the ministry of Jesus, they are important to address here. Two things are of significance for our purposes. First, the fact that Isaiah uses blindness metaphorically provides confidence that an ancient audience would have associated physical blindness with being spiritually lost. Second, the concept of blindness and its healing at the end of the age is, according to the Gospel writers, foundational for understanding Jesus' ministry. Let us briefly mention some of the more significant occurrences of blindness in Isaiah.

Isaiah uses blindness as a figure of speech for ignorance or hard-heartedness that prevents the message of God from being received by the people. The most well-known statement of this sort is Isaiah 6:9–10 when Isaiah is commissioned as a prophet.[72] God says to Isaiah, "Go

[72] Isa 6:9–10 is not the only example; in fact, blindness appears in a number of places throughout Isaiah as a significant theme of the prophet's message. Other significant examples include 43:8, 59:10, and the servant song of Isa 42, probably best taken as the blindness of the nation of Israel. For helpful and brief discussion of this theme in Isaiah, see the following works: Ronald E. Clements, "Beyond Tradition-history: Deutero-Isaianic Development of First Isaiah's Themes," *JSOT* 31 (1985): 95–113; Philip D. Stern, "The 'Blind Servant' Imagery of Deutero-Isaiah and Its Implications," *Bib* 74 (1994): 224–32; and Robert P. Carroll, "Blindsight and the Vision Thing: Blindness and Insight in the Book of Isaiah," in *Writing and Reading the Scroll of Isaiah: Studies in an Interpretive Tradition* (ed. Craig C. Broyles and Craig A. Evans; Leiden: E. J. Brill, 1997): 79–93. Among the commentary tradition, see especially John D. W. Watts, *Isaiah 1–33*

and say to this people: 'Keep listening, but do not comprehend; keep looking, but do not understand.' Make the mind of this people dull, and stop their ears, and shut their eyes, so that they may not look with their eyes, and listen with their ears, and comprehend with their minds, and turn and be healed." The blindness in this text is easily understood as figurative, for certainly Isaiah is not being sent on a quest throughout Israel to gauge out the eyes and puncture the ear drums of everyone he meets; rather, the people are going to be obstinate and oblivious to the message of God that Isaiah is to deliver. It is important to note that Isaiah 6:9–10 is one of the very few OT passages that is common to all four Gospel writers—it is found most directly in Mark 4:11–12; it is found in a somewhat softer form in Matt 13:13–15; Luke closes his two-volume work with it (Acts 28:25–28); and John offers it as explanation for unbelief in 12:37–40 (interestingly, John omits deafness and mentions only blindness). More will be said about the Gospels' use of this concept in the next chapter, but for now suffice it to say that the metaphor of blindness as spiritual ignorance is a defining and foundational concept, and one that communicated significantly to a wide audience.

Not only is blindness used metaphorically to signify spiritual ignorance in Isaiah, its healing is also an apocalyptic sign. In Isa 29:18 ("On that day the deaf shall hear the words of a scroll, and out of their gloom and darkness the eyes of the blind shall see"), the blind gain sight as a sign of the coming of the Kingdom or the Day of Yahweh. Likewise, we find this use in Isa 35:5–6 ("Then the eyes of the blind shall be opened, and the ears of the deaf unstopped; then the lame shall leap like a deer, and the tongue of the speechless sing for joy").[73] In these cases, the literal healing of blind eyes is the plainest meaning of the text. Additionally, however, it is worth noting that the healing of the blind can also be read metaphorically; that is, with the coming of the Kingdom of God, not only will the physically blind be healed but also the spiritually blind will gain sight. When readers come to the NT, it is common to understand the healing of the blind as a sign of the in-breaking of the Kingdom of God, but readers may do just as well to

(WBC 24; Waco, TX: Word Books, 1985), 75, and Clements, *Isaiah 1–39* (NCBC; Grand Rapids: Eerdmans, 1980), 76–77.

[73] In the prophetic tradition, we find an unusual injunction in Zeph 1:17—here the day of Yahweh is judgment, and Yahweh promises to blind people on that day, as opposed to the more usual healing of the blind on that day.

understand those texts as representative of the restoration of spiritual sight that comes with the Kingdom as well.

Conclusion

The Jewish writings are replete with examples of the physical body being used as an indicator of character. Specifically, sight and blindness are used to indicate one's spiritual aptitude or ignorance. This chapter contends that the stories of blindness in the Jewish writings should be read on two levels, both the literal level of lacking eyesight and as stories about spiritual blindness or obtuseness to the work of God. Though such a reading of the text is rare in the modern historical-critical environment, it is interesting to note that it is not without witnesses in the history of interpretation. These are the words of Augustine:

> O Thou Light, which Tobias [sic, read: Tobit] saw when, these eyes closed, he taught his son the way of life; and himself went before with the feet of charity, never swerving.... Or which Isaac saw when his fleshy 'eyes being heavy' and closed by old age, it was vouchsafed him, not knowingly to bless his sons, but by blessing to know them. Or which Jacob saw, when he also, blind through great age, with illuminated heart, in the persons of his son shed light on the different races of the future people, in them foresignified; and laid his hands, mystically crossed, upon his grandchildren by Joseph, not as their father by outward eye corrected them, but as himself inwardly discerned. This is the light, it is one, and all are one, who see and love it. (*Confessions* 10.52)

Here, Augustine believes that these characters who have lost their physical eyesight are able to be guided by a spiritual eyesight—the Light—which is far superior. I am suggesting quite the opposite, that physical blindness and spiritual blindness tend to occur in tandem. Nonetheless, what is important to notice about Augustine's reading is that he gives witness to a tradition of reading blindness and sight metaphorically, a tradition that we would do well to recover in reading the biblical material. Let us now turn to the Christian writings.

CHAPTER FIVE

PHYSIOGNOMY AND BLINDNESS IN THE NEW TESTAMENT AND OTHER EARLY CHRISTIAN LITERATURE

In the previous chapter, we surveyed some examples of Old Testament passages that can be read in light of physiognomics. In this chapter, we turn attention to the New Testament and other early Christian literature. We will withhold discussion of Luke and Acts until the final chapter, since Luke seems to make the most extensive use of physiognomics of any of the NT writers. This chapter will follow the same model as the previous chapter. First, we will survey several examples of physiognomics in general, of which there are surprisingly few within the NT canon. In the second half of the chapter, attention will be given to examples of blindness. These examples are relatively frequent, and they are highly significant in each case.

Examples of Physiognomy in the NT and Other Early Christian Literature

Now that the reader has learned to be physiognomically conscious as an ancient reader would have been, the first and most striking feature of the canonical Christian literature is the virtual *lack* of physiognomics for characterization. Aside from Luke-Acts, one is hard pressed to find examples of physical descriptions, especially in contrast to something like the Deuteronomistic History where examples abound. Perhaps most striking of all is the fact that nowhere in the Gospels does one ever find a physical description of Jesus, not even a passing reference to a single physical feature. With the one major exception of Paul in the *Acts of Paul*, none of the earliest followers of Jesus ever get a lengthy physical description either. While we can offer some guesses as to why there are no such descriptions, it is difficult to make an argument from silence. On the one hand, we need not be alarmed by the lack of descriptions and conclude that the Gospel writers are wholesale opposed to physiognomics in the way that some of the Patristic writers will be. Certainly there are plenty of narratives in the Greco-Roman literature that do not employ physiognomic descriptions either, but it does not warrant the conclusion that those authors are all anti-physiognomic in their thinking;

it merely means that they accomplished characterization in other ways. Nevertheless, the absence of physical descriptions in the NT is striking, and one would like an explanation. Let us offer some conjecture.[1]

One possibility is simply that the Gospel writers found other ways to do characterization of major characters, whether through dialogue, action, or comments from an omniscient narrator. A second possibility is that Christ cannot be given such a description because Christ cannot be contained in that sort of characterization. That is to say that when a physical description is offered, it says something about who a character is, but it also says much about who a character is *not*. In other words, to offer a description of Jesus is also to limit the characterization of Jesus, and it might well be the case that the Gospel writers refuse to constrain such an obviously limitless character. Whatever the case, it is no surprise that, as Albert Schweitzer warned in his epic work on the historical Jesus, we continue to create Christ in our own image, making a Jesus that looks like us and is comfortable to us.[2]

Indeed, physical descriptions are rare in the NT canon for whatever reason. In the section that follows, we will consider the possibility of some physiognomic overtones to the healing narratives. One might also find possibility in the Pauline writings[3] or in the Apocalypse,[4] but those

[1] I consider Luke and Acts a separate discussion in this case, as will be shown in the next chapter. To offer brief explanation here, Mikeal C. Parsons, *Body and Character in Luke and Acts: The Subversion of Physiognomy in Early Christianity* (Grand Rapids: Baker Academic Press, 2006), esp. 81, has made a compelling case that Luke is employing physiognomics for the purpose of overturning those conventions, making Luke something of an anti-physiognomist. In this case, Luke cannot possibly give a physical description of someone like Jesus. If Luke offers a positive physical description, then he cannot be an anti-physiognomist; yet he also cannot offer a negative description that makes Jesus ugly and implies bad things about him either. Thus in the case of Luke, a description must be left out altogether.

[2] Albert Schweitzer, *The Quest for the Historical Jesus: A Critical Study of Its Progress from Reimarus to Wrede* (Baltimore: John Hopkins University Press, 1998), especially his final chapter, 398–403.

[3] Parsons offers a good discussion of Paul's rhetoric concerning his own body. See Parsons, *Body and Character in Luke and Acts*, 48–51. See also the following articles and books that explore the nature of Paul's corporal rhetoric: Jennifer A. Glancy, "Boasting of Beatings (2 Corinthians 11:23–25)," *JBL* 123 (2004): 99–135; J. Albert Harrill, "Invective against Paul (2 Cor 10:10), the Physiognomics of the Ancient Slave Body, and the Greco-Roman Rhetoric of Manhood," in *Antiquity and Humanity: Essays on Ancient Religion and Philosophy Presented to Hans Dieter Betz on His 70th Birthday* (ed. Adela Yarbro Collins and Margaret M. Mitchell; Tübingen: Mohr Siebeck, 2001), 189–213; Jennifer Larson, "Paul's Masculinity," *JBL* 123 (2004): 85–97; Dale B. Martin, *The Corinthian Body* (New Haven, CT: Yale University Press, 1995); and Karl Olav Sandnes, *Belly and Body in the Pauline Epistles* (Cambridge: Cambridge University Press, 2002).

[4] Here one might think of the descriptions of the heavenly creatures in Rev 4 with their many eyes. One might also find meaning in zoological physiognomics given the

will not be explored herein. While examples of physical descriptions are rare within the NT, physiognomics is much more widely used in non-canonical literature and among the Church Fathers. Physiognomics, then, was still very much a part of the early Christian milieu and thus would be a part of the interpretive grid of the ancient auditor. Here, we consider in detail the examples of Paul's description in the Acts of Paul as well as Ambrose's use of physiognomics to read the character of current and potential ministers.

Healing Narratives

The New Testament contains a host of stories that involve Jesus healing various diseases and disorders of the body, and a word is in order about those healing stories as we begin the discussion of physiognomics in the New Testament. Several stories present themselves as possible examples of physiognomy. One might think of the mute found in Matt 9:32–33 and recall what Ps-Aristotle says concerning the voice. The voice is a prime indicator of manliness and bravery, and the best voice is the one that is strong and deep. Ps-Aristotle writes, "the strong voice must be confined to the brave and the slack and weak voice the cowardly" (807a). While the issue of an absent voice is not addressed directly, a mute certainly would fall into the category of the weak voice rather than the strong. One might also think of the many cases of lepers who are healed by Jesus. Ps-Aristotle (812a) talks about various problems of the complexion, although leprosy is not addressed specifically in his or any other handbook. If much more minor imperfections in the skin indicate bad character traits, however, it is not difficult to imagine that an ancient reader would have drawn very negative conclusions about the character of a leper as well. Perhaps an ancient auditor might also hear various character traits in the healing of the deaf, the paralyzed, or the man with a withered hand. Because of the belief that changes in the body will be reflected in the character and vice versa, the ancient auditor would have expected a character change in the healed person, whatever the auditor might have assumed about the person in the first place.

A cautionary word is in order here, though, lest we get too carried away with finding examples of physiognomics lurking in every healing

number of animals used in the Apocalypse, including the lamb, dragon, lion, ox, and eagle, just to name a few. In a book so heavily laden with symbolism, one would suspect that physiognomics would be an easy fit.

narrative. Coleen Grant makes this point well. The healing stories are generally not about the person being healed, but they are interested in the healing power of Christ. These stories teach Christological lessons by and large.[5] With this in mind, one must be careful when reading the stories in light of physiognomics because the goal of physiognomics is the characterization of the person whose body is being described. Since the person being healed is typically a secondary character in the story, however, very little is done in terms of characterization. The recipients of the healings tend to be flat, undeveloped characters. They rarely speak or act in the narrative, and they rarely make a second appearance in the story; they are usually little more than nameless, faceless recipients of the healing power of Christ, the one who is the proper object of attention in the story.

There are a few exceptions to this rule, however, and most of the blind healing stories seem to be of a completely different sort. The blind characters tend to be more developed, the narrative gives more attention to them, and they usually have speaking lines; the blind characters are significant characters rather than the necessary but undeveloped characters of most of the other healing narratives. They are more than mere passive recipients of a healing, and thus while we resist making too much of other healing stories in terms of physiognomic implications, the blind stories require more attention and care. So while one might perhaps be able to hear some physiognomic overtones in the healing stories, we will confine our attention here to the healing of the blind where we stand on much firmer ground.

The Acts of Paul

The apocryphal *Acts of Paul* begins with a rather famous description of the apostle Paul. The description is significant because it is rare—both the New Testament and the non-canonical Christian literature resist offering physical descriptions of main characters such as Jesus or the apostles. The description found in *Acts of Paul*, then, is significant both because it is rare and because it uses physiognomic conventions to characterize Paul. A certain Onesiphorus of Iconium, upon hearing that Paul was coming to his city, wished to welcome Paul into his home.

---

[5] Coleen C. Grant, "Reinterpreting the Healing Narratives," in *Human Disability and the Service of God: Reassessing Religious Practice* (ed. Nancy L. Eiesland and Don E. Saliers;. Nashville: Abingdon, 1998), 73.

Onesiphorus went out to meet Paul, armed only with the knowledge of the apostle's appearance as described to him by Titus. We then find the following physical description of Paul:

> And he saw Paul coming, a man small of stature, with a bald head and crooked legs, in a good state of body, with eyebrows meeting and nose somewhat hooked, full of friendliness; for now he appeared like a man, and now he had the face of an angel.[6]

This description, imbedded in a second-century work, is the only such literary depiction of Paul's appearance.[7] It is only in relatively recent years that scholarship has come to realize that the description of Paul is best understood not as a mere physical depiction, but instead as a rhetorical depiction that partakes in the conventions of physiognomics. That is, it is certainly possible that the author of the *Acts of Paul* thought that Paul actually looked as described; yet, if the text is understood as reflecting physiognomic conventions, one finds a deeper rhetorical significance to the description in which the physical characteristics point to the moral character of the apostle. Specifically, the description is presented near the beginning of the document in order to characterize the apostle and give the reader an indication of how the main character will behave throughout the story. Before examining the description, it is helpful to begin with a survey of the scholarship on this depiction since there is no real consensus as of yet.

Roughly a century ago, the scholarly consensus took the physical description of Paul as a literal depiction, a literary photograph of sorts, likely written by someone who knew the apostle firsthand. As that consensus crumbled in the early 1900s, a flurry of options was forwarded, helpfully chronicled by Malherbe's brief but immensely important article.[8] Paul's description was understood variously as ugly,

---

[6] The translation is that of Schneemelcher, *New Testament Apocrypha*, 2:239. The Greek text reads as follows: ἄνδρα μικρόν τῷ μεγέθει, ψιλὸν τῇ κεφαλῇ, ἀγκύλον ταῖς κνήμαις, εὐεκτικόν, σύνοφρυν, μικρῶς ἐπίρρινον, χάριτος πλήρη· ποτὲ μὲν γὰρ ἐφαίνετο ὡς ἄνθρωπος, ποτέ δέ ἀγγέλου πρόσωπον εἶχεν. It is interesting to note that absent from this description are any references to the scars of which Paul is so proud in his letters. On this point, see the recent article by Jennifer A. Glancy, "Boasting of Beatings (2 Corinthians 11:23–25)," *JBL* 123 (2004): 99–135.

[7] There are, however, several artistic representations throughout the centuries. Those have been gathered in E. von Dobshütz, *Der Apostel Paulus: II. Seine Stellung in der Kunst* (Halle: Buchhandlung des Waisenhauses, 1928) and in Giuseppe Ricciotti, *Paul the Apostle* (trans. Alba I. Zizzamia; Milwaukee: Bruce, 1953), 151–59.

[8] See notes 4–10 in Abraham J. Malherbe, "A Physical Description of Paul," in *Christians Among Jews and Gentiles: Essays in Honor of Krister Stendahl on his Sixty-fifth Birthday*

plain, small, unflattering, or as a typical portrait of the Jewish male. One author even took the description as a portrayal of Paul as the antichrist![9] The majority opinion though would probably have deferred to Martin Luther, who took Paul as contemptible and poor in appearance.[10] In the final decades of the twentieth century, however, many scholars began to understand the description of Paul as a physiognomic description. Since then, four significant interpretations of this description have been forwarded, and those interpretations have very little in agreement, particularly when it comes to understanding what sources lie in the background of the description and how the description is supposed to portray Paul.

Robert Grant began the current conversation when he argued that the description of Paul was not historical fact but was borrowing from the physiognomic tradition.[11] He argues that the description of Paul is taken directly from a passage from the popular poet Archilochus, who writes the following in his *Elegy and Iambus II*: "I love not a tall general nor a straddling, nor one proud of his hair nor one part-shaven; for me a man should be short and bowlegged to behold, set firm on his feet, full of heart."[12] Grant argues that the description of Paul comes directly from Archilochus, and thus the reader would understand that Paul is being depicted as the ideal general in the army of God based on familiarity with the work of Archilochus. Grant, however, failed to recognize how widespread these physiognomic conventions were, and thus erroneously connects the description of Paul with that of Archilochus's general rather than with the larger physiognomic consciousness. Grant was answered quickly by Malherbe,[13] who confirms Grant's assertion that the description is best understood in light of physiognomics, but

(ed. George W. E. Nickelsburg with George W. MacRae; Philadelphia: Fortress, 1986): 170–171.

[9] E. Preuschen, "Paulus als Antichrist" *ZNW* 2 (1901): 169–201, esp. pages 191–193.

[10] I do not wish to imply that modern scholars do not also hold this view. For one example, see E. Margaret Howe, "Interpretations of Paul in the Acts of Paul and Thecla," in *Pauline Studies: Essays Presented to Professor F. F. Bruce on His 70th Birthday* (ed. Donald A. Hagner and Murray J. Harris; Grand Rapids: Eerdmans, 1980), 44, who writes, "The canonical material parallels the *Acts of Paul and Thecla* in its suggestion that Paul's personal appearance was not outstandingly attractive, although the evidence is sometimes slight and open to other interpretations."

[11] Robert M. Grant, "The Description of Paul in the Acts of Paul and Thecla," *VC* 36 (1982): 1–4.

[12] Archilochus, *Elegy and Iambus II* 58 (LCL).

[13] Malherbe, "A Physical Description of Paul," 170–175.

he disputes the source of that description. Malherbe argues that the description of Paul is borrowed from the descriptions of Heracles that were well known in the ancient world, in particular the description found in Philostratus.[14] The rhetorical effect, then, is to portray Paul as a beautiful figure, a hero among the Greeks, and perhaps even as a semi-divine figure like Heracles who is something more than a mere human. Both Grant and Malherbe err by linking the description of Paul to this or that description in the ancient world rather than to the larger physiognomic consciousness.

A third approach is that taken by János Ballók.[15] Aside from the final statement about Paul having the face of an angel which Ballók connects to Valentinian Gnosticism, he takes the rest of the descriptors as decisively negative and representative of weakness, lack of intelligence, and the like. Ballók connects the description found in *Acts of Paul* with 2 Corinthians, where we find some evidence of how Paul is perceived by others. Ballók makes a one-for-one correspondence between charges against Paul stated or implied in 2 Corinthians and the description in the *Acts of Paul*, assuming that the author of the *Acts of Paul* worked backwards from the evidence in 2 Corinthians and a knowledge of physiognomy in order to derive what must have been the physical appearance of the apostle. Though Ballók takes the physiognomic tradition seriously, the oddity of this position is that it takes the description negatively, a reading that no other scholar seems to support.

A fourth approach is that of Malina and Neyrey, who have written the most thorough piece to date on the physiognomy of Paul.[16] They argue, somewhat similarly to Bollók though without the use of 2 Cor, that if one can go from the physical characteristics to the implied moral and personal characteristics, then it is a short step to run the process in reverse; that is, one should be able to go just as easily from the moral and personal characteristics that are known about a person backwards

[14] See Philostratus, *Lives of the Sophists*, 552. Malherbe writes, "Heracles and traditions associated with him were used extensively in early Christianity, and I suggest that the author of the *Acts* derived his description of Paul from these sources" ("A Physical Description of Paul," 175).

[15] János Ballók, "The Description of Paul in the Acta Pauli," in *The Apocryphal Acts of Paul and Thecla* (ed. Jan N. Bremmer; Kampen, Netherlands: Kok Pharos Publishing House, 1996), 1–15.

[16] Bruce J. Malina, and Jerome H. Neyrey, *Portraits of Paul: An Archaeology of Ancient Personality* (Louisville: Westminster John Knox Press, 1996), esp. ch. 4, "Physiognomics and Personality: Looking at Paul in *The Acts of Paul*."

to what that person must have looked like. They argue that this physiognomy-in-reverse, as it were, is precisely what has been done by the author of the *Acts of Paul*. The author of that document, then, knows traditions about Paul and most likely the writings of Paul, and is thus able to work backwards to reconstruct what the apostle looked like. Yet their interpretation, in the end, is less than helpful. They conclude that Paul, when all is said and done, is being portrayed simply as "the ideal male."[17] Such a conclusion, though undergirded by much that is useful, is ultimately unhelpful and overly reductionistic.

So what would an ancient auditor have likely heard in the description of Paul? I am suggesting that the auditor would have heard in this description a series of implied character traits and would have expected the apostle to in turn behave accordingly, which he does. It is a resoundingly positive description on the whole, with each of the constituent parts contributing to the overall portrait. Let us briefly examine each of the descriptors in light of the physiognomic traditions.

If there were any debate over whether the description is positive or negative, the final descriptor lays the discussion to rest, and thus we shall begin at the end. To describe Paul as full of grace and as having the face of an angel can be nothing but positive. Two New Testament echoes make the meaning clear. First, John 1:14 describes Jesus as full of grace. Second, the martyrdom of Stephen describes him as "full of grace and power" (Acts 6:8) and as having the face of an angel (Acts 6:15). One is hard pressed to find examples in Greek literature of the phrase "full of grace" or "face of an angel" that are used in any other context, giving the reader confidence that Paul is being cast in the mold of Jesus and Stephen.[18] Jesus and Stephen are the defining

---

[17] Malina and Neyrey, "Physiognomy and Personality," 146.

[18] There are 135 occurrences in all of Greek literature of "πλήρη" and "χάριτος", in their various forms and in close proximity to one another. Nearly without exception, the texts are speaking directly about either Jesus as the μονογενοῦς from the Father who is full of grace and truth (usually in commentaries on the Fourth Gospel or in homilies), or the martyrdom of Stephen. The only exceptions seem to be in cases where various saints are described as "full of grace," and such examples only strengthen our confidence (See particularly *Sancti Pachomii vita quarta* 452 [TLG #4373.007], *Vita sancti Fantini iunioris* 51 [TLG #5064.001], and *Vita Nicolai Sionitae* 5 [TLG #5066.001]). Likewise, when we search for uses of the words ἀγγέλου and πρόσωον, in their various forms and in close proximity to each other, we find less than 50 references. Nearly all of these references post-date the New Testament and are Christian writings speaking of Stephen. Particularly interesting is John Chrysostom's commentary *On the Epistle of 2nd Corinthians*, 61.449 where he makes a close link between Saul, who saw the face of Stephen shining like the face of an angel, and the effect the experience would have

examples of Christian martyrdom, and to describe Paul in language that conjures imagery of both Jesus and Stephen is to portray Paul as a faithful martyr in their same trajectory. Paul of course suffers the same fate and does so faithfully, and the reader can see this coming from the opening description.

As for the more conventional physical descriptors, Paul is first described as "small of stature" and "in a good state of body." To be short in stature can very easily be a negative characteristic; in the biblical material one might think specifically of Zacchaeus in Luke 19.[19] Additionally, given the value accorded to great height as a sign of courage, leadership, and military prowess, one might expect shortness to imply exactly the opposite and thus be a negative marker. Such a reading might be the case, except that "in a good state of body" occurs in conjunction. Shortness need not necessarily be a negative description if one's body is still proportional.[20] Particularly helpful here is Ps-Aristotle who links shortness to intelligence:

> Excessively small men are quick; for as the blood travels over a small area, impulses arrive very quickly at the seat of the intelligence [i.e., the heart]. But the excessively large are slow; for as the blood travels over a large area the impulses arrive slowly at the seat of the intelligence. (813b:8–12)

For Ps-Aristotle, then, to be short can mean that one is intelligent, and so the reader of the *Acts of Paul* might make a similar conclusion about Paul since "short" occurs in an overall positive description and in conjunction with "a good state of body." Certainly, Paul demonstrates great intelligence throughout the document, proving to be an effective orator who is able to construct persuasive speeches about the gospel and also able to construct moving defense speeches.

---

had on Paul the apostle. Chyrsostom may be giving witness to a tradition similar to that of the AP in which there is a tight exegetical link between Stephen and Paul. In the cases of both "full of grace" and "face of an angel" the reader, particularly a Christian one, would immediately recall the Stephen episode.

[19] See Mikeal C. Parsons, "'Short in Stature': Luke's Physical Description of Zacchaeus," *NTS* 47 (2001): 50–57.

[20] See especially Suetonius's Augustus, who is short in stature, but the shortness is disguised by the fine symmetry of his body. Short, in Augustus's case, is not a bad characteristic so long as his body has a good symmetry relative to his height. Such might also be the case for Paul.

Paul is also called bald in this description, a descriptor that is typically negative.[21] As has been discussed in previous chapters, having long hair is a sign of manliness, strength, and virility.[22] Paul lacks hair. While the descriptor would typically be negative,[23] we would like to suggest that in this particular context, it is given a positive spin. That is, if long hair is a sign of virility and baldness indicates a lack of virility, in a document that has sexual asceticism as a major theme it is important that Paul be portrayed as one who lacks—or better, controls—sexual appetites. Aristotle states in *Generation of Animals* that the cause of baldness is a "lack of hot fluid."[24] In the case of the human, "hot fluids" can be either the blood or, in the case of the male, semen. Following Aristotle, baldness can be an ambiguous description open to multiple interpretations.[25] Either one is *too* sexually active and has consequently lost too much semen, cooling the brain, and causing the hair to fall out; or, because of an insufficient amount of semen produced, one is not sexually active at all. Both the lack of adequate amounts of semen as well as the overactive secretion of semen would have the same effect—both would cool the body, cool the brain, and cause the hair to fall out, according to Aristotle.

The question as it concerns Paul is which of the two is he? Is Paul considered sexually promiscuous, making Thecla Paul's consort? Certainly some in the narrative suspect just that. Or is Paul being portrayed as having a low sex drive? The latter seems more likely in a story in which Paul is the hero, and if true, it is an important feature for an unwed traveling preacher who preaches sexual purity and has female companions. If this second option is accepted, then baldness in the

---

[21] Many are quick to conclude that the baldness is literally true of Paul, calling into evidence such passages as Acts 18:18 and 21:24 as well as the rich iconography that portrays Paul as bald with surprising consistency. Malherbe, "Physical Description," 175, is one such scholar. While Paul may well have been bald, it is of no consequence here. Instead, we are interested in what an audience would have thought when they heard this description, and if the historical Paul was actually bald, then so be it.

[22] See especially Maud W. Gleason, *Making Men: Sophists and Self-Presentation in Ancient Rome* (Princeton, Princeton University Press, 1995), 68–69, who asserts that "Hairiness in general is the mark of a manly nature" and gives the primary source material behind the assertion.

[23] Take, for example, Suetonius's Caligula who is said to have "hair thin and entirely gone on the top of his head" (*Caligula*, 50). Though the physiognomic handbooks are silent on baldness, there are very few descriptions in ancient literature in which baldness is a positive characteristic.

[24] Aristotle, *Generation of Animals*, 783b (LCL).

[25] See *Gen. An.* 783b–784a.

description of Paul would be a way of saying that despite that fact that Paul travels around with women such as Thecla, you can tell just by looking at him that the relationship is not sexually immoral. In this way, Paul being bald is a good feature.

Paul is next said to have "crooked legs," bowlegged. As we have already seen, bent legs can be a sign of strength, particularly in the general or warrior. Recall Archilochus's general[26] and Philostratus's Heracles,[27] both of whom are bowlegged. Thus we see a tradition in which to have curved legs shows that one is firmly planted on a strong foundation, demonstrating the desirable quality of one who is fearless and willing to stand his ground. Paul is certainly that.

Paul is also said to have meeting eyebrows. There is a lengthy tradition of the meeting eyebrows as a sign of beauty, including Philostratus,[28] Suetonius,[29] Anatolius.[30] He is also said to have a crooked nose, or better translated, a long nose (ἐπίρρινον). Unfortunately, the term is never treated in the physiognomic handbooks, and the dozen uses of the term in extant Greek literature are both too rare and too poorly defined for us to draw any solid conclusions.

When the entire description is put together, the *Acts of Paul* provides a heroic portrait of the apostle that conforms to the conventions of physiognomics. The description appears at the front of the narrative as if to foreshadow the kind of behavior that the reader can expect from the main character. It is a physiognomic description whose rhetorical value is to set the stage for the narrative that is to follow, and it is a description that a physiognomically-conscious auditor would have readily understood.

Ambrose and the Early Christian Tradition

In Ambrose's *On the Duties of the Clergy*, one finds a strange scene in which Ambrose refuses to allow a man to become a bishop on the basis of his gestures and refuses association with another clergy on

---

[26] Archilochus, *Elegy and Iambus II* 58.

[27] *Vit. Soph.* 552.

[28] See *Heroikos* 33.39 where the unibrow is found as a sign of beauty in a conversation between the Vinedresser and the Phoenician. See also Philostratus's description of Heracles in *Vit. Soph.* 552.

[29] Suetonius, *Aug.* 79.

[30] See Anatolius, *Περὶ γεννήσεως*, 8.188.13 (TLG #2577.003) for his description of Aphrodite in which the meeting eyebrows is a sign of her great beauty. This work is a first century work that gives descriptions of many of the gods.

the basis of the way he walks. In later paragraphs, Ambrose criticizes the voice in addition to the gestures. The passage from Ambrose bears quoting in full:

> 71. Modesty must further be guarded in our very movements and gestures and gait. For the condition of the mind is often seen in the attitude of the body. For this reason the hidden man of our heart (our inner self) is considered to be either frivolous, boastful, or boisterous, or, on the other hand, steady, firm, pure, and dependable. Thus the movement of the body is a sort of voice of the soul.
> 72. Ye remember, my children, that a friend of ours who seemed to recommend himself by his assiduity in his duties, yet was not admitted by me into the number of the clergy, because his gestures were too unseemly. Also that I bade one, whom I found already among the clergy, never to go in front of me, because he actually pained me by the seeming arrogance of his gait. That is what I said when he returned to his duty after an offence committed. This alone I would not allow, nor did my mind deceive me. For both have left the Church. What their gait betrayed them to be, such were they proved to be by the faithlessness of their hearts. The one forsook his faith at the time of the Arian troubles; the other, through love of money, denied that he belonged to us, so that he might not have to undergo sentence at the hands of the Church. In their gait was discernible the semblance of fickleness, the appearance, as it were, of wandering buffoons.
> 73. Some there are who in walking perceptibly copy the gestures of actors, and act as though they were bearers in the processions, and had the motions of nodding statues, to such an extent that they seem to keep a sort of time, as often as they change their step.
> 74. Nor do I think it becoming to walk hurriedly, except when a case of some danger demands it, or a real necessity. For we often see those who hurry come up panting, and with features distorted. But if there is no reason for the need of such hurry, it gives cause for just offence. I am not, however, talking of those who have to hurry now and then for some particular reason, but of those to whom, by the yoke of constant habit, it has become a second nature. In the case of the former I cannot approve of their slow solemn movements, which remind one of the forms of phantoms. Nor do I care for the others with their headlong speed, for they put one in mind of the ruin of outcasts.
> 75. A suitable gait is that wherein there is an appearance of authority and weight and dignity, and which has a calm collected bearing. But it must be of such a character that all effort and conceit may be wanting, and that it be simple and plain. Nothing counterfeit is pleasing. Let nature train our movements. If indeed there is any fault in our nature, let us mend it with diligence. And, that artifice may be wanting, let not amendment be wanting.
> 76. But if we pay so much attention to things like these, how much more careful ought we to be to let nothing shameful proceed out of our

> mouth, for that defiles a man terribly. It is not food that defiles, but unjust disparagement of others and foul words....
> 84. The voice, too, should not be languid, nor feeble, nor womanish in its tone,—such a tone of voice as many are in the habit of using, under the idea of seeming important. It should preserve a certain quality, and rhythm, and a manly vigour. For all to do what is best suited to their character and sex, that is to attain to beauty of life. This is the best order for movements, this the employment fitted for every action. But as I cannot approve of a soft or weak tone of voice, or an effeminate gesture of the body, so also I cannot approve of what is boorish and rustic. Let us follow nature. The imitation of her provides us with a principle of training, and gives us a pattern of virtue.[31]

To the twenty-first-century reader, it is offensive to modern sensibilities that one would be denied ordination on the basis of the way one walks or talks. Yet this is exactly what one finds at work in Ambrose. The reason, of course, that Ambrose would react so strongly to things so seemingly insignificant as walk, talk, and gestures is physiognomics. Ambrose believed that character was discernable in such things as the voice and gait.

Few of the examples of physiognomics seen so far are as overt as this text from Ambrose, who states plainly that he is making judgments based on physiognomics: "For the condition of the mind is often seen in the attitude of the body...Thus the movement of the body is a sort of voice of the soul" (*Duties* 71). Let us explore two specific physiognomic markers employed by Ambrose: the walk and the talk.

In the first case, a would-be clergy is rejected by Ambrose because his deportment or gestures were "unseemly." "Unseemly" for Ambrose implies ideas of sexual impurity or behaviors which violate the virtue of modesty.[32] In the second case, Ambrose avoids an already-ordained clergy because his gait portrays arrogance. Though the reader is not told exactly what these gestures looked like or specifically what sort of gait these men had, the reader does know Ambrose's interpretation of those signs. The reader also knows that Ambrose's diagnosis of both men was apparently correct, since both proved to be "faithless" in a time of trouble. It is helpful, then, to make a list of the charges levied

[31] Ambrose, *On the Duties of the Clergy*, 1.18.71–76, 84 (*NPNF*[2] 10). For two scholars who have treated this story see Gleason, *Making Men*, 60–62, and Parsons, *Body and Character*, 59–61.

[32] See especially Ambrose, *On the Duties of the Clergy*, 1.18.76 and 1.18.78.

against these men based on their gait and deportment: unseemliness, arrogance, faithlessness, and fickleness.

What can be deduced about the way they must have been walking? And what is the "correct" way to walk? The handbook traditions are helpful here, especially Ps-Aristotle. In his longest single treatment of gait, Ps-Aristotle writes,

> The man with a long, slow step is a slow starter but carries on to the end, for a long step implies a good beginning, and a slow one procrastination. The man with a short, slow step is a slow starter, but does not carry on to the end, for a short and slow movement is poor at accomplishment. A man with a long quick step is a slow starter, but carries on to the end, because swiftness ensures finishing, but length is not good at starting. The man with a short quick step starts well but does not last. (813a)

This paragraph reads much like a riddle, for there seems to be no true solution to be found therein. All four combinations seem to be bad, so what is the "correct" gait? A gait that avoids all of the extremes is probably preferred, since the physiognomists tend to prefer moderation over extremes when it comes to physical markers. Yet with the gait, Ps-Aristotle has already described the ideal, and it is the gait of the lion: "he moves slowly with a long stride, and swings his shoulders as he moves" (809b). A man of ideal character will have the swagger of a lion.

Clearly, the men to whom Ambrose refers do not walk like the lion. Using Ps-Aristotle's four options above, one might imagine that the men whom Ambrose rejects are guilty of taking "short steps;" that is, they fail to finish their goals or accomplish their purposes as evidenced by their falling away in a time of crisis. Likewise, one might imagine that Ambrose's men are guilty of walking too quickly. Recall that Ambrose later explains, "Nor do I think it becoming to walk hurriedly, except when a case of some danger demands it, or a real necessity. For we often see those who hurry come up panting, and with features distorted. But if there is no reason for the need of such hurry, it gives cause for just offence" (1.18.74). Likewise, he states in the following paragraph that, "A suitable gait is that wherein there is an appearance of authority and weight and dignity, and which has a calm collected bearing. But it must be of such a character that all effort and conceit may be wanting, and that it be simple and plain" (1.18.75). Thus it appears that Ambrose has in mind a leonine walk, and he rejects these men on the basis of something like a hasty gait and/or short steps.

When attention is turned away from the gait specifically and to deportment more generally, one finds new areas of concern that were concerns shared by, or at least similar to those shared by, Ambrose. Ps-Aristotle writes the following concerning deportment:

> As to the carriage of the hand, arm and forearm, the same principles apply. Those who swing from side to side with straight stiff shoulders are blustering; witness horses. But those who stoop forward and swing their shoulders are high-minded; witness the lions. Those who walk with feet and legs turned out are effeminate; this applies to women. Those who swing and bend the body from side to side are flatterers; this applies to the affection. Those who incline to the right in their movements are morbid [or effeminate]; this is appropriate. (813a)

This paragraph needs to be compared to what is perhaps the most significant negative character portrayed in Ps-Aristotle—the "morbid" character. Ps-Aristotle says of this character "he carries his hands palm upward and slack, and he has two gaits—he either waggles his hips or holds them stiffly" (808a). If this character or some similar character is in view for Ambrose, it would capture both of Ambrose's most significant problems—sexual impurity and immodesty. The "morbid" man, (Greek κιναίδου, later translated in the Latin as *cinaedus*) is better understood as an effeminate character.[33] The effeminate character is despised and is closely related to the confusing and consequently outcast characters of the eunuch and the androgen. These characters are despised not only for their effeminacy but especially because they blur the lines between what is masculine and feminine. The androgynous character is described in Polemo and the Anonymous Latin handbook as follows:

> You may recognize him by his provocatively melting glance and by the rapid movement of his intensely staring eyes. His brow is furrowed while his eyebrows and cheeks are in constant motion. His head is tilted to the side, his loins do not hold still, and his slack limbs never stay in one position. He minces along with little jumping steps; his knees knock together. He carries his hands with palms turned upward. He has a shifting gaze, and his voice is thin, weepy, shrill, and drawling.[34]

---

[33] See Gleason, *Making Men*, 65, who argues that the term *cinaedus* is a synonym for *androgynos*. I find her argument convincing and am following it here, choosing to understand "morbid" as "effeminate." Significantly for this paper, Gleason also cites Clement of Alexandria, *Paidagogos* 3.29.2–3, who launches a scathing attack on the *androgynoi* and *cunaedi*. Thus, it is not just Ambrose who despises an effeminate self-portrayal.

[34] This quote is somewhat of a textual mess. The quote is taken from and is the translation of Gleason, *Making Men*, 63. Gleason, however, has constructed the quote

Gleason argues that gender does not necessarily have to do with anatomy: "Masculinity in the ancient world was an achieved state, radically underdetermined by anatomical sex."[35] That is, gender is not an either/or question, but it is instead a point on a spectrum in which "masculinity" is one pole and "femininity" is the other pole, with a great deal of room in between. Gleason quotes Polemo in this regard:

> You may obtain physiognomic indications of masculinity and femininity from your subject's glance, movement, and voice, and then, from among these signs, compare one with another until you determine to your satisfaction which of the two sexes prevails. For in the masculine there is something feminine to be found, and in the feminine there is something masculine, but the name *masculine* or *feminine* is assigned according to which of the two prevails.[36]

Movements, then, are one way to tell how masculine or how feminine someone may be. Masculinity, as one might expect, is the goal in the ancient world, particularly for those in positions of authority. As Ambrose uses it, then, part of what is at stake is that the clergy should be thoroughly masculine, both in gait and in voice.

Is there evidence in the quote from Ambrose that the effeminate character may in fact be in view? Indeed, I think there is. Recall that one of the most significant problems with these clergymen was that their gestures were "unseemly," a term that for Ambrose implies sexual immorality or lewdness of some sort. It is possible that these unseemly gestures include some combination of those of the effeminate as described above—feet turned outward (Ps-Aristotle); movements inclined to the right (Ps-Aristotle); head turned to the side (Polemo); palms carried upward and slack (Ps-Aristotle and Polemo); either of two gaits—either excessively waggling the hips, or holding them too stiffly (Ps-Aristotle); a hesitant gait (Polemo); frequent short steps (Polemo); limp limbs that glide slowly along (Polemo); loins that do not hold still (Polemo); and/or jumping steps (Polemo).

Taken alone, connecting these "unseemly" gestures to the effeminate character type would be too speculative. But Ambrose adds further

as a composite of Polemo LXI, which is incomplete textually, and the Anonymous Latin treatise that follows Polemo and whose text completes the missing portion of Polemo. The basic trajectory of the text, however, is intact.

[35] Gleason, *Making Men*, 59.

[36] Foerster, 1.192. The translation is that of Gleason, *Making Men*, 58.

light to the discussion several paragraphs later.[37] In that paragraph, he criticizes many things, including movements, gestures, and voice types that are effeminate. He criticizes the voice that is "languid," "feeble," or "womanish." Instead, the voice should "preserve a certain quality, and rhythm, and a manly vigour." He then exhorts "all to do what is best suited to their character and sex." He closes the paragraph by voicing his disapproval for "a soft or weak tone of voice, or an effeminate gesture of the body."

The issue of a voice that has "manly vigour" is crucial for Ambrose, as it is also for Ps-Aristotle. Ps-Aristotle writes, "In the matter of voice the deep and full voice denotes courage, when high and slack it means cowardice" (806b). As with deportment, voice can communicate something of one's courage or cowardice. The same sorts of stereotypes exist in the modern era as well, and are not a far stretch for the modern reader to conceive—the man with the deep voice is considered strong and manly; the man with the high voice is considered soft and, sometimes, effeminate. Certainly in the context of the Ambrose quote with clergy who abandon the faith in a time of trouble, cowardice is in view. Suffice it to say, then, that voice, as with deportment, has much to do with the politics of masculinity. Even the slightest violation of the masculine norm would open one to attacks against one's manhood.

When the evidence is all taken together, it is difficult to imagine that Ambrose would not have in mind some sort of effeminate gestures or manner of walking and talking that caused him to despise these lewd clergymen, solely on the basis of the way they carried themselves. The appearance of these men indicated at least four major problems for Ambrose: unseemliness, arrogance, faithlessness, and fickleness. Though one might deduce any number of gaits or gestures on their part, one thing is absolutely clear: however these men were carrying themselves, they failed to carry themselves in a way that is suitable for the man of God, and on the sole basis of appearance Ambrose rejects them and refuses any association with them. His conclusions are made for physiognomic reasons.

Ambrose, of course, is not alone in the early Christian tradition in his use of physiognomics. Many of the Fathers rejected the use of physiognomics, perhaps because it became too closely tied to astrology,

[37] The references to Ambrose in this paragraph are all found in *On the Duties of the Clergy* 1.18.84.

and its use came to look too much like sorcery.[38] Yet many who wrote in the Patristic era made use of physiognomic conventions, and we will mention some of those examples here. We have already noted Origen's statement, "And if there be any truth in the doctrine of the physiognomists, whether Zopyrus, or Loxus, or Polemon, or any other who wrote on such a subject, and who profess to know in some wonderful way that all bodies are adapted to the habits of the souls..." (*Cels* 1.33). Similarly, Clement of Alexandria (*Strom.* 1.21.135) classifies physiognomists into doctors and seers. Clement also talks about spotting an effeminate by the noises made with the nose, claiming that he can recognize such a person even if he is trying to conceal his true character (*Paed.* 3.5.29). Basil talks about voice, eyes, and gait in a letter to Gregory of Nazianzus.[39] Eusebius even offers a physiognomic description of the emperor Constantine:

> Constantinus Magnus was of medium height, broad-shouldered, thick-necked, whence his epithet Bull-necked. His complexion was ruddy, his hair neither thick nor crisp curling, his beard scanty and not growing in many places, his nose slightly hooked, and his eyes like the eyes of a lion. He was joyous of heart and most cheery of countenance. (*Vit. Const.*, Prolegomena, 2.3, NPNF)

In addition, a widely popular treatise among early Christians, often erroneously attributed to Ambrose or even Jerome, was the *The Physiologus*. In this work, characteristics of animals are discussed along with the corresponding moral traits.[40]

Examples could certainly be multiplied, but these are sufficient to illustrate the point. Whether for or against the use of physiognomics, what is clear is that the early Christian writers were well aware of these conventions and their audiences were conditioned to think in these terms. The point is that if the Fathers are using physiognomics, and if the Fathers give us evidence that early Christians also thought in these terms, then we are further justified in reading the biblical texts through those lenses. In fact, if authors and audiences thought in these terms, then we as modern readers of ancient texts are obligated to learn to

[38] On this point see especially Hippolytus, *Haer.* 4.15.

[39] *Saint Basil: The Letters I.2* (LCL, 20–21). Apparently, Gregory was fond of using physiognomics as well, according to Evans, *Physiognomics in the Ancient World*, 77–78. She cites several uses of physical descriptions in invectives.

[40] For an excellent recent discussion of this work, see Parsons, *Body and Character*, 56–58.

hear these texts as the ancients would have heard them, with all of the moral implications that these physical features would carry.

As we have seen, the early Christians were well aware of the conventions of physiognomics, even if such detailed descriptions were not canonized. Just as general physical descriptions are uncommon within the canon, however, instances of blindness abound. We now turn attention to some of those texts.

Examples of Blindness in the NT and Other Early Christian Literature

Examples of blindness are found frequently in the New Testament. One can quickly think of several examples of blind characters in the NT narratives, and one can think of many non-narrative uses of blindness where people are said to be blind to the gospel (consider Rom 2:19, 2 Pet 1:9, and Rev 3:17, among others). Blindness plays a prominent role in the New Testament, and in the pages that follow we will explore several key texts from the Gospels. Examples could be multiplied, but we will discuss four significant texts here. First, we will look at the man born blind in John 9, a character who follows the expected *topos* of a blind character. Second, we will look a Bartimaeus in Mark 10, a character who seems to break the expected *topos*, presumably for the purpose of highlighting the blindness of the disciples and others who fail to see and understand Jesus for who he is. Finally, we will explore the use of Isaiah 6 in the Gospels as a means of understanding Jesus' ministry. In all of these cases, properly understanding blindness is the key to interpreting the text, and it is clear that the freight carried by the concept of blindness is apparent in the texts. Before turning to those texts, however, a word is in order regarding the concept of vision in the New Testament world, and to this end we need to consider the statement by Jesus that the "eye is the lamp of the body" found in both Matthew and Luke.

"The Eye is the Lamp of the Body" (Matt 6:22–23 // Luke 11:34–36)

In the Sermon on the Mount, Jesus makes the following statement regarding the eyes: "The eye is the lamp of the body. So, if your eye is healthy, your whole body will be full of light; but if your eye is unhealthy, your whole body will be full of darkness. If then the light in you is darkness, how great is the darkness!" (Matt 6:22–23). The statement is paralleled, although not exactly so, in Luke 6:34–36: "Your eye is the lamp of your body. If your eye is healthy, your whole body is full of light; but if it is not healthy, your body is full of darkness. Therefore consider whether the light in you is not darkness. If then your whole body is full of light, with no part of it in darkness, it will be as full of light as when a lamp gives you light with its rays." The issue is whether the eye is healthy/good (ἁπλοῦς) or unhealthy/wicked (πονηρὸς). The eye is without question the "lamp of the body," a notion that we have seen repeatedly already. What is in question here is what sort of light or darkness is being sent out. Several good studies have been devoted to this text and are worth summary here. Works by Allison,[41] Betz,[42] and Elliott[43] have brought valuable insights to the table that must be understood.[44] Allison treats the Jewish background for Jesus' statement, Betz treats the Greek background, and Elliott looks specifically at the "Evil Eye" tradition.

Allison is of the opinion that the Jewish background of the statement is sufficient to understanding the text. Allison begins by outlining four ancient theories of vision, three of which carry some notable following in the ancient world.[45] Those three theories are intromission (light comes into the eyes to produce images), extramission (the eye emits or channels light in order to see), and a theory that assumes both. It is widely agreed that the extramission theory of vision is the theory at work in Jesus' proverbial statement about the eyes here. Allison cites a host of examples for the extramission theory and argues that this theory is the popular theory for most in the culture.[46] He follows with examples of this theory outside of the Greek world in various places, and finally lists numerous Jewish sources that assume this theory.[47] He then argues for the Jewish background as the most logical background

[41] Dale C. Allison, "The Eye Is the Lamp of the Body (Matthew 6:22–23 = Luke 11:34–36," *NTS* 33 (1987): 61–83.

[42] Hans Dieter Betz, "Matthew vi.22f and Ancient Greek Theories of Vision," in *Text and Interpretation: Studies in the New Testament Presented to Matthew Black* (ed. Enest Best and R. McL. Wilson; Cambridge: Cambridge University Press, 1979), 43–56.

[43] John H. Elliott, "The Evil Eye and the Sermon on the Mount: Contours of a Pervasive Belief in Social Scientific Perspective," *BibInt* 2 (1994): 51–84.

[44] Recently, Mikeal C. Parsons (*Body and Character in Luke and Acts: The Subversion of Physiognomy in Early Christianity* [Grand Rapids: Baker Academic Press, 2006], 76–81) has written both a summary of these three works and an exegesis of the Lukan passage specific to physiognomics.

[45] Allison, "The Eye is the Lamp of the Body," 62–63.

[46] For his examples see Allison, "The Eye is the Lamp of the Body," 62–63.

[47] See Allison, "The Eye is the Lamp of the Body," 64–69 for these two sets of examples.

for this statement found in the Gospels. What is especially significant for our purposes is the theory of vision that is assumed.

Betz devotes his entire essay to the exploration of the Greek theories of vision, and he includes a heavy list of examples.[48] He finds the background to the Jesus saying to be one of Greek philosophy, and while he explores other theories of vision, he concludes that Jesus' statement is ultimately assuming a theory of extramission. The sheer volume of his examples where such a theory can be seen in Greek texts makes his case compelling and difficult to dispute.

Finally, Elliott is concerned specifically with one strand of this theory of vision, the tradition of the "evil eye" in ancient cultures. He studies these traditions from a sociological perspective. In short, the evil eye tradition holds that if the eye emits light (assuming an extramission theory of vision), then a person can send out either good or bad light and affect the person upon whom such a light is cast. He lists a number of examples of the evil eye, and even discusses attempts to ward off the effects of this malicious attack, including magic spells, incantations, or even charms.[49] Elliott specifically notes that the blind were believed to be especially capable of wielding the evil eye,[50] and such a statement might seem odd at first. That is, if no light is coming out of the eye at all, how can a person use the "evil eye"? Upon further review, however, it is not the case that in an extramission theory of vision the blind person sends out no light at all; rather, the blind person is sending out darkness. In a physiognomic world, of course, the person who is physically blind is also spiritually blind, but there is more to say. That is, the person who is blind is also full of darkness, and the eye is emitting this very darkness. Such a physiognomic assumption would further contribute to the rejection and fear of the blind in the ancient world.

Here again, the beliefs about physical features that reflect inner character are apparent, and those assumptions are foundational to this particular saying of Jesus. If the eye is healthy, it is because the body is full of light; if the eye is not healthy, it is because the body is full of darkness. If one has a light-filled soul, then one's eyes emit good, healthy light; but if one's soul is darkness, then the eyes send out that darkness and the eye is evil. The character of the eye reflects the character of

[48] Betz, "Theories of Vision," 43–56.
[49] Elliott, "Evil Eye," 53.
[50] Elliott, "Evil Eye," 56.

the soul. Thus in this saying, we find the positive aspects of the eye. In most of the cases of blindness that we are about to encounter, the negative aspects of the eye are invoked.

John 9

As far as texts about blindness are concerned, none have received as much scholarly attention as the man born blind in John 9. Since so many excellent studies exist on this passage,[51] there is no need to critically analyze every aspect of this text as that would be to reinvent the wheel. It should be noted, however, that the preponderance of recent work on John 9 has been dominated by the concern over being put out of the synagogue and what that might have meant for the Johannine community that produced this Gospel.[52] In the present study our goal is to explore this text with specific attention to how an ancient auditor would have understood the element of blindness in the story and how both the blindness and its healing would have served as windows into the character of the man born blind. To give away the conclusion, this man follows the expected pattern—he is spiritually blind when he lacks physical sight, but the gift of his physical sight also grants him spiritual insight as well. At the same time, he is set up as a foil to the religious leaders who, though having healthy eyes, fail to see the truth of Jesus that is plainly before them. This text is significant for our study of blindness because it overtly spells out the imagery within the text

[51] In addition to the shelves of excellent commentaries on the Gospel of John, a number of studies have been devoted specifically to John 9. For studies specific to this text, see especially the following: Felix N. W. Just. "From Tobit to Bartimaeus, from Qumran to Siloam: The Social Role of Blind People and Attitudes Toward the Blind in New Testament Times," (Ph.D. diss., Yale University, 1997); Dorothy A. Lee, *The Symbolic Narrative of the Fourth Gospel: The Interplay of Form and Meaning* (JSNTSup 95; Sheffield: JSOT Press, 1994); James L. Resseguie, "John 9: A Literary-Critical Analysis," in *The Gospel of John as Literature: An Anthology of Twentieth-Century Perspectives* (ed Mark W. G. Stibbe; Leiden: Brill, 1993): 115–22; Jeffrey L. Staley, "Stumbling in the Dark, Reaching for the Light: Reading Character in John 5 and 9," *Semeia* 53 (1991): 55–80; J. Warren, Holleran, "Seeing the Light: A Narrative Reading of John 9," *ETL* 69 (1993): 354–82.

[52] On this topic most commentators defer to J. Louis Martyn and Raymond Brown. See in particular J. Louis Martyn, *History and Theology in the Fourth Gospel* (New York: Harper and Row, 1968) and Raymond Brown, *The Gospel According to John I–XII: A New Translation with Introduction and Commentary* (AB 29; New York: Doubleday, 1966), esp. 380, along with Brown's *The Community of the Beloved Disciple* (New York: Paulist Press, 1979).

itself (9:39–41), making it clear that physical blindness was linked to spiritual blindness in antiquity.

This text is also significant because of its strong history of interpretation, a history that runs up to the modern era with a song as well known as "Amazing Grace." The first verse of the hymn famously states that "I once was lost but now I'm found, was blind but now I see." The meaning is self-evident: no one sings this song and means that their physical eyesight was lacking until they met Jesus. No, the meaning is clearly that Jesus has opened the spiritual eyes of the believer. The lyric for the hymn, of course, is drawn from John 9:25 where the man who was formerly blind proclaims, "One thing I do know, that though I was blind, now I see." That blindness and sight are metaphors for one's spiritual insight has a longstanding interpretive tradition indeed.

The passage begins with a theological question from the disciples: "Who sinned, this man or his parents, that he was born blind?" The first thing that ought to be noticed is that the disciples assume one of the elements of the blind *topos*, namely, that blindness is a divine punishment. Their question was not *if* someone sinned to cause the blindness, but *who* sinned; it is assumed that someone must have.[53] The Gospel's audience would have been conditioned to make the same assumption.[54] A good deal of scholarly attention is then focused on Jesus' answer to the question. The answer is cryptic and difficult to understand, and even the syntax of the sentence obscures the meaning.[55] Additionally, as has often been pointed out, the ἵνα clause can either be purpose or result—was he born blind *so that* the works of God might be revealed

[53] As Brown (*John*, 371) notes, the theory that physical disorders are linked to sin was still very pervasive in the first century world, even with works like Job testifying to the contrary. See also C. K. Barrett, *The Gospel According to St. John: An Introduction with Commentary and Notes on the Greek Text* (London: S.P.C.K., 1955), 294–95; George R. Beasley-Murray, *John* (WBC 36; Nashville: Thomas Nelson Publishers, 1999), 154–55; Gerald L. Borchert, *John 1–11* (NAC 25A; Nashville: Broadman and Holman Publishers, 1996), 312–313; D. A. Carson, *The Gospel According to John* (Grand Rapids: Eerdmans, 1991), 361–62; Ernst Haenchen, *John 2: A Commentary on the Gospel of John Chapters 7–21* (*Herm*; trans. Robert W. Funk; Philadelphia: Fortress, 1984), 37; Andreas J. Köstenberger, *John* (Baker Exegetical Commentary on the New Testament; Grand Rapids: Baker Academic, 2004), 281; Rudolf Schnackenburg, *The Gospel According to John* (New York: Seabury Press, 1980), 2:240–41; Talbert, *Reading John: A Literary and Theological Commentary on the Fourth Gospel and the Johannine Epistles* (New York: Crossroad, 1994), 158.

[54] For the best brief discussion of the notion of the "sins of the parents" in the ancient world, see Garland, *Eye of the Beholder*, 59–61.

[55] See Charles Talbert, *Reading John*, 158–59 for a brief discussion of two different ways to punctuate Jesus' answer that give two different readings of the passage.

in him, or was he born blind *with the result that* the works of God might be revealed in him? The syntax is elusive, as is Jesus' answer. Jesus does not offer a complete rebuttal of the theology assumed by his disciples, at least not the kind of rebuttal that we in the modern era tend to expect or even claim to find in the narrative. Jesus does say the blindness is not caused by sin, but he continues by attributing a divine purpose to the blindness nonetheless—"so that/with the result that God's works might be revealed in him." This statement is only a partial break with the expected *topos*—the man is not being divinely punished, but his blindness does serve a divine purpose in some fashion or another, and those are not altogether different. Thus, the *topos* is still very much in play here, not only with the erroneous assumption of the disciples, but also in the explanation given—his blindness is by divine appointment, however that may be understood.

This unnamed man also fits the expected *topos* in that he is pitied and helpless. It is presumed that he is sitting by the road begging when Jesus spots him, and he is identified by the crowd later as a beggar (9:8). Not only is he in need of charity when Jesus finds him, but he is also utterly helpless. Note that he does not come to Jesus on his own; he is merely discovered. He is passively sitting by the road, presumably waiting for charity, and taking no initiative so far as the text tells us. He also does not ask Jesus to heal him. In fact, the blind man says nothing. He is but a passive recipient of the healing, and the only thing the blind man does is obey by going to the pool to wash the mud from his eyes. Thus the man born blind is an excellent example of one who fits the *topos*—he is helpless, pitiable, and both the Pharisees and disciples assume that he is being divinely punished. Therefore, it would be logical to conclude that one might also assume the rest of the *topos*, that he is spiritually or morally blind as well.

Jesus heals the man's physical condition. One major question surrounding this text, however, is at what point the man's *spiritual* sight is healed? Does he gain sight immediately, gradually, or only when Jesus finally encounters him after the man's expulsion from the synagogue? How one answers that question has a great deal to do with how one understands the trail scenes that comprise the bulk of the passage. I argue that an ancient audience would have expected the man to gain his spiritual sight in the same moment that he gained his physical sight, but let us examine the passage to see if such a reading can be maintained.

Certainly not everyone whom Jesus heals comes to immediate faith in him. A glance at some of the other healings in this Gospel demonstrates that fact. For example, one might think of the lame man in John 5. There is no indication that he understands Jesus. He readily reports Jesus to the religious leaders and offers no defense of Jesus, and he shows very little gratitude for the healing. He may have been healed, but there is no indication that his eyes had been opened to who Jesus was, nor would a reader have readily expected the healing of lame legs to be tied to spiritual vision. But when a *blind* man is healed, his spiritual vision is tightly tied to his physically sight, and a reader would expect both to be restored—remember Ps-Aristotle's maxim that a change in character will result in a change in the body and vice versa. Thus when the blind man ceases to be blind, one would have also expected that his spiritual darkness would have likewise been lifted.

The blind man has his physical sight healed, and people immediately begin to question him. He knows very little, only the name of the man who healed him and the method. He does not know where Jesus is, nor is there much indication that he really understands Jesus' divine identity. In fact, when the Pharisees, who are themselves divided as to Jesus' identity, question the man and ask him who he says Jesus is, the man merely answers "He is a prophet" (9:17). This answer is difficult for the reader. It is not wrong, but it is incomplete; the reader knows that Jesus is in fact a prophet, but he is so much more than that, and thus it is difficult to know what to make of the man's statement.[56]

In many ways, the man seems like he is still very much blind. Notice also that while the narrator typically refers to the man as the one who was formerly blind (9:13, 34), he is anachronistically referred to as "the blind man" when the Pharisees first interrogate him (9:17). Just notes that this is not an accident, rather, it indicates the unfair judgments that the Pharisees continue to make about this man.[57] They refuse to see him as anything but a blind man, and thus as one who is spiritually blind too. The fact that the man is sighted is all the more stinging

[56] Beasley-Murray, *John*, 157 sees this title as a progressive step in the man's gradual spiritual growth. So also Carson, *John*, 368, and Köstenberger, *John*, 287. To the contrary, however, Brown, *John*, 373, seems to think the title means nothing more than that the man thinks Jesus has divine power or blessing but does not represent a faith statement of any sort. So also Barrett, *John*, 298–99, Schnackenburg, *John*, 248.

[57] Just, "From Tobit to Bartimaeus," 258.

to the Pharisees when the man begins to mock them and offer them enlightenment. In their minds, a blind man can no more teach them spiritual truth than a sinner who works on the Sabbath can be sent from God. Yet this is exactly their problem—the blind man is no longer blind, and the man they think is a sinner is anything but. Thus, the use of the title "blind man" after the man has gained his sight serves to further underscore the spiritual blindness of the Pharisees and their refusal to see the truth that stands plainly before their eyes.

The question still remains though, if the man now has his spiritual sight restored, why does he offer an incomplete answer to Jesus' identity, and why is he not more forthright? One obvious answer is that the man simply does not know any more than that because his insight is still only partial. Given the conventions of physiognomics, however, one would expect him to have spiritual vision. An interesting answer is offered by Staley, who applies some of the concepts of reading OT narrative proposed by scholars like Alter and Sternberg.[58] He argues that the formerly blind man is seeking to defend Jesus when he is interviewed by the Pharisees, and he lists several reasons. First, the man does not use Jesus' name as he had previously done when talking to the crowd, as if to protect his healer. Second, while the narrator used terms like "made mud" and "anointed his eyes," two things that would be apparent violations of the Sabbath law, the man simply states that Jesus "put mud on my eyes." Phrasing it this way, the man may be shielding Jesus from the potential violations of the Sabbath. In a final defense, the man even takes responsibility himself by saying "then *I* washed and *I* received my sight" instead of Jesus' command to go and wash. If Staley is correct, then the man had his spiritual vision restored when his eyes were opened, much as an ancient auditor would have expected, and he plays coy in the story in order to protect his benefactor.

After the first interrogation of the man, the parents are brought in. They are interviewed and it appears that they want to give the least amount of information possible since they are afraid of the Jewish leaders. 9:22 implies that they *would* confess that Jesus must be the Messiah, but they stop short of that out of fear.[59] We are not told specifically

[58] Staley, "Stumbling in the Dark, Reaching for the Light," 67.

[59] So most commentators. See Beasley-Murray, *John*, 157, who helpfully notes that parents who knew that their son was born blind would be just as likely to accept the identity of Jesus as the healed man would have, but they nevertheless feared reprisal. So also Köstenberger, *John*, 287–88.

how much they truly understand of Jesus. The recent scholarship on this passage has not dealt adequately with what the parents understand of their son's healing or the man responsible for it. Instead, the scholarship derails on 9:22 and to what extent being "put out of the synagogue" reflects a real concern of the Johannine community which had been expelled from the synagogue for its belief in Jesus as Messiah. North American scholarship in particular has become enamored with such a reading, following the works of J. Louis Martyn and Raymond Brown. Scholars in this vein often argue that 9:22 is out of place in the narrative, and is thus a clear indication of the *Sitz im Leben* of the Johannine community. Since the parents are not asked about Jesus, it is argued, there is no reason for this statement to be in the narrative unless it is indicative of the situation of the original audience. To the contrary, Resseguie argues that there is no need to posit such a reading. Instead, says Resseguie, the statement is very much appropriate to the text because rhetorically the parents are now established as the foil to the now-sighted son. "While the parents are fearful of the authorities and are fearful to confess Jesus as Messiah, the man born blind is fearless and bold in his confrontation with the authorities."[60] If Resseguie is correct, then this is support for the case that the blind man has gained spiritual vision already.

After the parental interview, the man is brought back in for a second and more confrontational interrogation. During the second interview, the formerly blind man gets bolder. He delivers the signature line of the passage in 9:25, "This one thing I know, though I once was blind, now I see," and then he mocks his interrogators by asking them if they would like to become Jesus' disciples also. He then gets even bolder in 9:30–33, declaring that Jesus is in fact divine as evidenced by his ability to open the eyes of one born blind. It appears that at least by this point, the man has gained his spiritual vision. One can read this passage as a gradual gaining of spiritual sight, or one might also conclude that he has been spiritually sighted all along and what is growing is his boldness. The latter seems to be the more likely conclusion for a physiognomically-conscious audience. Also interesting in this exchange is the response of the Pharisees in 9:34 to the man's proclamation: they still assume the *topos* and declare that the man was born entirely in sin. Their evidence? He was born blind. Here we find the *topos* clearly

[60] Resseguie, "John 9: A Literary-Critical Analysis," 118.

assumed by the Jewish leaders once again, and assumed so forcefully that even the opening of the man's eyes cannot overturn it.

Finally, in 9:35–38, Jesus finds the man after he is expelled from the synagogue. The man still does not recognize Jesus' face, and in all fairness it must be noted that he never saw Jesus in the first place because he was still blind when he parted ways to wash his eyes. Lee is typical of those who take this encounter as evidence that the man does not gain spiritual vision until Jesus finds him late in the story. Lee argues that in 9:35 the man "both sees and 'sees' Jesus for the first time in the narrative,"[61] and much of the basis for this conclusion is that the healing took place without Jesus around in the first place since sight was not restored until the mud was washed off the eyes. Yet what is striking in this encounter is that not only does the man come to identify Jesus' face in this passage, but he already seems to readily recognize Jesus' identity. It takes no convincing, no fancy ontological arguments, no theological lesson on the divine purpose of the Messiah healing blind eyes; it simply takes the man putting a face with what he already knows to be true—the one who opened his eyes must be the Son of Man. The man's question, "Who is he, so that I may believe?" is not a request for a theological explanation; it is a simple request to put a face with a name and with a miracle.

One significant debate in this paragraph is over the proper translation of κύριε, which occurs in 9:36 and 9:38 and can mean either "sir" or "lord." Most commentaries and translations translate the term in 9:36 as "sir," but translate the same word in 9:38 as "lord," as if some sort of salvific shift has taken place in between.[62] Such a translation assumes that the now-sighted man is still spiritually blind in 9:36 and is only able to recognize Jesus as "sir," but then he gains his spiritual sight when Jesus identifies himself as the Son of Man. However, there is no reason in the text to come to such a conclusion; rather, the fact that the blind man has had his eyes opened would already imply that

---

[61] Lee, *The Symbolic Narrative of the Fourth Gospel*, 179. So also Barrett, *John*, 302; Beasley-Murray, *John*, 159; Carson, *John*, 376–77, Haenchen, *John 2*, 40; Köstenberger, *John*, 294; and Francis J. Moloney, *The Gospel According to John* (SP 4; Collegeville, Minn.: Liturgical Press, 1998), 295–96. Cf. Brown, *John*, 375, who merely notes the man's question as "curious."

[62] So the NRSV, NIV, and New Jerusalem Bible, along with translations in the commentaries by Brown, Beasley-Murray, Carson, Haenchen, Moloney, and Schnackenburg, among others. Köstenberger, *John*, 294, takes the same view, as does Borchert, *John*, 325. Note to the contrary that the NASB chooses "Lord" in both places.

his spiritual eyes were opened simultaneously. Coupled with his spirited defense of Jesus against the Pharisees, the reader would more likely conclude that κύριε in both 9:36 and 9:38 bears the christological weight "lord" for the man who now sees. To translate the term as "sir" in one place and "lord" in the other is to unfairly bias the interpretation. When both verses are translated as "lord," it is much clearer that the man has been spiritually since his healing.

Likewise, Just argues that the man recognizes Jesus as Lord, contrary to the debate over the meaning of his question "who is he?"[63] Just argues that the man would already recognize Jesus—blind people naturally recognize others and do not require sight to do so, plus the man has already declared the name of the one who healed him and has boldly defended that man before the Pharisees. He knows who Jesus is, and Just then argues that his question to Jesus, "who is he?" must mean something else. What he is doing instead is trying to understand more fully who Jesus is. His understanding of Jesus is maturing, but this scene is not the beginning of that understanding. Similarly, Talbert argues that it is the man's *christology* that is developing,[64] but his belief in Jesus is already established. The reader of the Fourth Gospel would recognize that he began to have such spiritual insight the moment Jesus healed his blindness—literally and figuratively.

Given the ambiguities and playfulness of the narrative, how then do we determine at what point the man gained his spiritual insight? Did his vision grow gradually, reaching its apex in this final scene? Or was his spiritual vision healed immediately, and it is merely his boldness that the reader watches as it grows throughout the story? The latter seems to fit best with the expected *topos*, for once his eyes are opened, his spiritual sight should be restored as well, and as has been demonstrated, the narrative can sustain such a reading. The man is evasive with the Pharisees to protect his healer, yet bold enough to proclaim Jesus as one who is "from God," even when faced with being put out of the synagogue. When he finally meets Jesus in person, he readily proclaims him as both Lord and as Son of Man, insights that he probably gained when his eyesight was healed but which only lacked a face to which to attach the insight.

---

[63] Just, "From Tobit to Bartimaeus," 300–01.
[64] Talbert, *Reading John*, 161.

With the story now complete, Jesus drives home his point in a final speech aimed at exposing the blindness of the religious leaders. Jesus' statement in 9:39 is a pointed attack and would likely carry a double meaning to the ancient reader. Jesus has come "so that those who do not see may see, and those who do see may become blind," echoing the prophet Isaiah. The first phrase, "so that those who do not see may see," if taken by itself could simply mean that part of Jesus' ministry is to heal blind eyes, and certainly this is true. Yet when the second phrase is added, "and that those who do see may become blind," the meaning becomes more complex since the literal meaning is not all that likely to be correct. That is, while part of Jesus ministry might be to compassionately grant eyesight to the blind, Jesus clearly has not come in order to gauge out eyes or place curses of blindness on people just because they have two good eyes. Indeed, with the addition of this second phrase, the meaning of the entire statement becomes clearly metaphorical—the spiritually blind will be given sight, and those who *think* they have spiritual vision will be exposed as utterly blind.

The Pharisees—perhaps shockingly—are perceptive enough to understand that Jesus is calling them blind to the work of God. Then Jesus condemns them one more time in the final verse. It is the very fact that they *think* they see that makes them guilty. If they were simply ignorant and blind to the truth, that might be forgivable; but since they *claim* to have sight, Jesus says, their sin remains. Thus Jesus flips the imagery of sight and blindness—it is the blind who have come to see the work of God, but it is those who claim to be sighted who are exposed as blind. As Brown points out, it is noteworthy that the man who was blind but who now sees three times attests his ignorance, while the Pharisees three times boast their knowledge.[65] Yet the reader knows that it is the blind man who is anything but ignorant, and it is the Pharisees who are truly blind.

The interplay between blindness and sin returns again too. The Jewish leaders have assumed the entire story that blindness equals sin. When they perceive that Jesus is calling them blind, they of course protest because as disciples of Moses they are by no means sinners. What is clear from Jesus' statement, however, is that it is the ones who claim to have spiritual sight—but who are now exposed as utterly blind

---

[65] Raymond Brown, *The Gospel According to John I–XII: A New Translation with Introduction and Commentary* (AB 29; New York: Doubleday, 1966), 377.

by virtue of failing to recognize Jesus for who he is and where he is from—that are sinners. Thus it is not physical blindness that marks one as a sinner; rather, it is spiritual blindness that exposes one as a sinner. The true sin is the failure to see Jesus for who he is, and the Pharisees are representative in this story of all who fail to see, while the blind man is typical of all true believers, since he (and we) are all blind until Jesus opens our eyes and grants us true vision.[66] Lee succinctly sums up the punch line of the narrative: "What appears to be unalterable blindness (the man born blind) turns out to be receptive to sight, and what appears to be sight (the 'Jews') turns out to be finally an irredeemable blindness."[67]

Blind Men Along the Way: Mark 8:22–26 and 10:46–52

Mark features two blind characters in the narrative. The first one, like the character in John 9, follows the expected pattern and measures up to the *topos*. The character is unnamed, helpless, and presumably spiritually blind. The second one, however, seems to break out of the *topos*. He has a name, he acts independently, and he seems to recognize Jesus and speaks correctly about him. In the biblical writings, Bartimaeus seems to be the lone character that breaks the *topos* of the blind character. These two characters, then, function in a type-antitype relationship in order to underscore some of this Gospel's most central points. Let us explore these stories.

There is a good deal of debate as to whether or not these two stories are to be read together and what they might mean in the context of Mark's Gospel. Scholarship ranges from those who suggest, as I will, that the two stories form a literary bracket that serves to underscore the blindness of those who are following Jesus on the one hand, all the way to scholars like Robert Gundry who insist that there is no such underlying symbolic meaning in Mark.[68] While Gundry is correct to

---

[66] On this point, see Just, "From Tobit to Bartimaeus," 297.

[67] Lee, *The Symbolic Narrative of the Fourth Gospel*, 189.

[68] Robert H. Gundry, *Mark: A Commentary on His Apology for the Cross* (Grand Rapids: Eerdmans, 1993). The first page of his commentary makes clear his point that interpreters are reading too much symbolic meaning into the text that simply is not there: "The Gospel of Mark contains no ciphers, no hidden meanings, no sleight of hand.... No messianic secret...No Christology of irony that means the reverse of what it says. No back-handed slap at Davidic messianism. No covert attack on divine man Christology.... No ecclesiastical enemies lurking between the lines or behind the twelve apostles...*No symbolism of discipular enlightenment in the miracles*..." (1, emphasis mine).

say that at times scholars tend to make *too much* of texts, Gundry falls into the opposite ditch—making *too little* of texts. With an awareness of "blindness" in the Greco-Roman milieu, Mark's first-century audience would have been predisposed to understanding just such a symbolism of physical sight versus spiritual sight when reading the stories of blindness.

Some scholars see no connection between 8:22–26 and 10:46–52. Some see 8:22–26 working more closely with 7:32–37 as a doublet, a position popular among form critics.[69] Other scholars take the position that 8:22–26 is the close to the first half of the Gospel and 10:46–52 is the close of the next section, and the two stories are not particularly related to each other. E. S. Johnson is one of few recent scholars who fall into this camp.[70] Another group of scholars see 8:22–26 as a "hinge" story. Read in this way, the passage is understood as a bridge between the first half of the Gospel and the second half, functioning both to close the first half of the Gospel and to point forward to the second half.[71] A fourth position is to understand the two blind stories as forming an inclusio, and this position has recently become a fashionable way to read Mark, particularly among more recent literary commentators.[72]

---

[69] Typical of this position are C. S. Mann, *Mark: A New Translation with Introduction and Commentary* (AB 27; Garden City, N.Y.: Doubleday, 1986) and E. Wendling, *Die Entstehung des Marcus Evangeliums* (Tübingen: Mohr, 1908), esp. 77. Robert A. Guelich, *Mark 1–8:26* (WBC 34a; Nashville: Thomas Nelson Publishers, 1989) takes a similar position, arguing that the two stories most likely circulated as a paired set of healing stories in the pre-Markan tradition

[70] E. S. Johnson, "Mark 10:46–52: Blind Bartimaeus," *CBQ* 40 (1978): 191–204. He writes, "Just as 8:22–26 terminates a series of pericopes in which the blindness of the disciples is graphically depicted, so the story of Bartimaeus concludes a portion of the gospel which shows that despite Jesus' patient instruction, his disciples are still unprepared for his journey to the cross" (198). See also Norman R. Petersen, "The Composition of Mark 4:1–8:26," *HTR* 73 (1980): 185–217, who sees 8:22–26 as the end of the section that began in chapter 4.

[71] Guelich, *Mark 1–8:26*, 430, is typical of this position also. See also the position of Augustine Stock, "Hinge Transitions in Mark's Gospel," *BTB* 15 (1985): 27–31. He sees Mark falling into five parts, marked off by geography: Wilderness, Galilee, On the Way, Jerusalem, and the Tomb. This structure, of course, is a macro-level chiasm and points to the centrality of the Way. The blind stories serve as hinges between the second-third and third-fourth sections in this scheme, but are not to be read together themselves.

[72] See the following: Mary Ann Tolbert, *Sowing the Gospel: Mark's World in Literary-Historical Perspective* (Minneapolis: Fortress, 1989), esp. 191; Paul J. Achtemeier, "And He Followed Him: Miracles and Discipleship in Mark 10:46–52," *Semeia* 11 (1978): 115–45; Sharyn Dowd, *Reading Mark: A Literary and Theological Commentary on the Second Gospel* (Macon, GA: Smyth and Helwys, 2000), esp. 83; David Garland, *Mark* (NIV Application Commentary; Grand Rapids: Zondervan: 1996), 313; presumably, Joel

This position sees the two stories as bracketing a section dealing with the blindness of the disciples, and the blind stories serve as a kind of interpretive key to the stories in between.

Given what has already been demonstrated about physiognomics in the ancient world and about blindness specifically, it is difficult to imagine that an ancient auditor would not have connected the two stories, and thus I find the position of many of the modern literary critics to be most compelling. What has not been said clearly enough, however, is how an ancient auditor would have thought about these blind stories and how that would affect the interpretation. Let us explore these two Markan texts.

Let us begin with the first of the two blind stories, a story that appears to follow the *topos* of the blind character very well. The introduction to the blind man illustrates the *topos* well: "Some people brought a blind man to Jesus and begged him to touch him" (8:22). The blind man is pitiable and helpless. He lacks the most basic marker of human significance—he has no name. Beyond that, he is utterly dependant upon others. It is other people who bring him to Jesus, and it is other people who beg Jesus on his behalf. Even when Jesus takes the man, he leads him by the hand, again illustrating the helplessness of this man. The unnamed blind man is a typical example of the blind character in the ancient world, and any reader would instinctively conclude that the man is spiritually blind as well. The blindness of this man is so severe, it would seem, that it takes two attempts on the part of Jesus to heal it. The first attempt renders partial sight, but it takes a second touch before vision is fully restored. Many recent scholars have noted that the two-touch healing is typical of the disciples in this story—it takes Jesus several attempts to make these disciples understand his mission as Messiah, and their spiritual vision is not fully healed until some point after the resurrection, after the Gospel of Mark ceases to narrate the story. What is certain, however, is that the ancient reader would have found nothing out of the ordinary with this blind man as he plays the role of the blind character perfectly.

Marcus (*Mark 1–8: An New Translation with Introduction and Commentary* [AB 27; New York: Doubleday, 2000]) sees 8:22–26 as a bracket story in some way, since he ended the first commentary on Mark 1–8 with 8:21. Presumably he intended to begin the second volume w[illegible]22 for literary reasons of some sort. Francis J. Moloney, *The Gospel of Mark: A C[illegible]y* (Peabody: Hendrickson, 2002), 163, hold s a hybrid position, seeing 8:22–26 a[illegible] a hinge and a bracket with 10:46–52.

The second blind man, however, breaks the expected mold and would be a shocking character in the mind of an ancient auditor as he shatters the expected *topos*. We have no example in the biblical writings of the type-breaking "blind seer" that occurs on rare occasions in Greco-Roman literature, but Bartimaeus probably comes the closest. He is by no means a prophet, but he is a blind character who seems to have spiritual insight, and he is set up in direct contrast to the physically sighted disciples who are spiritually in the darkness. Let us look at how Bartimaeus shatters the *topos*.

The first thing the reader learns about Bartimaeus is his name, and only after his name comes his occupation—a blind beggar. When we first meet Bartimaeus, we are struck by his independence, a feature that is certainly atypical of the blind in the ancient world. Unlike his predecessor in chapter 8, he is not led to Jesus by others but instead comes screaming to Jesus on his own, refusing to be deterred. He is also independent in the sense that he ignores the advice given to him to remain quiet, ignoring his social superiors. If Bartimaeus so flagrantly violates the conventional character type thus far, then one might also expect him to violate it in other ways—perhaps even fitting into the category of the "the blind person who sees clearly."

I would argue, though certainly there is wide disagreement in the scholarly literature, that Bartimaeus sees clearly who Jesus is *before* his physical sight is restored—his initial location in the story is said to be παρὰ τὴν ὁδόν, "along the way", he correctly applies a title to Jesus ("Son of David") thus recognizing his true identity, and when he is healed he "follows him on the way" (10:52). Bartimaeus breaks the conventional type of the pathetic and helpless blind man and instead functions as someone in the "blind who sees clearly" trajectory. He is physically blind yet sees clearly, and he is set up in the narrative in direct opposition to the disciples who see nothing of who Jesus is.

There is some debate in the secondary literature as to whether or not "Son of David" on the lips of Bartimaeus has any significance.[73] Does Bartimaeus recognize Jesus as the Messiah? Is Bartimaeus using this

---

[73] For a succinct, thorough, and helpful survey of the scholarship on the "Son of David" phrase in Mark 10:47, see James H. Charlesworth, "The Son of David: Solomon and Jesus (Mark 10:47)," in *The New Testament and Hellenistic Judaism* (ed. Peder Borgen and Søren Giversen; Peabody, Mass: Hendrickson Press, 1997): 72–87, but esp. 72. Charlesworth himself argues that the "Son of David" cry is not a recognition of Jesus as Messiah, but is rather a recognition of Jesus as a Solomon figure. Solomon (mostly citing the Testament of Solomon) is considered not only a wisdom teacher but also

title to manipulate Jesus into healing him? Is Bartimaeus, like Peter in chapter 8, using a title for Jesus but filling it with the wrong meaning? Is the title a creation of the author that is inserted here because of the proximity to Jerusalem?[74] Or is "Son of David" a throwaway line that is essentially meaningless?

It would seem most likely, in light of the use of blindness in the ancient literature, that the audience would place great value in the words of blind Bartimaeus. It is entirely significant here that Bartimaeus actually speaks (as opposed to the man in 8:22–26 who only speaks when spoken to, and only then in order to give a progress report). The simple fact that Bartimaeus is speaking, especially when he is hurling titles and accolades, would likely lead the reader to think of what is said as some sort of prophetic utterance. This conclusion is especially likely in light of the lack of attention given to the actual healing, implying that whatever else is going on in this story, it is more than a simple healing story. Though he is not called a prophet by any means, he speaks prophetically, as he is the first human character in the narrative to apply a Christological title to Jesus *correctly* (I do not count Peter who, though he gets the title correct, by no means understands what he just said).

The question, of course, is *how* does one know that Bartimaeus is using the title correctly, especially with such widespread disagreement within the scholarship? I understand Bartimaeus to be speaking correctly for two significant reasons. First, his initial location in the story is "along (παρα) the way" and once he is given sight and able to follow, he continues "on the way" with Jesus. He not only follows Jesus *after* he is healed, but he is also *along* the way prior to his healing. This terminology would seem to characterize Bartimaeus quite positively. Second, there is no rebuke of Bartimaeus. When Peter (ch. 8) uses the correct title χριστός but uses the title *in*correctly, Jesus rebukes him. There is no such rebuke here, and instead Jesus beckons Bartimaeus and asks him to speak. Especially when contrasted with the Peter episode, the fact that Jesus neither rejects the title nor rebukes the one who speaks it would lead one to conclude that the title is being used correctly.

---

a healer and exorcist, and it is in this tradition that Charlesworth thinks Bartimaeus understands Jesus.

[74] Robbins, *New Boundaries in Old Territory*, 57. He suggests that Mark inserts the title here because of the proximity to Jerusalem, as Jesus is about to enter the city as David, and the meaning of the title need not be stretched beyond that.

With the blind man speaking correctly about Jesus' identity, it is likely that the ancient auditor would hear similarities to the traditions of the blind seer here.

The location of this story in the narrative is helpful to note as well. It occurs between Jesus' third passion prediction and his entry into Jerusalem where the passion will begin. Thus, what Bartimaeus "sees" and what the disciples fail to see—and what the reader is *supposed* to see—is that Jesus' life and mission is his suffering, death, and resurrection. The disciples in Mark never see this.[75] Bartimaeus sees it as he both recognizes Jesus before he is able to physically see and as he is said to follow Jesus "along the way" after he is healed; likewise, the audience of Mark, it is hoped, will see this as well. Significantly, it is this story that ends the section on Jesus' public ministry and journey to Jerusalem. Thus the positioning of the story serves to underscore the blindness of the many who encountered Jesus but failed to see who he truly was, highlighted first by the helpless and unnamed blind man in chapter 8, and on the other hand by Bartimaeus who manages to see things clearly even without his eyes. Thus, the value of having the type-breaking blind man here is to highlight the blindness of Jesus' followers and to simultaneously jar the reader, seeking to deter the reader from making the same mistake. That is, the reader is supposed to recognize the danger of being spiritually blind to the true messianic mission of Jesus and will instead be the kind of sighted follower who truly understands how to pick up the cross and follow Jesus on the way.

Isaiah, Blindness, and the Gospels

One further example of blindness that is crucial to the New Testament is the commonly found quotations of and allusions to blindness from the prophet Isaiah. All four of the Gospels as well as Acts make use of Isaiah's concept of spiritual blindness, and each of these works appropriates blindness as a way of understanding Jesus' mission and the response to him on the part of those who see his ministry and hear

[75] Gundry (*Mark*, 597) writes, "Nor does the healing of blindness [of Bartimaeus] join with the healing of blindness in 8:22–26 to form an inclusion, everything in between being a kind of healing of blindness, i.e. an opening of the disciples' eyes to the full dimensions of Jesus messiahship and of their own discipleship... much of the material between betrays just the opposite of a symbolic healing. That is to say, the disciples' eyes remain closed." Yet, I would argue, the fact that the disciples' eyes remain closed is *precisely* the point that the blind stories underscore.

his teachings. Since Luke and Acts will be treated in the next chapter, this section will attend to the other three Gospels with particular attention to Mark.

In Isaiah 6:9–10 one finds Isaiah's commissioning scene. As part of the commissioning, Isaiah is told the following: "Go and say to this people: 'Keep listening, but do not comprehend; keep looking, but do not understand.' Make the mind of this people dull, and stop their ears, and shut their eyes, so that they may not look with their eyes, and listen with their ears, and comprehend with their minds, and turn and be healed." Part of Isaiah's ministry, then, will be marked by the inability of the people to comprehend the message from God, and that lack of comprehension is talked about in terms of eyesight and blindness. Each of the Gospels uses either a quotation of or an allusion to this text as a way of understanding Jesus' ministry. Mark quotes this text in 4:11–12 as a way to explain why the parable of the sower is difficult to understand. Matthew uses it in 13:13–15, likely following Mark's example. Luke has the quote in 8:10, also following the parable of the sower, and Acts 28:26–27 employs the quote as a means of concluding Luke-Acts. John paraphrases Isaiah 6 in 12:40.[76] A few other texts in the Gospels employ the imagery of blindness as well, most notably among those texts are John 9 discussed above, Matthew 23 and the woes to the Pharisees that label them as blind, and Jesus' self-introduction to his ministry as found in Luke 4:18 where sight to the blind is part of the messianic mission (to be discussed in the next chapter). Clearly, all of the Gospel writers understand a concept of spiritual blindness and employ that concept in order to help explain the ministry of Jesus and the response he received. Since the Synoptics all use the Isaiah 6 quotation in conjunction with the parable of the sower, we will focus our attention on the singular example of Mark 4.

In Mark 4, Jesus finds himself surrounded by a large crowd, and he begins to teach them in parable form. The parable that anchors the chapter is the parable of the sower. After Jesus tells the parable to the crowd, the disciples find a private moment to ask about the parable and to expression their confusion. Before Jesus offers an allegory as an

---

[76] Craig Evans (*To See and Not Perceive: Isaiah 6:9–10 in Early Jewish and Christian Interpretation* [JSOTSup 64; Sheffield: Sheffield Academic Press, 1989], 81) also suggests that while Paul does not quote this text directly, it might be in the background of texts like Rom 11:7 and 2 Cor 3:14. If so, then it would give all the more weight to the importance of the blindness imagery in the NT.

interpretation, he quotes Isaiah in order to explain why the parable fell, as it were, onto rocky soil, and it is here that the Markan Jesus employs Isaiah. Jesus says, "To you has been given the secret of the kingdom of God, but for those outside, everything comes in parables; in order that 'they may indeed look, but not perceive, and may indeed listen, but not understand; so that they may not turn again and be forgiven'" (4:11–12).

Mark 4 has received enormous amounts of scholarly attention, most of it dealing with the perplexing quotation of Isaiah 6. Mark uses Isaiah in such a way that makes it sound as if Jesus is talking in riddles on purpose, in order to confound outsiders and prevent non-insiders from understanding his message—intentionally blinding the audience.[77] Famously, William Wrede calls this verse cruel, odd, and useless.[78] Jeremias has also offered a now famous interpretation, arguing that both the allegorical interpretation of the parable as found in Mark as well as the Isaiah quote are Markan additions and not original to Jesus, and that Mark inserted the quotation here because of the catch word παραβολή.[79]

What is clear is that the verse makes most readers of Mark uncomfortable because Jesus appears to be saying something that few interpreters can stomach—is God really *causing* spiritual eyes to be blinded to the truth? Most interpreters understandably try to offer explanations for why the plain sense of the text is not what is really meant. Most of the debates about this verse center around the ἵνα clause and how to best translate that tiny conjunction. A plurality of scholars show great

[77] A good deal of attention has been given to who is meant by "outsiders" and "insiders" in Mark. Are the outsiders just non-believers in general? Are outsiders anyone who does not understand Jesus in this Gospel, including the disciples? Both the crowds and the disciples seem to enjoy his teachings, even if they do not fully understand them. One interesting suggestion comes from Michael Douglas Goulder ("Those Outside [Mk 4:10–12]," *NovT* 33 [1991]: 289–302), who argues that the Gospel of Mark is dealing with Christian factions, and much like Paul in Galatians, the conflict is with the Jerusalem church and the Jewish Christian group found there. Specifically, Goulder argues that the Jerusalem church is Jesus' own family church, headed by his brothers and their descendants, and that given the poor portrayal of the family of Jesus in Mark (think especially of the family being called "outside" when they come to talk to him), Mark must be carrying on a polemic against the Jerusalem church. His reading, then, claims that the "outsiders" are this group of Jewish Christians who have misunderstood Jesus.

[78] William Wrede, *The Messianic Secret* (trans. J. C. G. Greig; Cambridge: J. Clarke, 1971), 62.

[79] Joachim Jeremias, *The Parables of Jesus* (Upper Saddle River, NJ: Prentice-Hall, 1954), 18.

reticence to translating the phrase "*in order that* they may look but not perceive," and a number of solutions have been forwarded in hopes of finding a more palatable way of understanding this clause. Craig Evans offers a good summary of six popular positions which we will briefly relay here.[80] 1) Mark has misunderstood the Hebrew and incorrectly used a purpose clause; 2) Mark has truncated the formula ἵνα πληρωθῇ to just ἵνα; 3) the phrase is causal rather than purpose; 4) the phrase is a result clause rather than purpose; 5) the clause is imperatival "let them see"; 6) the clause is telic. Any of these options, of course, would soften the meaning of the verse and would make it more acceptable to most readers. While all of these readings are permissible by Greek syntax, the most natural reading is still as a purpose clause, and this fact is what gives fits to commentators—what the text seems to say quite plainly is a conclusion that our theological sensibilities often cannot allow.

Even amidst the debate, this current project does not stand or fall on what one decides about this troublesome clause. Whether or not this is a statement about God's sovereign election of only a few to understand the message of Christ is not our concern, and our reading of this text is not affected either way. Instead, what is the larger concern here is the blindness imagery. In other words, whoever may be at the cause of the blindness, the fact remains that blindness is used as the primary imagery for those who fail to believe the gospel of Jesus Christ, whether it is by divine will or by human stubbornness or ignorance.

The more pressing question here is not one of the agency of the blindness; rather, the question is what is meant by the blindness and how it is to be understood in the context of this Gospel. I would like to suggest that the imagery of spiritual blindness is the most appropriate of images for the Gospel of Mark to use because, as is well documented in scholarship, this Gospel more so than any other has as a major theme that Jesus is a misunderstood Messiah. It is a natural fit, then, for Mark to point to the blindness of those who encounter Jesus. Let us offer a few brief examples.

The Gospel opens with the title line: "The beginning of the Gospel of Jesus Christ, the Son of God." The phrase, "Son of God," however,

[80] Evans, *To See and Not Perceive*, 92–96. See also R. T. France, *The Gospel of Mark: A Commentary on the Greek Text* (Grand Rapids: Eerdmans, 2002), 199–200, who summarizes four positions.

only appears on the lips of two other characters in this Gospel. The first is a demon in Mark 5:7, and the second is the Roman centurion who witness Jesus' death in 15:39. The only characters that manage to recognize Jesus by the correct title are a demon and a Roman soldier, two characters who are prototypes for what the average Jew would think of as "outsiders." These two examples stand in stark contrast to the many characters in Mark who are *supposed* to recognize and understand Jesus. The Jewish religious leaders certainly fail to recognize his identity since they have a hand in putting him to death. The Isaiah quote in Mark 4 tells the disciples that the so-called "outsiders" will not understand Jesus' teachings, and this is by no means the only time that people are said to fail to understand Jesus. The disciples are said to fail to understand his parables in 4:13 and 7:18. In Mark 8 Peter, chief among the disciples, gets the christological vocabulary right when asked who Jesus is, but clearly does not have the right understanding of the vocabulary, since Jesus immediately offers a rebuke and an explanation that the Messiah must suffer. The disciples fail to understand the feeding miracle and Mark tells us their hearts were hardened (6:52). In 8:17–18 the disciples are concerned about physical bread and Jesus berates them for having hard hearts and blind eyes. Finally, of course, these disciples abandon Jesus at the moment of his arrest and in Mark, never return in the narrative; instead, the story ends with three scared women who say nothing to anyone, and thus the story ends with those who *should* understand Jesus still blind to what has happened. Evans's conclusion here is helpful: "prior to Easter all, Jesus' friends and enemies alike, suffered from the wrong concept of messiahship. The explanation for this consistent misconception, Mark tells us, is due to the biblical problem of the hardened heart."[81]

Certainly more examples from Mark could be amassed, but the point is clear: the Markan Jesus is misunderstood by nearly everyone in the story, or said another way, nearly everyone is spiritually blind to the message and mission of Jesus.[82] The disciples should understand him but do not, and it appears that Jesus may be intentionally obscuring his message from the crowds, according to Mark 4. He is misunderstood by design, apparently, and the misunderstanding of Jesus only further

---

[81] Evans, *To See and Not Perceive*, 102.

[82] This theme accents all the more the scene with Bartimaeus who is physically blind, but who is one of the few human characters that actually seems to have any sort of spiritual insight.

highlights the spiritual blindness of his audience, whether disciples, crowds, or otherwise. Why do this? I would suggest that this Gospel intends to caution the would-be believer who *thinks* he understands Jesus but who still very much risks misunderstanding Jesus just as his original audience had. Jesus cannot be whatever kind of Messiah we want him to be, but he must be the suffering Messiah, according to Mark. Furthermore, to be a follower of this Messiah cannot take just any form, but the follower must also take the form of one who suffers, who picks up a cross and follows. Anything else is simply blindness to Jesus' message, mission, and demand. Thus, when read in the context of the Gospel as a whole, the blindness imagery in Mark 4 is an ideal fit for this Gospel that so heavily emphasizes the misunderstood Messiah and that seeks to prevent future followers from continuing in blindness to the mission and message of Christ.

Conclusion

As this chapter has demonstrated, the New Testament and other early Christian writings make frequent use of physiognomics. In particular, the imagery of blindness is a significant way of speaking of a spiritually obtuse audience. Within the pages of the NT, however, no author makes more extensive use of physiognomics than does the writer of Luke-Acts, as it offers multiple examples of physiognomic descriptions as well as examples of blindness specifically. It is to those writings that we now turn.

CHAPTER SIX

PHYSIOGNOMY AND BLINDNESS IN LUKE-ACTS

To this point, we have explored the presence of physiognomy in the Greco-Roman world, the Old Testament and Jewish traditions, and the early Christian writings. What remains is to examine Luke-Acts. Having seen physiognomics at work in the literature of the milieu of Luke-Acts, it is no surprise that Luke-Acts would also reflect some knowledge of physiognomic conventions. Indeed, Luke knows these conventions and, among biblical writers, is probably the most rhetorically adept at using them. As we shall see in this chapter, Luke uses and often subverts them. When it comes to blindness, we shall see that Luke uses the conventions concerning blindness in a programmatic way that offers at least one key or heuristic for reading the Gospel. Let us begin with physiognomics in general.

Physiognomy in Luke-Acts

Whereas in previous chapters we have rehearsed a number of examples of physiognomics, no such exercise is needed here; an excellent treatment specific to physiognomic scenes in Luke-Acts has already been written recently by Mikeal Parsons.[1] What follows is mostly a distilled summary of that work.

That Luke knows the conventions of physiognomics is clear, as he uses examples from all three categories of physiognomics—zoological, racial/ethnographical, and bodily features. In zoological terms, two examples will suffice. In 3:7, John the Baptist refers to the crowds as a "brood of vipers," and the meaning here is self-evidently negative and insulting.[2] Polemo, for example, says the viper is characterized by such thing as being dangerous, quick to run away, and hypocritical or inconsistent in character.[3] In this same verse, we find that the crowds

[1] Mikeal C. Parsons, *Body and Character in Luke and Acts: The Subversion of Physiognomy in Early Christianity* (Grand Rapids: Baker Academic Press, 2006).

[2] For a discussion of "brood of vipers," see Parsons, *Body and Character*, 73–76.

[3] Foerster 1.188.

are apparently "fleeing the coming wrath," exactly the sort of behavior that the physiognomist might expect from a brood of vipers. The crowds are likewise fickle and inconsistent in their character. A second example is 13:32, where Jesus is warned that Herod is out to get him. Jesus answers, "Go and tell that fox..." (13:32).[4] Polemo's characterization of the fox is primarily that of being cunning and deceptive.[5] Certainly Herod rules in such a manner, and the physiognomic convention is very much at work in this text to add a layer of meaning that is often unnoticed.

Racial or ethnographical physiognomics are also present in Luke-Acts. Whether or not *all* geographical designations are significant to characterization is yet to be demonstrated. One might think of references like Jesus the Nazorean, Peter of Galilee, Simon of Cyrene, or Saul of Tarsus. Yet some indeed carry great ethnographical significance. The parable of the Good Samaritan takes as the hero of the story a man who is unnamed, known only by his geographical designation—he is a Samaritan. The audience expects for a Samaritan to behave in a certain way, and assumptions are made about his character based solely on his geographical designation as the audience has no other information with which to work. The shock of the parable, of course, is that the Samaritan is the only one who behaves mercifully, something that was not expected based on his ethnic characterization. A second example would be the Ethiopian Eunuch of Acts 8. He also lacks a name and is known only by his two characteristics—he is Ethiopian, and he is a eunuch. As an Ethiopian, he is quite literally from the farthest corner of the earth.[6] He is also a descendant of Ham (Gen 10:6), which would carry negative connotations in the Jewish world. Ps-Aristotle lists the Ethiopians specifically, labeling them wooly and cowardly (812a), and thus the ethnographical characterization is far from positive. Yet it is just such a person who comes to receive the gospel and is baptized,

[4] See Parsons, *Body and Character*, 69–71. See also John Darr, *Herod the Fox: Audience Criticism and Lukan Characterization* (JSNTSup 163; Sheffield; Sheffield Academic Press, 1998). Darr's work is a study of the characterization of Herod in the Gospels, and that characterization as a fox includes both the wily nature of the fox as well as effeminacy. The effeminacy angle has been captured even as recently as Mel Gibson's *The Passion of the Christ*.

[5] Foerster 1.174.

[6] Most ancient Greeks and Romans considered themselves to be the center of the world, and when the so-called four corners of the earth were labeled, Ethiopia was typically the southern corner. Consider for example Herodotus, *Hist.* 1.134.

and part of the significant here is that the gospel has literally reached the "ends of the earth" (Acts 1:8) as Jesus had commissioned.

When we turn to the bodily features method of physiognomy, however, we notice something striking in Luke. Luke often introduces physical features, allowing the audience to make conventional assumptions about the character of the person, only to later subvert those characterizations. Specifically, as Parsons points out, these subversions of the expected physiognomic conventions have to do with the Abrahamic covenant and who is included and excluded from the eschatological community of God.[7] That is, no one is to be excluded based on physical appearance in a world where physical appearance is assumed to say something about one's character. No, in the community of God all are to be included, and for the Lukan Jesus, this especially includes the people least likely to get in by human standards. Parsons sees this subversion of physiognomics in at least four texts, and we will briefly summarize each in turn here.

The first example is the bent woman of Luke 13:10–17.[8] Jesus encounters a woman who is unable to stand up straight, a condition with which she has suffered for eighteen years. Jesus heals her, but since it took place on the Sabbath, Jesus is attacked. His response is simple: "And ought not this woman, a daughter of Abraham whom Satan bound for eighteen long years, be set free from this bondage on the sabbath day?" (13:16). Ps-Aristotle says that those who have a weak back are feeble and weak of character (810b), and that those whose back is bent are of "evil disposition" because "the parts in front which should be visible disappear" (810b). In addition, she is also female which is, for the physiognomists, universally a characterization of weakness. Yet, this woman, who by cultural standards was of weak character, is healed by Jesus and declared to be "daughter of Abraham," a part of the covenant people. In her case, she is healed of her bent condition, and the physiognomists would readily note that with a change in the physical appearance comes a change in the moral character as well. Such is not the case with the second example, Zacchaeus.

Zacchaeus has an emphatically negative introduction: "A man was there named Zacchaeus; he was a chief tax collector and was rich. He

[7] See especially Parsons, *Body and Character*, 82, but this is the sustained thesis of the book as a whole as well.

[8] For a full treatment of the physiognomics of this text, see Parsons, *Body and Character*, 83–95.

was trying to see who Jesus was, but on account of the crowd he could not, because he was short in stature" (19:2–3).[9] Being a tax collector and being rich are already clearly negative in the context of this Gospel, but to call Zacchaeus short is to invoke physiognomic implications beyond that. That is, his stature is far more than a literary necessity in order to put him into a sycamore tree where Jesus will spot him. To be short is typically negative in the physiognomic handbooks. For Ps-Aristotle, short stature is the mark of a small-minded person (808a), and if the tall person is considered to be courageous, valiant, and a good leader as we saw with Saul, the short person might be exactly the opposite. Yet Jesus singles out this man of seemingly deficient character, and ultimately declares, "Today salvation has come to this house, because he too is a son of Abraham. For the Son of Man came to seek out and to save the lost" (19:9–10). He is declared to be a son of Abraham and is included in the kingdom of God, despite his obviously deficient inner character. The surprising part of the story, at least to the physiognomist, is that his character is changed—he sells his possessions and changes his ways—but his outward features never change. The bent woman was healed of both her physical and spiritual condition; Zacchaeus has a changed character, but at the end of the story he is still short. For both, the physical marker is deceptive because in Christ's eyes, both are children of Abraham already and the physical marker is hiding their true status. Thus, physiognomic assumptions about one's character are ultimately not a guide for inclusion in God's kingdom.

As one turns to Acts, two more stories emerge. The first is the lame man at the Temple gate in Acts 3.[10] Ps-Aristotle says that feet which are weak or poorly-jointed are markers of one who is weak of character (810a). Polemo adds that such a person is weak and lazy.[11] The lame man certainly fits these characteristics. Note that he is carried to the gate and laid there by others (3:2). He is also a beggar, which is not the only field open to the lame in the ancient world, as one needs only to think of Hephaestus who was lame but also the master craftsman of the gods. The lame man is healed of his lameness, and thus he would

[9] For a full treatment of this story, see Parsons, *Body and Character*, 97–108, or Parsons, "'Short in Stature': Luke's Physical Description of Zacchaeus," *NTS* 47 (2001): 50–57. One might also consider the interesting work of J. Rendel Harris, "On the Stature of Our Lord," *BJRL* 10 (1926): 112–126, who argues that it is Jesus, not Zacchaeus, who is short of stature.

[10] For a full treatment, see Parsons, *Body and Character*, 109–22.

[11] Foerster, 1.200.

be expected to have a healed character as well. Yet when he is healed, he jumps up, walks, and leaps (3:8). While no doubt he is excited to be able to do such things, the physiognomists as we have seen would encourage a lion-like gait that is slow, deliberate, and with a certain swagger.[12] Yet this man is *leaping*, which is more deer-like than lion-like, and the physiognomists would likely frown upon such a gait. Yet this man is also to be included in the covenant community of God.

A fourth scene is the Ethiopian eunuch of Acts 8.[13] As Parsons notes, this scene is the only scene of the four that is not explicitly a part of the Abrahamic covenant, but it is logically very much a part of that covenant as a Gentile is converted in fulfillment of the promise that Abraham's seed will be a blessing to all the peoples of the earth.[14] We have already mentioned the ethnographical aspects of this scene. What the physiognomists might make of a eunuch is also significant. In a world where gender is like a continuum and the male wants to be as far on the male pole as possible and the female as far on the female pole as possible, those who blur the lines of gender are despised. The androgen is perhaps the most harshly criticized of any character in both Ps-Aristotle and Polemo, and one might expect the same treatment of a eunuch. Yet it is exactly such a person who, though probably not even allowed in the Temple itself, is welcomed into the kingdom of God, finding that there is nothing to prevent him from believing and being baptized. Here, Jesus' commission to carry the gospel to the ends of the earth is fulfilled, and the Abrahamic covenant finds fulfillment as well.

In each of these four scenes Luke introduces physiognomic markers only to later subvert them. Sometimes the physical deficiency is healed—the bent woman stands upright again and the lame man can walk—but sometimes the physical shortcoming is not corrected—Zacchaeus is still short and the Ethiopian is still a eunuch. Each case, however, does indicate that the community of God in Christ will not be hindered by physical barriers, and constituents in that community will not be judged by bodily characteristics.

Luke does not, however, always subvert the physiognomic conventions. To take one such example, consider the man with dropsy

[12] Remember especially Ps-Aristotle 809b.

[13] For a full treatment see Parsons, *Body and Character*, 123–41.

[14] Parsons, *Body and Character*, 123.

in Luke 14.[15] Dropsy is a disease having to do with the retention of water. The sufferer thirsts for more water, yet the more water that is consumed, the more water that is retained, eventually leading to death. Thus one dies from the very thing for which one thirsts. In the ancient world, dropsy often became symbolic of the plight of the wealthy.[16] The wealth for which one thirsts is often one's undoing. Though the physiognomic handbooks do not address dropsy, it is treated in ancient literature in the same way as other physiognomic markers.

Blindness is another such example where Luke seems to employ physiognomics in a way that is consistent with the expected conventions. It is to an exploration of blindness in Luke-Acts that we now turn.

Blindness in Luke-Acts

Blindness is highly significant to Luke-Acts. In fact, "sight to the blind" becomes an interpretive heuristic to the work from start to finish. Following the birth stories, the ministry of Jesus begins with a quotation from Isaiah through which Jesus announces that he will, among other things, bring sight to the blind (4:18). Acts ends with a similar quotation of Isaiah, declaring that some of the Jews in Rome are blind to the work of God, and thus the message will go to the Gentiles (28:26–28). Along the way, a blind man is healed near Jericho, Saul will be blinded on the road to Damascus, and Elymas the magician will be blinded as punishment. Luke will maintain the standard *topos* for the blind throughout Luke-Acts, and the "blind" becomes a metaphor that extends to all of those who are spiritually obtuse and in need of Jesus' healing touch. Jesus as the healer of blindness becomes a defining aspect of his ministry and the subsequent ministry of the apostles. Unlike the examples dealing with the Abrahamic covenant, Luke maintains the standard *topos* for blindness. While in the former cases, physical deficiencies are not indicative of unworthiness for the kingdom, blindness seems to be logically different. That is, if the blind are assumed to be spiritually blind as well, one cannot very well enter the kingdom with blind eyes;

[15] Charles H. Talbert, *Reading Luke: A Literary and Theological Commentary on the Third Gospel* (New York: Crossroad: 1982), 172 has an excellent brief discussion of this text, including several Greco-Roman references not recited here. Also, see Willi Braun, *Feasting and Social Rhetoric in Luke 14* (SNTSMS 85; Cambridge: Cambridge University Press, 1995).

[16] Consider, for example, Stobaeus, *Flor.* 3.10.45.

the spiritual sight must be healed, and that healing is the very essence of the ministry of Jesus in this Gospel. Let us look at the examples of blindness in Luke-Acts, beginning with Jesus' self-introduction.

Jesus' Self-Introduction to His Ministry (Luke 4:18–30)

The very first occurrence of "blind" in the Gospel of Luke is a highly significant one. It occurs as part of a quotation from Isaiah that Jesus reads during his self-introduction in this Gospel, and it is a passage that is particular to Luke. The significance of this passage is almost universally recognized by commentators, but a thorough treatment of blindness as part of the passage is still largely lacking. In this section, then, we shall explore the import of this keystone passage in Luke, and we shall do so with an eye in particular to the significance of the blindness.

The first element that catches the attention of the reader is the placement of this passage. Luke's Gospel, of course, begins with a birth story, followed by the baptism, a genealogy, and the temptation narrative. After these introductory matters, Luke immediately takes the reader to Nazareth where Jesus reads from the scroll of Isaiah in his local synagogue before being rejected in his own home country. Thus, this story is placed as the first story in the public ministry of Jesus. In this regard Luke has deviated from the structure of Mark of Matthew,[17] who both have other stories such as the calling of the disciples fronted, while the rejection at Nazareth comes several chapters later. Mark, who lacks a birth story, does not mention this rejection until chapter 6, while Matthew has the story almost into the center of his Gospel in Matt 13. For Luke to locate this episode at the front of the narrative right behind the baptism and temptation is to give it a place of prominence, a location in the narrative that makes it a defining text for understanding the ministry of Jesus. Talbert says as much, saying that Luke has fronted this scene because "this scene does not simply relate one event among others but has programmatic significance for

[17] The Lukan version differs in several significant ways from the versions of Mark and Matthew, most notably in the inclusion of the Isaiah reading, causing source theorists to debate whether Luke's story is dependent upon Mark, part of Luke's special source, or just heavily redacted by the author. Whether or not Luke is literarily dependent upon Mark at this point is of no consequence; what is significant is that Luke has fronted the rejection in order to give it a defining position in the narrative.

the whole."[18] Commentators are nearly unanimous in calling this text programmatic for understanding the Gospel of Luke. Kimball, for example, says that this passage "is likely the most important passage in Luke-Acts; it is almost universally held to be programmatic for the two-part work,"[19] and Fitzmyer says that "the Lucan story, transposed to this point in the Gospel, has a definite programmatic character."[20] Tannehill, makes an even stronger case for the prominence of this text. He argues that four factors indicate a text that is central to the narrative: "major Old Testament quotations, statements of the commission which an important character has received from God, previews and reviews of the course of the narrative, and disclosures of God's purpose by characters presented as reliable."[21] This Isaiah quote does all of these things.

As any literary theorist would note, beginnings matter a great deal since beginnings often offer an interpretive guide to the rest of the work. This passage is programmatic in exactly this way, offering a heuristic for reading the rest of the Gospel, and this, too, has not escaped the notice of commentators. Consider just two examples. Tannehill says of this text, "At the beginning of Jesus' ministry, Luke presents to the reader in one representative scene the meaning which he sees in this whole event [of Christ], thereby giving the reader the key to understanding what follows,"[22] and Fitzmyer adds that "Luke has deliberately put this story at the beginning of the public ministry to encapsulate the entire ministry of Jesus and the reaction to it."[23] There is no question that this

---

[18] Talbert, *Reading Luke*, 57.

[19] Charles Kimball, "Jesus' Exposition of Scripture in Luke 4:16–30: An Inquiry in Light of Jewish Hermeneutics," *PRSt* 21 (1994): 180.

[20] Joseph A. Fitzmyer, *The Gospel According to Luke* (AB 28; Garden City: Doubleday, 1981), 529. For other commentators who see this text as programmatic, see also the following: Darrell L. Bock, *Luke* (The IVP New Testament Commentary Series; Downers Grove, Ill: InterVarsity, 1994), 86–87; David Hill, "Rejection of Jesus at Nazareth (Luke 4:16–30)," *NovT* 13 (1971): 170; John Nolland, *Luke 1–9:20* (WBC 35A; Dallas: Word Books, 1989), 195; and Robert Tannehill, "The Mission of Jesus According to Luke 4:16–30," in *Jesus in Nazareth* (ed. Erich Grässer, et al.; BZNW 40; Berlin: de Gruyter, 1972), 51. Frans Neirynck, "Luke 4:16–30 and the Unity of Luke-Acts," in *Unity of Luke-Acts* (ed. J. Verheyden; BETL 142; Leuven: Leuven University Press, 1999), 357–95, not only calls this text programmatic, but he also gives a series of examples from Luke and Acts where Luke 4 serves to foreshadow what will happen in those texts.

[21] Tannehill, *The Narrative Unity of Luke-Acts: A Literary Interpretation* (FF; 2 vols.; Philadelphia: Fortress, 1986), 1:61. (All subsequent references to this work assume that all references to the Gospel are volume 1 and all references to Acts are volume 2.)

[22] Tannehill, "The Mission of Jesus According to Luke 4:16–30," 73.

[23] Fitzmyer, *Luke*, 529.

text is a hermeneutical key for understanding the rest of the Gospel. What meaning, then, is this passage to unlock for us?

Jesus, led by the Spirit, returns to his hometown and enters the synagogue, a place which was customary for him to go (4:16). He stands to read, and the reading is from the scroll of Isaiah. Jesus reads the following: "The Spirit of the Lord is upon me, because he has anointed me to bring good news to the poor. He has sent me to proclaim release to the captives and recovery of sight to the blind, to let the oppressed go free, to proclaim the year of the Lord's favor" (4:18–19). He then proclaims, "Today this scripture has been fulfilled in your hearing" (4:21).[24]

The poor, blind, captives, oppressed—all are named in the Isaiah reading. The poor and the blind recur several times in Luke-Acts, sometimes in a literal sense, sometimes in a figurative sense, and probably sometimes as both. Literal blindness is found in Luke 14:13, 7:21–22, and 18:35. The captives and the oppressed never occur again.[25] This

---

[24] There is a great deal of debate concerning the meaning of "the year of the Lord's favor" in regards to the Year of Jubilee (Lev 25:10), a debate which will not be engaged here except to say that whatever Jesus means, he is proclaiming some sort of end to oppression for the poor and the outcast. Opinions vary. For example, Robert B. Sloan (*The Favorable Year of the Lord: A Study in Jubilary Theology in the Gospel of Luke* [Austin, Schola Press, 1977], 146) argues that the Lukan Jesus intends to announce a year of Jubilee. So also Asher Finkel, "Jesus' Preaching in the Synagogue on the Sabbath (Luke 4:16–28)," in *The Gospels and the Scriptures of Israel* (ed. Craig A. Evans and W. Richard Stegner; JSNTSup 104; Sheffield: Sheffield Academic Press, 1994), 337, who is following John Howard Yoder on this point (Yoder, *The Politics of Jesus* [Grand Rapids: Eerdmans, 1972]). Tannehill (*Narrative Unity*, 68) disputes such a conclusion as going too far. Still other scholars say that the Jubilee is typological, referencing a figurative deliverance from sin and darkness through salvation in Christ. See for example the following: Bock, *Luke*, 90; Fitzmyer, *Luke*, 533; Kimball, "Jesus' Exposition of Scripture in Luke 4:16–30," 193; and Nolland, *Luke 1–9:20*, 197. It is also notable that the Lukan Jesus stops reading in the middle of the sentence in Isaiah, omitting the clause about impending judgment. On this point, see Nolland (*Luke 1–9:20*, 198) who says this reflects Luke's "two-stage eschatology for Jesus—salvation now, judgment in the future," and Fitzmyer (*Luke*, 532) who simply says that this is "deliberate suppression of a negative aspect of the Deutero-Isaian message." Perhaps Tannehill ("The Mission of Jesus According to Luke 4:16–30," 71) is more nearly correct when he says that "the context in the quotation makes quite clear that this refers to the time of salvation." He continues to say that this quote is all the more important because Luke chose to end the quote here rather than to continue on with a statement of judgment, and thus the time of salvation is the climax of the quote.

[25] For a good discussion on these groups, see Nolland, *Luke 1–9:20*, 197. See also John S. Roth, *The Blind, The Lame, and the Poor: Character Types in Luke-Acts* (JSNTSup 144; Sheffield: Sheffield Academic Press, 1997), who treats these three characters in Luke while setting them against their Jewish and Roman backgrounds. Notice that the captive and oppressed have fallen out of his work as well.

places special emphasis, it would seem, on the poor and the blind. The poor have been thoroughly discussed especially in light of Luke's Gospel and the proclamation of the good news to the poor and oppressed as one of its major themes—one might think of such stories as the Good Samaritan, the Rich Man and Lazarus, Zacchaeus, or the thief on the cross to name only a few. Yet the blind have been largely unnoticed, and it is this shortcoming that needs to be corrected if we are to understand the text as its original auditors would have understood it. That is, this text would seem to underscore the role of the blind in understanding the message of this Gospel in a way that is largely unappreciated.

Fitzmyer, for example, devotes only a single sentence to the blind.[26] Tannehill says only that "captives... blind... and broken... probably have some metaphorical range,"[27] but he only offers explanation for how the "poor" might be understood metaphorically. The blind, for Tannehill, are simply a part of "the poor" since disabled persons were most often poor also. Talbert says that 4:18–19 outlines Jesus' threefold ministry of preaching, physical healing, and exorcism.[28] While this is true, I am suggesting that a Greco-Roman audience would have heard even more in this passage and its reference to blindness. It is not just the healing ministry of Jesus typified by the healing of the blind that is programmatic here; it is also the healing of spiritual blindness that is shared by all whom Jesus encounters that is programmatic in this text.

Part of the reason for the silence on blindness is the ambiguity of the Hebrew text of Isaiah. Most English translations of the Isaiah text lack the phrase "recovery of sight to the blind" and instead have a second phrase about freedom to the prisoner. The LXX clearly uses the language of blindness (τυφλοῖς ἀνάβλεψιν). The Hebrew text, however, is more ambiguous, reading פְּקַח־קוֹחַ. This phrase in Hebrew can either mean the setting free of one who is in a dark prison, or it can be figurative of the opening of blind eyes. Most English translations of Isaiah have chosen the former, more literal meaning, while the LXX and Luke have both chosen the latter, more figurative meaning. Why not retain the ambiguity? Perhaps it is because blindness holds a

[26] Fitzmyer, *Luke*, 533.
[27] Tannehill, *Narrative Unity*, 64.
[28] Talbert, *Reading Luke*, 58.

special significance in this milieu that Luke wishes to invoke.[29] That is, part of what is programmatic in this text is not just the good news to the poor, but also that blind eyes will be opened. Those whom Jesus will encounter are spiritually blind and in need of healing, a point that will be illustrated before the pericope is finished, and a point that will be illustrated over and over again in this Gospel in both a literal and figurative sense.

After Jesus finishes his reading, the town people respond, "Is this not Joseph's son?" This question has sparked a great deal of confusion among interpreters, unsure of whether the question is one of anger and rejection,[30] a positive statement showing pride,[31] or one of mere confusion.[32] Tannehill notes that Luke is clear that Joseph is not the father of Jesus (see especially 3:22–23), and that this question from the crowd perhaps indicates ignorance and confusion, not hostility.[33] In a different work, Tannehill says the following: "Hidden in the hearts of his townsfolk are attitudes of which they, perhaps, are not yet conscious: resistance to God's purpose combined with jealous possessiveness."[34] Said a different way, the question merely illustrates the blindness of the crowd since they are people who *thought* they knew Jesus. To the contrary, they are blind to Jesus' true identity, and this on the very heels of Jesus' proclamation of the kingdom of God to the blind. Read in this way, the people themselves are spiritually blind, already typifying the Isaiah quotation and already demonstrating Jesus' fulfillment of the passage. Jesus has come to open blind eyes such as these.

As the narrative continues, of course, Jesus talks the people into a rage, and he is rejected by his own people who chase him to the edge of a cliff before he covertly slips through the crowd. Notably, Jesus escapes by going right through the midst of the crowd who—blindly?—fail to

[29] On this point, see Nolland, *Luke 1–9:20*, 193, and Kimball, "Jesus' Exposition of Scripture in Luke 4:16–30," 184.

[30] See, for example, Nolland, *Luke 1–9:20*, 199. He says that while the exact force of the phrase is uncertain, it is clear from the unfolding narrative that there is some hostility and criticism in the question, "Is this not Joseph's son," a strong statement of unbelief or rejection of his claim to fulfill the scriptures.

[31] Fitzmyer (*Luke*, 535) acknowledges that it could be hostile, but prefers to think of it as "pleasant surprise and admiration." So also Bock, *Luke*, 91 and Talbert, *Reading Luke*, 59.

[32] See for example Hill, "Rejection of Jesus at Nazareth (Luke 4:16–30)," 164, who takes this question not as an expression of hostility, but as one of disbelief.

[33] Tannehill, "The Mission of Jesus According to Luke 4:16–30," 53.

[34] Tannehill, *Narrative Unity*, 69.

notice him as he passes through them. Jesus is, just like the prophet from whom he read, rejected. In fact, it is in Isaiah's own call story where the prophet is told that his message will not be understood because of the hard-heartedness of the people. The people will see but not perceive, hear but not comprehend (Isa 6:9–10). The story of Jesus goes in much the same way—the people do not perceive and comprehend, beginning here in Nazareth but continuing all the way to Golgotha. Yet Jesus announces in this narrative that his purpose is to bring sight to the blind, to open spiritual eyes such that people would understand the grand plan of God at work. In Luke-Acts, the gospel is ultimately going to the Gentiles, but it is only able to do this when the Jews reject the gospel.[35] Thus, by having Jesus and his mission rejected by his own people at the outset, and by connecting that rejection to the good news that he proclaims from the scroll of Isaiah, then we even have something of the annunciation of a Gentile mission here in this passage that is programmatic for Luke-Acts. The case is made all the stronger when we notice that Isaiah is quoted again in the end of Acts (28:26–28) when the gospel has in fact done exactly what Jesus said it would do. Thus the quotes from Isaiah, which both concern blindness, bracket the narrative of Luke-Acts from its inauguration in Luke to the unhindered spread of the Gospel in the end of Acts.

How, then, are we to understand this use of blindness in this passage? Nolland writes, "The rejection in Nazareth is a 'dress-rehearsal' for the passion, and sets up theological categories which prepare the reader for Jesus' prophetic destiny in Jerusalem."[36] He continues to argue for several points of parallelism between the rejection of Nazareth and the death of Jesus in Jerusalem, but I would add one more—the opening of blind eyes. Until Jesus' death, he is unable to be fully recognized, his mission not entirely understood. It is only with his death that spiritual eyes will be fully opened. Jesus has healed the eyes of those who are physically blind; but it is in the death and resurrection of Jesus that the spiritual eyes can be healed. Indeed, Luke gives an example of exactly

[35] Tannehill ("The Mission of Jesus According to Luke 4:16–30," 62) sees a connection "between man's rejection and the unexpected fulfillment of God's plan through that rejection." He explains further: "4:25–27 shows that Luke is not simply saying that Jesus will have to work elsewhere because of bad conditions in Nazareth; rather he is saying that it is God's plan that Jesus work elsewhere and that eventually the benefits of his work be given to the Gentiles."

[36] Nolland, *Luke 1–9:20*, 200.

such a scenario in the post-resurrection stories when he narrates the journey to Emmaus. It is there that Jesus is recognized in the breaking of bread, the eyes of two of his followers being opened to the truth about Jesus' life, death, ministry, and ultimate fulfillment of scripture. Such episodes are anticipated at the beginning of Jesus' ministry in Luke 4. That is, the reader finds in Jesus' self-introduction some categories for understanding the unfolding ministry of Jesus and subsequent mission of the church. This gospel is good news for the poor and oppressed, and this Christ is going to open blind eyes. That Jesus' mission is good news to the poor and the oppressed is well documented in Luke; we would do well to add to that a more thorough understanding of how Jesus opens the eyes of the blind and grants spiritual vision since the sight to the blind is likewise programmatic for this Gospel. Let us follow along in the narrative as this key image unfolds further. We will proceed in canonical order.

Luke 6:39—Blind Guides

At the end of the Sermon on the Plain, the Lukan Jesus offers several parables, one of which involves the imagery of blindness: "Can a blind person guide a blind person? Will not both fall into a pit? A disciple is not above the teacher, but everyone who is fully qualified will be like the teacher" (6:39–40). The answer to this question is self-evidently "no," and the obvious point is made by the rhetorical question. The absurdity of such a question is only further reinforced by our *topos* for blindness. The blind are helpless and usually accompanied by a guide; therefore, it is absurd that a blind person would serve as a guide to another blind person, since both are helpless and both need guidance. Such a situation will cause both parties—the blind leader and the blind follower—to fall into a pit. The same is true on the metaphorical level. The blind person is assumed to be spiritually blind, and thus the spiritually blind person cannot lead anyone, not even another spiritually blind person. The result will be misguidance.

It is notable in this text that the person being guided is assumed to be blind. If the follower needs guidance, his own spiritual vision is, logically, incomplete or insufficient—he is blind and in need of a guide. This particular text at the end of the Sermon on the Plain concerns Christian leadership and the disciple's influence over others, and as such it is concerned with the one doing the guiding rather than the one being guided.[37] The Sermon on the Plain has been concerned with ethics through the transformation of one's character. Here, the transformed character can serve as the light to others, but the untransformed character will serve only to mislead. The untransformed character, then, is labeled as one that is "blind," and the one whose character is blind and whose spiritual eyes are not yet open cannot serve as the much-needed guide to others.

Luke 7:21–22—The Witness to John the Baptist

John the Baptist, incarcerated and soon to be executed, sends messengers to Jesus to ask a question that is plaguing him: "Are you the one who is to come, or are we to wait for another?" (7:19). The answer to this question is for the disciples of John to go and report what they see and hear. Luke 7:21–23 says the following: "Jesus had just then cured many people of diseases, plagues, and evil spirits, and had given sight to many who were blind. And he answered them, 'Go and tell John what you have seen and heard: the blind receive their sight, the lame walk, the lepers are cleansed, the deaf hear, the dead are raised, the poor have good news brought to them. And blessed is anyone who takes no offense at me.'"

As the question was posed to Jesus, he had "just then" healed many, literally "in that hour." When those healings are described though, there is a striking feature—"he gave sight to many who were blind" gets its own independent reference apart from those who were cured of "diseases, plagues, and evil spirits." The healings are described in general terms, not stating which diseases were healed; but the healing of the blind is labeled specifically. Such a designation might indicate that the healing of blindness holds special significance in this Gospel.

Jesus then instructs John's disciples to return and report what they see and hear.[38] Included in the list of things to report are several familiar items. The giving of sight to the blind, of course, is fronted here, which may also indicate a special significance. The list of things that the messengers are to report is a list that is already familiar to the

[37] Note the parables that follow, concerned with self-judgment (removing the plank from one's own eye before helping others), producing good fruit, and wise house-building, all of which are concerned with the Christian leader rather than the one who is following.

[38] Fitzmyer (*Luke*, 667) makes an interesting observation that the witness of the messengers back to John "will depend on their own seeing and hearing."

reader though, as most of them have already been listed in 4:18–19 when Jesus introduced his own mission, and both this text and Luke 4:18–19 echo the text of Isaiah 61. Fitzmyer explores the connection between this text and Isaiah 61:1 and Luke 4:18.[39] He also notes that to this point, no specific report is yet made of a blind person being healed in this Gospel. Nolland also notes the lack of blind healings thus far, taking the specific mention of healing the blind in verse 21 as necessary to make verse 22 make sense. He also notes that at this point in Matthew, two blind men had already been healed.[40] Indeed, Luke has not yet narrated the healing of blindness, and I might suggest that this is nice artistry on the part of Luke. By not specifically narrating the healing of a blind person to this point, this Gospel pushes us towards the metaphorical level of meaning that blindness carries. That is to say that while no one has yet specifically been said to have their physical blindness healed, eyes have indeed been opened metaphorically at every turn, and this is worth reporting to the Baptizer.

In this text, the reader is reminded of the purpose of Jesus' mission in the first place as described in the programmatic text of Luke 4—to open the eyes of the blind. The messengers are told that blind eyes have been opened, but the reader has not yet seen such a story, at least not on a literal level. Thus, the reader should take pause and consider the metaphorical layer of meaning, and when this is considered, it is quite clear that Jesus has been healing blindness of the spiritual variety throughout the narrative so far. The messengers can report this to the Baptist with confidence.

Luke 14: 12–24—The Parable of the Banquet

In this text, Jesus finds himself at the dinner table at the home of a Pharisee. During the meal Jesus gives the following instructions regarding meals and guests: "When you give a luncheon or a dinner, do not invite your friends or your brothers or your relatives or rich neighbors, in case they may invite you in return, and you would be repaid. But when you give a banquet, invite the poor, the crippled, the lame, and the blind. And you will be blessed, because they cannot repay you, for you will be repaid at the resurrection of the righteous" (14:12–14). The list of guests is, of course, the same poor and outcast people whom

[39] Fitzmyer, *Luke*, 667.
[40] Nolland, *Luke 1–9:20*, 329.

the Lukan Jesus has sought out throughout the Gospel. In the ensuing parable, when invited guests do not show up for the banquet, the host sends a servant to invite the poor, the crippled, the blind, and the lame to the meal.[41] The parable is painting a picture of the eschatological banquet in the kingdom of God, and the shock of the parable is that those who are expected to be a part of that banquet refuse to come, while those that no one expects to be invited are the very ones who are present in the end.

The list here—poor, crippled, blind, lame—is very similar to what appeared in 7:22, and shares many similarities to Luke 4 as well. Nolland simply remarks, "The list matches pointedly those who were targeted by Jesus' ministry."[42] This observation is noting the similarity between this story and what has preceded it, specifically in 4:18–19 and in 7:22. In this text in particular, it is easy to read the text metaphorically. Parables naturally have a metaphorical layer of meaning to them, and therefore it is not a far leap to recognize the blind in this text as something more than just those who are literally blind.

As Fitzmyer notes, these same groups of people were specifically excluded from ritual meals in the Qumran Scrolls.[43] Thus on one level, this text finds Jesus encouraging his listeners to invite the very people who were not welcomed in the eyes of many in that culture as Jesus instructs them to invite to dinner those who cannot reciprocate. Yet on another level, Jesus is speaking of an eschatological banquet in the kingdom of God where expectations are reversed. In this case, the servant of God has gone to find, among others, those who are blind. As we have seen throughout this Gospel, those who are blind are the ones to whom Christ is announcing the kingdom, and these are the ones to whom Christ intends to grant true vision.

Luke 18:35–43—A Blind Beggar

This story is not unique to Luke, and it is nearly identical to the Markan story of Bartimaeus.[44] The reader will recall from the previous chapter

[41] Notably, the list is the same in verses 13 and 21, except the order has changed. In verse 13, the blind are listed last. In verse 21, the blind and lame are reversed.

[42] Nolland, *Luke 1–9:20*, 757.

[43] See specifically 1QSa 2:5–7. Also see Fitzmyer, *Luke*, 1057 and his helpful discussion of the parallels between these texts.

[44] For a list of the various theories that try to harmonize the Synoptic accounts of the blind healings at Jericho, see Fitzmyer, *Luke*, 1212. Since defending historicity

that, in my estimation, Bartimaeus is the closest example we have in the New Testament of the "blind who sees clearly" anti-type. That is, Bartimaeus was independent and seems to recognize Jesus, two things that topple the expected *topos* of the blind person, which then leads one to conclude that he may indeed have spiritual vision and speak correctly about Jesus. Though Bartimaeus may not be a blind seer on the level of, say, Teiresias, he does seem to topple the expected conventions. The Lukan version of the story, to the contrary, does not seem to partake in the "blind who sees clearly" anti-type. There are differences in the Lukan story that, though being admittedly subtle, prevent the reader from shattering the expected *topos* in the way the Bartimaeus story does. Though Luke uses the same basic story, he tells it in such a way that the reader is led to completely different conclusions.

There are notable differences from the Bartimaeus story. For example, Bartimaeus immediately knew who Jesus was; this unnamed blind man in Luke does not know. In fact, Luke specifically states, "When he heard a crowd going by, he asked what was happening" (18:36). The Lukan character needs information from others. Additionally, Luke's blind man is much more helpless than Bartimaeus, in keeping with the *topos*. He is said to be sitting by the roadside begging when Jesus passes by. Bartimaeus is called "a blind beggar," but he is not actually said to be begging in Mark's text. That nuance is subtle, but Luke has changed the story to show that the unnamed blind man is in the act of begging when Jesus passes by, highlighting more emphatically his helplessness. Furthermore, in Mark Bartimaeus is very independent. Notice that when he is summoned by Jesus, "throwing off his cloak, he sprang up and came to Jesus" (Mark 10:49). Luke, however, has the blind man brought to Jesus rather than coming on his own (Luke 18:40). Nolland remarks that the blind man being brought to Jesus is more appropriate, and that "he will not be able easily to find his own way."[45] It should also not escape notice that the name of the beggar has dropped out in the Lukan version. The Lukan text is certainly more in keeping with the expected blind *topos*.

The Markan story and the Lukan story are not very different, but the differences are significant. That the name of the blind man is

---

or explaining literary dependence are not our concerns here, these issues will not be explored.

[45] Nolland, *Luke 18:35–24:53*, 900–01.

omitted by Luke and that Luke paints the blind man as more helpless and dependant prevents us from thinking of the Lukan blind man as anything but one who fits the standard *topos*. He is a blind man seeking physical sight. He has only enough spiritual sight to know that he is in fact spiritually blind. He finds in Jesus the cure to both ailments. Bock takes the story the other way, seeing the cry for mercy from the blind man as evidence of his recognition of Jesus' true identity. He writes, "So as the blind man calls for Jesus he reveals the extent and clarity of his spiritual vision."[46] Talbert is more typical, noting that "the healing opens the door to a perception of yet another problem," that is, that his spiritual condition needs healing as well.[47] Fortunately, Jesus brings healing to both conditions.

For Luke, the significance of this story would be undercut if the blind man were to be understood as one who fits the "blind who sees clearly" category as seems to be the case in Mark. Instead, Jesus has come to bring sight to the blind, and this man is a literal example of Jesus doing just that. More significant is the metaphorical level of this man's healing—his spiritual eyes are opened as well, and as one who now both sees with his eyes and "sees" with his spirit, he is ready to be a part of the kingdom that Christ is building. The story of this man's physical healing becomes a physical manifestation of what Jesus is doing on a spiritual level in his ministry.

The Blinding of Saul: A Look at Acts 9

There is no doubt that Saul's encounter with Christ on the Damascus Road is a pivotal story in the book of Acts. Prior to Saul's experience—whether it be termed a conversion or a calling, as is frequently debated in the scholarly literature[48]—the focus of the story in Acts has been on the original disciples of Jesus, mostly centered in the Jerusalem church and the spread of the gospel in the immediate vicinity. The gospel has reached an Ethiopian as well as an Italian centurion,

---

[46] Bock, *Luke*, 305.

[47] Talbert, *Reading Luke*, 204.

[48] See Barrett, *The Acts of the Apostles* (ICC; 2 vols.; Edinburgh: T&T Clark, 1994), 1:442–43; James D. G. Dunn, *The Acts of the Apostles* (Valley Forge, PA: Trinity Press International, 1996), 119–120; Fitzmyer, *The Acts of the Apostles* (AB 31; New York: Doubleday, 1998), 420–21; William J. Larkin, *Acts* (IVP New Testament Commentary Series; Downers Grove, Ill: InterVarsity Press, 1995), 137; and Talbert, *Reading Acts: A Literary and Theological Commentary on the Acts of the Apostles* (Macon, GA: Smyth & Helwys, 2005), 95–97.

but the gospel is still waiting to be carried to the Gentile world on a larger scale. This task will fall to Paul, whose story will consume the remainder of Acts. Thus, the encounter between Saul and Christ that changes Saul from a persecutor of the church to its greatest missionary is foundational, not only for Saul himself but also for the Gentile mission as a whole.

To paint Saul's story using large brushstrokes, Saul begins as a zealous adherent to the Pharisaical Judaism in which he is trained, positive that the religion he knows and fights for is the truth. It is the truth as he knows it, but the reader knows that Saul is in actuality blind to the truth—he fails to recognize the Messiah who has been in their very midst. Saul, then, is spiritually blind to the work of God in his world, and when he encounters Christ, the world as he knows it is shattered and his error is exposed. Everything he *thought* to be true is no longer true. To make things worse, his physical condition is made to mirror his now-exposed spiritual condition—he is blind on both counts. He will remain blind, in fact, until Ananias is sent by God to open his eyes. As Saul's eyes are opened physically, so also are his spiritual eyes. This is the broad story; let us follow the narrative in more detail to see how it plays out.

Saul is first introduced into the story at the end of chapter 7, and his characterization is decisively negative. He is introduced at the stoning of Stephen where the reader is told, "the witnesses laid their coats at the feet of a young man named Saul," and that "Saul approved of their killing him." Saul's characterization is already made clear—his is one of the many who are misguided about the Christian Way. He approves of the stoning of their first martyr, and it seems clear that he approves because this new heresy known as the Way is a threat to the pure Jewish faith to which he has devoted his life. Yet Saul is not content merely to approve of the killing of Stephen, for in the next few verses we are told that "Saul was ravaging the church by entering house after house; dragging off both men and women, he committed them to prison" (8:3). Saul is so certain that the Jewish faith as he understands it is the truth, and so certain that the Christian Way is a dangerous heresy, that he is willing to personally seek after these Christians house by house in order to stomp them out and protect the true faith. Saul is certain that he has clear spiritual sight; and the reader is certain that he could not be more blind.

After the narrative briefly turns to Philip and the Ethiopian eunuch, it returns to Saul again in chapter 9. The negative characterization of

Saul is resumed: "Meanwhile Saul, still breathing threats and murder against the disciples of the Lord, went to the high priest and asked him for letters to the synagogues at Damascus, so that if he found any who belonged to the Way, men or women, he might bring them bound to Jerusalem" (9:1–2). This time, the narrator adds to the characterization of Saul the vivid characterization that Saul is "breathing threats and murder." His desire to root out the Christians has become so strong that it is as natural as breathing to Saul. In fact, as will be discussed later in this section, this imagery of "breathing threats and murder" may well be a way of characterizing Saul as a much-feared dragon. Here, as the reader stands on the precipice of Saul's encounter with Christ, the reader is just as certain that Saul is blind to the truth as Saul is certain that he sees the truth.

The encounter between Saul and Christ is recounted three times in the narrative of Acts. Here in Acts 9, the story is told by the narrator. In 22 and 26, Paul retells the encounter himself. It has often been noted that many of the details in those stories differ from one account to the next, and the overwhelming flow of recent scholarship is in agreement that these variations are not the result of different sources used by Luke, nor do they represent carelessness on the part of the author; rather, the variations are intentional and significant in that Paul retells his own story with variations in each case that are rhetorically appropriate based on the points he is trying to score in each of the defense speeches. Since a large body of literature exists that explores these differences, we will not get into those here.[49] Suffice it to say that for our purposes, we will consider primarily the Acts 9 story as the base story, following the many literary theorists who note that the version of a story told by the narrator tends to be the authoritative version, while characters within the story may tell shaded versions of a story for various reasons.[50]

---

[49] In addition to nearly all recent commentaries that include a discussion on the comparison of these chapters, see especially the following helpful articles and essays: Dennis Hamm, "Paul's Blindness and Its Healing: Clues to Symbolic Intent (Acts 9, 22, and 26)," *Bib* 71 (1990): 63–72; Daniel Margeurat, "Saul's Conversion (Acts 9, 22, 26) and the Multiplication of Narrative in Acts," in *Luke's Literary Achievement: Collected Essays* (ed. C. M. Tuckett; JSNTSup 116; Sheffield: Sheffield Academic Press, 1995): 127–55; and Ronald D. Witherup, "Functional Redundancy in the Acts of the Apostles: A Case Study," *JSNT* 48 (1992): 67–86.

[50] See for example Alter, *Art of Biblical Narrative*, chapter 8 "Narration and Knowledge," and Sternberg, *Poetics of Biblical Narrative*, 409–419. Also, see Marguerat ("Saul's Conversion," 138), who helpfully notes that the retellings in 22 and 26 on the lips of

In the Acts 9 story, the narrator tells us that while on the road, suddenly a light flashed around Saul—a light that presumably no one traveling with Saul sees. Saul falls to the ground and hears a voice. His travel companions hear the voice but see no one, and it may well be that Saul himself hears a voice but sees no one either. He is presumably blinded by the light. The narrator does not specify how it happened in 9, but Paul's version of the story in chapter 22 notes specifically that he was immediately blinded due to the brightness of the light. The significance is that as of this point in the story, Paul has not actually seen Christ, and he is still very much spiritually blind.

It is particularly noteworthy, then, that the entire encounter between Saul and Jesus takes place while Saul is blind; thus, it is more of an auditory encounter than a vision. Horne is one of several scholars who argues that the blindness is an indication that Paul has encountered the Lord,[51] drawing on the OT tradition that those who meet Yahweh are often disabled after the encounter. He cites in particular Isaiah, Daniel, and Micah, but one might also think of Jacob's limp in this category as well. While such a reading is very much the case, my issue here is that this makes too *little* of the blindness; it could apparently be any disability in this mode of thinking, and as we have seen so many times already in the biblical narratives, blindness carries a more specific meaning on its own merit.

As the encounter ends and Paul stands up, the narrator relays the following line, a line which is highly symbolic and loaded with double meaning: "Saul got up from the ground, and though his eyes were open, he could see nothing" (9:8). On a literal level, Saul has his eyes open, but no images were being received by his brain; his eyes were wide open but he was blind. On a metaphorical level though, a whole new layer of meaning is apparent. Saul's spiritual eyes have to some extent been opened as he now realizes that he has been persecuting the Christ; yet, he is still blind because he does not understand this Christ or anything

the main character are best read in light of the ancient rhetorical exercise of *prosopopeia*, which is defined as a speech in character. That is, a rhetorician would practice telling a story as if it were to be told from the perspective of different characters in the story.

[51] Simon Horne, "'Those Who Are Blind See': Some New Testament Uses of Impairment, Inability, and Paradox," in *Human Disability and the Service of God: Reassessing Religious Practice* (ed. Nancy L. Esland and Don E. Saliers; Nashville: Abingdon Press, 1998): 92. See also Barrett, *Acts* (ICC), 452; Ernst Haenchen, *The Acts of the Apostles: A Commentary* (Philadelphia: Westminster, 1971), 323; and Larkin, *Acts*, 138–39.

about him. His spiritual eyes have been opened, but his spiritual vision is still lacking—his eyes are opened, but he is blind.

Saul's physical condition is made to match his spiritual condition. Now that Saul is described as blind, what might an ancient reader assume about his character? Saul has already been characterized as one who terrorizes the Church; now, an ancient reader would likely conclude a number of other things about Saul based on his physical description of being blind. The reader would likely assume the three things that make up the blind *topos*: Saul would be assumed to be helpless and pitiful; Saul would be assumed to be under some sort of divinely-decreed punishment; and Saul would be assumed to be spiritually blind. Indeed, this characterization is sustained in the narrative. Notice that Saul is clearly pitiable and in need of assistance—immediately after the reader is told of Saul's blind condition, the reader is told that his servants take him by the hand and lead him to the city. Saul cannot find his own way; he is blind and in need of assistance. Additionally, as Margaurat helpfully notes, most of the verbs used to characterize Paul following his blinding are passive, having the effect of demonstrating his total helplessness.[52] Immediately after the blindness, then, the first element of the blind *topos* is invoked by the narrator. Second, there is little doubt that Saul's blindness has a divine origin, presumably as punishment,[53] since it is as a result of a divine encounter that his eyesight is taken away, even if only temporarily. Given these two elements of the *topos* that are present already in the narrative, the reader would also be likely to assume the third element, that Saul is spiritually blind as well—"though his eyes were opened, he saw nothing." His eyesight, and likewise his spiritual sight, will not be restored immediately. He will need Ananias to come to him; he will need to spend time with the disciples to understand more fully; he will need time and assistance before he will see the spiritual world clearly enough to carry out his

---

[52] Margaurat, "Saul's Conversion," 142.

[53] There is some debate as to whether the blindness should be seen as divine punishment. Most scholars tend to recognize that there is an element of divine punishment involved. Fitzmyer (*Acts*, 426) for one, disagrees, saying that it is not an issue of punishment, but is instead emphasizing the helplessness of the very person who had previously been the aggressor against Christ and his Church. Larkin (*Acts*, 141) chooses a more nuanced position. He writes, "it is not a punishment nor an indication of divine disfavor nor simply a concrete proof of the vision. An acted parable, it shows Saul the spiritual bankruptcy of his pre-Christian condition."

mission as the apostle to the Gentiles.[54] It is in this vein that Hamm says, "Before Paul can embody the vocation of Israel to be light to the nations, he must be converted from his condition of embodying Israel's blind resistance to the straight way of God."[55]

As an interesting side note, it is worth mentioned that Paul's retelling of the events in chapter 26, both the blindness and the Ananias scene fall out of the story altogether; the two elements seem to go hand in hand, since it is in the Ananias scene that Paul finds healing for both his physical and spiritual blindness. Instead, the eyesight imagery shifts to a completely metaphorical sort, and Christ says that Saul is being sent to the Gentiles "to open their eyes so that they may turn from darkness to light and from the power of Satan to God, so that they may receive forgiveness of sins and a place among those who are sanctified by faith in me" (26:18). In the words of Hamm, "Paul's own experience of loss and recovery of physical vision is transmuted to a metaphor describing the end-time mission of Israel, Jesus and Paul."[56] In 26, then, Paul appears to gain full insight and spiritual awakening at the moment of the encounter, thus making it logically impossible for him to describe himself as "blind" *after* his spiritual vision was restored.[57]

Saul spends the next three days in Damascus, now both physically and spiritually blind ("for three days Saul was without sight" 9:9), and while he is there he neither eats nor drinks according to the text. Many commentators have traditionally read this as an act of penance, usually in light of the pre-baptismal fast that was often practiced in the early church.[58] While this story fits nicely if one is seeking a story where a

---

[54] That Paul does not learn of the gospel in the vision but has to be directed to the church in Damascus is noted by Hans Conzelmann, *Acts of the Apostles: A Commentary on the Acts of the Apostles* (Hermeneia. Philadelphia: Fortress, 1987), 71.

[55] Hamm, "Paul's Blindness and Its Healing," 70.

[56] Hamm, "Paul's Blindness and Its Healing," 71.

[57] In Paul's own narration of the events in chapter 22, he is also less helpless than in chapter 9. On this point see Witherup ("Functional Redundancy," 76), who argues that the addition of another speaking line ("What shall I do, Lord?") indicates a Saul who is not as helpless as he was portrayed in 9; however, he still talks of being led by the hand into the city, something that might have been left out if Paul were trying to portray himself as independent despite the blindness. Witherup (84) argues that the point of these redundant stories that have variations with each retelling ("functional redundancy") is in large part to show the developing character of Saul. In his words, "Luke allows the reader to watch Paul change from a persecutor, to a blind and helpless convert, to an eloquent spokesperson for the faith."

[58] For example, see Conzelmann, *Acts*, 72; Dunn, *Acts*, 122; Fitzmyer, *Acts*, 426; Haenchen, *Acts*, 323; Luke Timothy Johnson, *The Acts of the Apostles* (SP 5; Collegeville, Minn: Liturgical Press, 1992), 164; and Larkin, *Acts*, 141, although Larkin seems to

fast precedes baptism, there is no indication whatever in the text that this fast is an act of penance or that it is related to baptism in any way, as Gaventa has helpfully argued.[59] I would add also that the fact that he is not eating or drinking is only further contributing to the *topos* of blind Saul as helpless, pitiable, and pathetic.

After three days, God appears to Ananias and sends him to Saul. Ananias is, not surprisingly, reluctant, not fully convinced that the former persecutor of the church will not arrest him and drag him off too. Yet God commissions Ananias to go and lay hands on Saul so that "he might regain his sight" (9:12). It is not until this scene that Paul's sight is restored, both physically and spiritually. Physically, "something like scales" fall off and he is able to see again. Spiritually, he gains sight as well. Spencer is among the few commentators that recognize this. He argues that Paul does not gain his spiritual sight until after his eyes are physically opened: "The rhetorical effect of delineating Saul's future through Ananias's vision stresses Saul's limited knowledge (blindness) at this stage and dependency on the assistance of other believers."[60]

Again, we would do well to remember Ps-Aristotle's rule: "It seems to me that the soul and body react on each other; when the character of the soul changes, it changes also the form of the body, and conversely, when the form of the body changes, it changes the character of the soul" (808b). When the body changes, so does the character, and vice versa. This pattern indeed holds true in the case of Saul's blindness—his physical and spiritual state match in that he is blind on both counts; the one blindness is not healed until the other is healed, and thus when the physical blindness is removed, so also the spiritual blindness. Saul's physical state as well as his character have been radically reversed in this narrative, a change made complete only now that his physical and spiritual sight are simultaneously granted. Marguerat is again helpful here: "The narrative of Acts 9:1–30 . . . is dominated by *the reversal of Saul's identity*. From being the persecutor with schemes of death, Saul becomes the persecuted one, threatened with death. From being a foe

---

instead favor the notion that the shock of a lightning strike would cause muscle contractions rendering it impossible to swallow. Talbert (*Reading Acts*, 98) says that it is unlikely that such a prebaptismal fast existed at that point, but that this scene would provide a scriptural basis for such a fast when it does develop in later decades.

[59] Beverly Roberts Gaventa, *The Acts of the Apostles* (ANTC; Nashville: Abingdon, 2003), 150.

[60] F. Scott Spencer, *Acts* (Readings, A New Biblical Commentary; Sheffield: Sheffield Academic Press, 1997), 99.

to the disciples, he becomes a master of disciples. From being a denier of Christ, Saul becomes a preacher of the Messiah."[61]

Note that in 9:17, Ananias says that Paul will regain his sight *and* be filled with the Holy Spirit, and the two events seem to work in conjunction with one another. That is, his spiritual blindness will be cured in the moment that he receives the Spirit, since the moment that the Spirit enters is the moment that he will be able to see/understand the truth of the Christian gospel. Also, note that in 9:18 Paul regains his vision and then immediately gets up and is baptized. Both the filling of the Holy Spirit and the baptism take place only after the eyesight has been restored, and it would seem that the spiritual sight is not gained until that moment either. Thus, following the rules of the physiognomists, the change in the physical body is reflected in a change in the spiritual character, and vice versa—both the physical blindness and the spiritual blindness change simultaneously.

In some sense, Paul's eyes had been opened to the truth on the Damascus road, but he was lacking in spiritual sight still yet. His eyes were opened to the fact that his current understanding of his faith was wrong, and that somehow the Christians were right; his vision had been changed. Yet it is not until Ananias shows up that the full spiritual insight is granted.

To fully understand this scene, one must also catch the overtones that would be carried by the "scales" that cover Paul's eyes. Over a century ago, Hobart suggested in his now famous book that argued for Luke as a physician that the term for "scales"—λεπίς—is medical terminology.[62] He lists a host of examples from Hippocrates and Galen for λεπίς, but all of his examples deal with things like scaly skin, scabs, cuticles, and other flaky particles that sometimes fall from the body. His

[61] Marguerat, "Saul's Conversion," 141. See also Spencer, *Acts*, 96–97, who notes some interesting plays between the Stephen episode and the Saul scene. Previously, Saul was among those who "covered their ears," but now he is hearing the message from the one he was persecuting. Previously, Stephen looked into the heavens and saw Christ, but now Saul has been struck blind by a similar theophany. Saul was the persecutor, but now he is the one being sought by Christ. In some sense, Spencer argues, this scene is the fulfillment of Stephen's prayer that God might forgive those who were killing him, noting that Yahweh does not punish Saul retributively with death, but instead mercifully finds the chief persecutor and wins him over to the Christian side. Finally, whereas Stephen was dragged outside of the city to be killed, Saul is being led into the city to await a further commissioning.

[62] William Kirk Hobart, *The Medical Language of St. Luke* (Grand Rapids, Baker Book House, 1954 [originally printed 1882]), 39.

examples are by no means specific to the eyes and blindness, nor does this term seem to bear any particular medical significance. In fact, the term appears in Greek literature more often than not in reference to fish and/or reptiles which are covered with "scales." I wish to suggest that when Acts states that "something like scales" fell from Saul's eyes, that this is not an invocation of medical language but is an invocation of zoological language. Zoological language, of course, is significant in the world of physiognomics and would be a common means of characterization, and this seems to be what the narrator is doing here. Specifically, the narrator seems to be characterizing Saul as a dragon that has ultimately been tamed and defeated, finally noted by the falling off of the scales.

While it should be noted that λεπίς, nor its Latin equivalent, does not occur in any of the physiognomic handbooks, it does seem to be most frequently used to describe animals and thus warrants attention as a potential example of zoological physiognomics. Most frequently, "scales" is used with respect to fish.[63] Less often, "scales" can be used when describing lizards.[64] Occasionally, the word can also be used more broadly to describe inanimate objects. For example, Josephus uses it to describe the plates of gold in the house of worship (*Ant.* 3.117.1), and Theophrastus even uses it to reference the flaky bark on a tree (*Hist. plant.* 4.14.13.10). These broader uses make it clear that λεπίς is not specifically medical; to the contrary, the overwhelming majority of the uses are zoological in nature. Fish and lizards were not entirely different categories in the ancient world since both have similar bodily features in the form of scales. Likewise, the ancients of nearly every culture had a robust fear of sea monsters, and these sea monsters were almost invariably seen as some sort of reptilian beast that lived in the waters, further blurring the lines between fish and reptile.

If all we had in Saul's narrative was the description of "something like scales" falling from his eyes, there would not be enough evidence to conclude anything more than just that Saul's eyes were covered with something flaky that is now removed. To an audience that thinks in

---

[63] In the Hebrew tradition, note especially Lev 11:9–12 and Deut 14:9–10 where the people are allowed to eat from the water only those animals that have scales. In the Greek literature, see for example Aristotle, *de an.* 419a and Aristotle, *Hist. an.* 490b for common references. One might also note Herodotus, *Hist.* 7.61 where the Persians are "wearing a coat of mail [λεπίδος], looking like fish."

[64] See for example Aristotle, *Part. an.* 691a where he says that scales on lizards are similar to scales on fish.

terms of physiognomics, however, this term λεπίς might trigger thoughts of fish and reptiles, and when the narrative is read again with zoological overtones, a more sinister and fearful characterization of Saul is revealed—Saul as a dragon. Note again the first verse of the episode: "Now Saul, still breathing threats and murder against the disciples of the Lord..." Read in light of reptilian imagery, Saul suddenly sounds like a fire-breathing dragon![65] At least some in the early Christian tradition read Saul's story in this way as well. Consider for example Bede, who writes the following in his commentary on 9:18:

> Every dragon's body is said to be covered with scales. Therefore, because the Jews were called serpents and brood of vipers, this man, who had been an eager follower of their lack of faith, covered over the eyes of his heart, so to speak, with a serpent's skin. With the falling of the scales from his eyes under the hands of Ananias, however, his face showed that he had received the true light in his mind.[66]

Could the narrator be characterizing Saul as a serpent or dragon? The evidence seems to indicate as much. The term for dragon in Greek, δράκων, is a very elastic term and can be used to describe any type of scaly reptilian creature. The term can be used to describe a simple snake. For example, see Diogenes Laertius (*Vit. soph.* 5.90) or Aesop's Fables which include about half a dozen stories where δράκων is a snake and not any other type of lizard. Likewise, Plutarch (*Alex.* 2.6) describes the δράκων that accompanied Olympias into her bedroom, which is clearly a snake. Homer (*Il.* 2.308) talks of a δράκων slithering beneath the alter, and he also describes a coiled snake in *Il.* 22.93. Philo's *Life of Moses* 1.77 and 1.91 describe the sign to Pharaoh where Moses throws down his staff and it becomes a δράκων.

The term can also describe something more dragon-like: see for example Apollonius Rhodius (*Argon.* 2.405) where a δράκων that never sleeps keeps guard over a sacred fleece. Similarly, Homer (*Il.* 11.39) tells of a δράκων that has three heads, and in *Il.* 6.181 he describes a creature with the front of a lion, the back of a δράκων, the middle of a goat, and which breathes fire, perhaps giving us the earliest Greek reference to a fire-breathing creature that is dragon-like. Philostratus

---

[65] For this suggestion regarding Saul's characterization as a dragon, and for much of the work finding references to make the case, I am indebted to my colleague Barbara Hawk. Thanks are expressed here.

[66] The Venerable Bede, *Commentary on the Acts of the Apostles* (trans. Lawrence T. Martin; Kalamazoo, MI: Cistercian Publications, 1989), 88.

(*Imag*. 2.17.6) describes a δράκων that guards a treasure of gold, and Plutarch (*Caes*. 9.5) describes a sacred δράκων that attends a goddess, perhaps a snake or perhaps something more dragon-like that keeps guard of something treasured. Likewise, the reader will also think of Revelation 12, where Satan is described as the δράκων. Here, he is described as a "great red dragon" and the color may well be symbolic of the bloodshed which he brings with him. Notably, Rev 12:9 makes the connection between dragon (δράκων) and serpent (ὄφις) as well.

An ancient dragon, then, was threatening, menacing, and, significantly, typically kept guard over something of great value. Saul of Tarsus fits nicely into this characterization. He is threatening as he breathes threats and murder against the disciples of the Way, and he is keeping guard over the pristine Jewish faith as he understands it. Added to that is chapter 7 where we recall that Saul was introduced as guarding the coats of those who stoned Stephen. In many ways, then, it is altogether appropriate to characterize Saul as a δράκων as he is a menace to the disciples and as he seeks to keep a violent watch over the treasured Jewish faith that he holds so dear.

If the δράκων of the Greek world is menacing and a guard, we must also consider the Hebrew notion of a δράκων that, like many Mesopotamian cultures, considers the creature to be synonymous with chaos and evil. The most obvious reference to the δράκων in Hebrew literature is Bel and the Dragon. Here the δράκων is not described in detail, so it is unclear whether it is more of a serpent or some sort of 4-footed lizard or even a dragon, but it is revered as a living god. One might also think of the Leviathan, the giant sea creature often found in creation myths. Leviathan is translated in the LXX as δράκων in several places, including Ps 103:26, Job 7:12, and Ez 32:2.[67] Though the Leviathan is variously described, it is typically understood as some sort of gigantic sea monster, usually a sea lizard, and its defeat by Yahweh is representative of Christ taming chaos. Perhaps the most sensational example is found in Job 41, where the sea monster is even said to breathe fire. Given the Hebrew notion of a δράκων or even Leviathan, it is noteworthy that these creatures are enemies of God that God consistently conquers and tames. In the story of Saul, this

[67] On the notion of the "dragon" in Hebrew literature see especially the helpful article by Nicolas K. Kiessling, "Antecedents of the Medieval Dragon in Sacred History," *JBL* 89 (1970): 167–77.

is exactly what we find God doing to the menacing persecutor of the Way—Christ defeats Saul and conquers him, even bringing him under the rule of God as a vessel for God's use.

Saul, then, appears to be characterized as a dragon. He is "breathing threats and murder," and he is keeping guard over a religious tradition that he considers of utmost value. He is even said to have his eyes covered with "something like scales." These features add up to a characterization of Saul as a dragon that God must tame and bring under his domain, using Saul as the vessel for the impending Gentile mission.

One other piece of evidence is worth considering in this scene. It is a well-known element of literary theory that the biblical narratives often tend to follow certain type-scenes.[68] One of the many type-scenes is the commissioning or calling narrative.[69] Though the components of the type-scene are variously labeled,[70] the type-scene for a commissioning typically follows a five-step pattern. First, there is an appearance of the divine messenger (whether God himself, an angel, or simply an undefined messenger). Second, there is a reaction on the part of the human, most typically one of fear or of "Woe is me." Third, there is the actual message or task to which the person is called. Fourth, there is typically some sort of objection on the part of the one being commissioned. Fifth, some sort of sign is given to reassure the human. This type scene can be seen throughout the biblical narratives, and one might take as examples the calling of Moses at the burning bush, the calling of Gideon in Judges, the calling of Samuel in the temple, or even the commissioning of Mary to give birth to the Messiah.

When the type scene is applied to Saul's encounter in Acts 9, it only further supports our reading that Saul is spiritually blind until the point

---

[68] On type-scenes, see especially Alter, *Art of Biblical Narrative*, 47–62, who enumerates a number of significant type-scenes in the Old Testament.

[69] For a good treatment of the commissioning as a type-scene, see N. Habel, "The Form and Significance of the Call Narratives," *ZAW* 77 (1965): 297–323 and E. Kutsch, "Gideons Berufung und Alterbau Jdc 6 11–24," *TLZ* 81 (1956): 75–84. Habel, drawing heavily on the work of Kutsch, discusses the scenes involving Gideon, Moses, and the major prophets. See also Robert E. Morosco, "Matthews Formation of a Commissioning Type-Scene Out of the Story of Jesus' Commissioning of the Twelve," *JBL* 103 (1984): 539–56, who applies the type-scene model to the commissioning of the disciples in Matthew.

[70] Habel, "The Form and Significance of the Call Narratives," uses six categories, as follows: 1) divine confrontation; 2) introductory word; 3) commission; 4) objection; 5) reassurance; 6) sign.

at which his physical eyesight is opened. The type scene begins just as expected. There is a divine appearance, in this case a flash of light. There is a reaction on the part of Saul in that he falls to the ground and cries out to know the identity of the one who is responsible for the blinding light. But it is here that something odd happens—the actual commissioning is begun but is left incomplete. That is, Christ identifies himself—"I am Jesus, whom you are persecuting"—and he gives Saul instructions—"Get up and enter the city." What is unusual though is that the instructions are incomplete, suspended until a later time—"enter the city and you will be told what you are to do." The actual commissioning will have to wait for a few days before it is completed. Why? I am suggesting that the commission is suspended because of the blindness. He cannot receive the full commission while he is blind because that also implies that he is spiritually blind; to give him the full commission would be to open his eyes, and this does not yet happen. Instead, the rest of the commission is delayed. Interestingly, the full commission is given to Ananias in the narrative, and likewise it is Ananias who offers the objection. It is presumed by the reader that Ananias relays this commission to Saul, although it is not directly narrated. Thus, when Saul's commissioning scene is read in light of the conventional type scene, we see that because of Saul's physical and spiritual blindness, the full commission is delayed until his eyesight is restored, and furthermore is given to one who has spiritual insight on Saul's behalf.

What then shall we say about the blinding of Saul? When an ancient reader encounters a ravenous Saul who is blinded by an encounter with the divine, a reader would easily assume that Saul's physical condition has been made to match his obvious spiritual condition. Saul fits all of the markers of the typical blind character—he is helpless and pitiable being led around by others; he is blind as a punishment from the divine world; and he is spiritually blind. It is not until Ananias lays hands on him that the scales fall from his eyes and both his physical and spiritual sight are healed, and it is not until those scales fall from his eyes that dragon-like Saul is exposed as the conquered and defeated monster that the disciples had long feared. At the same time, he is filled with the Holy Spirit and immediately moves to be baptized, and then he spends time with the disciples of Jesus learning. The message that the reader must see, then, is that God's healing arm is not too short to reach even the most monstrous enemy of the church, and God's arm is not too short to heal one who is the most desperately blind to the spiritual world that is unfolding right before his eyes. The mission to open the eyes of the Gentiles will move forward, and it will move forward in the person of Saul who was once blind—both physically and spiritually—but who now sees clearly.

Acts 13:4–12: The Blinding of Bar-Jesus / Elymas

Chapter 13 begins with the commissioning of Paul and Barnabas by the church at Antioch. The two men, along with John Mark, are sent out to spread the gospel. The chapter quickly lists their travels, pausing to tell the story of the evangelization of the Roman proconsul Sergius Paulus. He is assisted by a certain Jewish magician (μάγος) named Bar-Jesus.[71] What follows is the story of the showdown between Paul and Bar-Jesus, a showdown that ends with the blinding of Bar-Jesus as punishment for misleading the proconsul and for opposing Paul and the gospel.

With this story, we have a textbook example of what we have described as the Greco-Roman *topos* for blindness. Bar-Jesus is punished by Paul and thus also by God. His opposition to the work of God is the direct cause of his blindness, and there is no question that the blindness is for punishment ("the hand of the Lord is against you," 13:11). Bar-Jesus is also immediately said to be helpless, looking for someone to lead him by the hand, and groping around in the darkness. As we have noted numerous times already, one element of the blind *topos* is helplessness, often marked by the blind person being led around by others, and it is just such an aid that Bar-Jesus seeks as soon as he is blinded. He goes from advisor to the proconsul to a pitiable and helpless character. Thirdly, without question he has demonstrated his spiritual blindness as well. Only now, by making him blind, Paul has exposed that spiritual blindness for all to see as the standard Greco-Roman person would easily conclude that the physically blind man is also spiritually blind, unable to render good advice or adequate spiritual guidance. Thus we find with Bar-Jesus an example that follows the *topos* perfectly.

Notably, very few commentators on this text take much notice of the role of the blindness in the text. Instead, most commentators devote their discussion to the strange array of names in this text. Three sets of names detain scholars. First, much attention is given to Bar-Jesus who

---

[71] That [illegible] man official would be assisted by such a magician is not unusual. Talbert (*[illegible] ts*, 127) gives an extensive list of magicians commonly found in the service o[illegible] an officials.

is also called Elymas.[72] After introducing the magician as Bar-Jesus—an odd name, no doubt, since the "son of Jesus" would not be expected to be a villain at first glance—Luke says that "the magician Elymas (for that is the translation of his name) opposed them…" (13:8). The simple fact of the matter is that Elymas does not translate Bar-Jesus, nor does it translate μάγος, so what Luke means here is entirely unclear. Luke does, of course, offer a third name in this passage that is completely clear: Paul names the so-called "son of Jesus" the "son of the devil" instead (13:10). Second, this is the first time in the narrative that Saul is also called Paul, as Luke writes, "but Saul, also known as Paul,…" (13:9), and much has been made of the potential significance of the shift in nomenclature here.[73] Third, a number of scholars spend time on the name of the Roman proconsul, Sergius Paulus. Most of this discussion has to do with situating this proconsul as an actual historical figure, especially making note of inscriptional evidence that might support the historicity of the text.[74]

There are, however, a few notable commentators who have noted the significance of the blindness itself to the story. Tannehill observes, "[The blindness] serves as a revelation to the proconsul, and perhaps to Elymas himself, of the blindness of this supposed seer."[75] Susan Garrett remarks, "Bar-Jesus claimed to be a prophet (or so Luke implies): as

[72] Fitzmyer (*Acts*, 502) spends time exploring the meaning of the translated name, but can make no final decision. So also Barrett (*Acts* [ICC], 613 and again 615–16), and Dunn (*Acts*, 176) dismisses the name, saying "its point is too obscure for us." Several others devote healthy discussions to the name, including F. F. Bruce, *The Book of Acts* (The New International Commentary on the New Testament; Grand Rapids: Eerdmans, 1956), 264; Larkin, *Acts*, 194; Johnson, *Acts*, 223; Haenchen, *Acts*, 398–99; Conzelmann, *Acts*, 100; and John J. Kilgallen, "Acts 13:4–12: The Role of the Magos," *EstBib* 55 (1997): 226–27. Rick Strelan, "Who Was Bar Jesus (Acts 13, 6–12)?" *Bib* 85 (2004): 65–81, is entirely devoted to the name and identifications of Bar-Jesus.

[73] Fitzmyer (*Acts*, 502–03) lists several options but rejects them all: name change at conversion, name change at commissioning, name change to match the name of the first Gentile convert Sergius Paulus, or just that Saul and Paul are his two names, which is clearly the case but does not explain why both would be used in this particular text. Fitzmyer (*Acts*, 503) also rightly notes that *saulos* as a Greek adjective carries the connotations of "loose, wanton," and is used to describe the way that effeminate males walk, and this alone is reason enough to switch away from that name in the Roman world. Most other commentators spend a good deal of time on the name shift as well, including the following: Barrett, *Acts* (ICC), 609 and 616; Conzelmann, *Acts*, 100; Dunn, *Acts*, 176; Gaventa, *Acts*, 194; Haenchen, *Acts*, 399–400; and Larkin, *Acts*, 195.

[74] Since the historicity of Acts is not our concern here, we will omit this discussion. For the best discussions on this question though, see the following: Fitzmyer, *Acts*, 501–02; Barrett, *Acts* (ICC), 613–14; and Johnson, *Acts*, 222.

[75] Tannehill, *Narrative Unity*, 163.

such he would have been a source of divine light and leadership, one who made paths straight so that others could follow. But Luke shows that the magician was, despite his claim, a fount of darkness and corruption."[76] In addition, Barrett rightly notes that the term used in verse 11 for the blinding (ἀχλὺς) is commonly used in Homer concerning the loss of sight at the moment of death.[77] Such a connection between death/darkness and life/light was well-documented in chapter three and need not escape our notice here. Also noteworthy is the observation of Kilgallen, who sees the blindness of Bar-Jesus, who is a *Jewish* magician, as an example of the Isaiah quotation that ends Acts concerning the blindness of many of the Jews to the gospel.[78]

What then is to be made of this episode? Let us first take note of the narrative location of the story, for that is significant to its interpretation. This episode is the first encounter Paul has on his career as a missionary. He sets out from Antioch, and in his first narrated attempt at spreading the gospel, he encounters a false prophet who must be physically blinded in order to expose the spiritual blindness that is already obvious to Paul. Garrett notes the importance of this narrative location, noting that Paul is sent to open the eyes of the Gentiles, and it first must be shown that he has power greater than the Enemy who blinds the spiritual eyes that God will soon open. Such a showdown is apparent here as Paul encounters one called "son of the devil" (13:10). It will be the enemies of God, then, in the end who are exposed as truly blind.[79] As Paul's first act as a commissioned missionary, it is significant that he begins with an episode regarding blindness, and this should be no shock to the reader—Jesus began his ministry by announcing that the gospel brings sight to the blind (Luke 4); Paul was blinded when he first encountered Christ on the road to Damascus (Acts 9); and the whole of Luke-Acts will end with a proclamation that the eyes of some of the Jews are blind and thus the message will be taken to the Gentiles (Acts 28). Here, Paul begins his career by encountering a magician who is misleading the proconsul, and Paul must expose the magician as spiritually bankrupt, a task which is accomplished by blinding Bar-Jesus.

---

[76] Susan Garrett, *The Demise of the Devil: Magic and the Demonic in Luke's Writings* (Minneapolis: Fortress, 1989), 83.

[77] Barrett, *Acts* (ICC), 618.

[78] Kilgallen, "Acts 13:4–12: The Role of the Magos," 230.

[79] Garrett, *Demise of the Devil*, 84.

Also noteworthy is the form of this story. Talbert says the story is a type-scene, in the form of what he terms "a prophetic response to a resister of God." He identifies five components to the scene: resistance to God's word, a prophetic indictment, a prophecy, its fulfillment, and the result.[80] Talbert also terms this scene as a "power encounter," a showdown between the power of God and the power of someone else.[81] In a culture where power matters, the superior power of the God of Paul must be demonstrated and that victorious power often leads to conversion. In the midst of such a showdown, it is also significant that the enemy of God must be demonstrated to be spiritually bankrupt, a characteristic that is easily demonstrated with blindness so often in the text of Luke-Acts. This story is one such example.

The showdown between Paul and Elymas, God and Satan, also serves other functions in the text as well. Tannehill says the attention is on the Elymas showdown as a means of legitimizing the work of Paul.[82] That is, Jesus and Peter have been shown to work signs and wonders, and now Paul does the same thing in his first scene as a missionary. Tannehill also draws several parallels between this scene and the first scenes of Jesus in Luke 4, illustrating the similarities between the two.[83] While this feature of the text is noteworthy, we need to go further—it is significant not only that Paul is being portrayed like Jesus or Peter in his authority over the spiritual world, but it is also important that the scene shows Paul as spiritually sighted and the magician/false prophet as spiritually blind.

Thus we find in this scene a power showdown between two human players, a kind of representative combat of a much larger cosmic battle between God and Evil. We also find in this text that Paul blinds his enemy as punishment from the divine world, the sort of punishment that a Greco-Roman auditor might have expected. In fact, we find that the character of Bar-Jesus is a perfect example of the standard Greco-Roman *topos* of the blind character—he is helpless, he is being punished by the divine world, and he is spiritually blind. Such a story has the effect of exposing the magician as a spiritually blinded false

[80] Talbert, *Reading Acts*, 127–28.

[81] Talbert, *Reading Talbert*, 128. Susan Garrett's *Demise of the Devil* is a sustained treatment of exactly this thesis, that Acts must demonstrate that the power of God is greater than the power of Satan.

[82] Tannehill, *Narrative Unity*, 161–62.

[83] Tannehill, *Narrative Unity*, 162. So also Johnson, *Acts*, 226.

prophet, while holding up Paul as a spiritually-sighted mouthpiece for the message of God. Garrett notes that Paul, like Jesus, has as his mission to open blind eyes, yet Paul is doing exactly the opposite here by bringing blindness.[84] I would suggest that Paul is in fact opening blind eyes—specifically those of the proconsul—and he does so, ironically, by blinding the one whom the Roman official *thought* was spiritually sighted. Likewise, this episode is also aiming to open the eyes of the reader to the true messenger of the gospel, and any Greco-Roman auditor familiar with the physiognomic conventions pervasive in that world would quickly recognize Paul as a true messenger of God and the blind Elymas as a spiritually-blinded and spiritually bankrupt false prophet.

Acts 28:23–31: The End of Acts and Isaiah 6:9–10

The book of Acts ends in much the same way that the public ministry of Jesus began: with a fulfilled quotation from Isaiah concerning blindness. In Luke 4, Jesus begins his public ministry by quoting Isaiah 61:1–1–2 and announcing that the coming of the kingdom of God meant the healing of blind eyes. Jesus did that, both literally and metaphorically, and now in Acts the story of the expanding church has been a story of the opening of blind eyes. As so many commentators note, the Isaiah quotation in Luke 4 is programmatic for Luke-Acts. Thus, it should come as no surprise that we find Acts ending in a similar way. It is not Isaiah 61 that is quoted, but Isaiah 6:9–10. Both quotes, however, are concerned with blindness and use blindness as a metaphor for spiritual obstinacy. It is highly significant, then, that Luke-Acts is bracketed by quotes from Isaiah concerning blindness. Let us look at this closing episode of Acts.

The final chapter of Acts narrates Paul's journey to Rome where he has appealed his case to Caesar. Upon his arrival in Rome, Paul is allowed to live under house arrest. He soon summons the Jewish leaders, as has so often been his starting point on his missionary journeys. After briefly presenting his case, the curiosity of the Jewish leaders was such that they set up a day to hear Paul explain this sect in more detail. On that appointed day, Paul explains the gospel to them all day long, but at the end of the day his results are mixed: "Some were convinced

[84] Garrett, *Demise of the Devil*, 81–82.

by what he had said, while others refused to believe" (28:24). As they turned to leave, still disagreeing with one another, Paul proclaims one final statement, the final spoken word narrated in Acts:

> The Holy Spirit was right in saying to your ancestors through the prophet Isaiah, 'Go to this people and say, You will indeed listen, but never understand, and you will indeed look, but never perceive. For this people's heart has grown dull, and their ears are hard of hearing, and they have shut their eyes; so that they might not look with their eyes, and listen with their ears, and understand with their heart and turn—and I would heal them.' Let it be known to you then that this salvation of God has been sent to the Gentiles; they will listen. (28:25–28)

Thus we find Paul declaring the people to be blind. The force of the quotation, of course, is to justify the Gentile mission. The Jews are intentionally blind to the Gospel—"they have shut their eyes" (28:27)—and a Gentile mission is announced instead—"let it be known to you then that this salvation has been sent to the Gentiles, they will listen" (28:28).

The first issue that must be addressed is the quotation itself. The quote is unquestionably from the LXX rather than the Hebrew text, and that difference is significant here. In the Hebrew text, the verbs are imperatives: "Go and say to this people: 'Keep listening, but do not comprehend; keep looking, but do not understand.' Make the mind of this people dull, and stop their ears, and shut their eyes, so that they may not look with their eyes, and listen with their ears, and comprehend with their minds, and turn and be healed." In the Hebrew text, the blindness does not seem to be their own fault entirely as it is presumably God's doing that they are blind. The LXX has softened the text considerably by changing the imperatives to finite verbs in the third person ("they have made themselves blind..."). Paul's quotation follows the LXX in this case, and that is significant to the text because Paul is announcing that the gospel will go to people who are willing to open their eyes rather than the so-called chosen people who refuse to have their eyes opened. The responsibility for the blindness, in this case, has shifted very definitively to the unbelieving Jews themselves.[85]

[85] Most modern scholars make note that this text puts the responsibility for the blinding on the Jews themselves. See, for example, Fitzmyer, *Acts*, 795; Haenchen, *Acts*,

Notably, this text is not to be read as Paul's or Luke's total abandonment of the Jewish people. To the contrary, some were convinced by Paul's presentation (28:23). Thus not all the Jews were unbelieving and blind, a scene which Fitzmyer terms as "divided Judaism."[86] Talbert rightly notes that the language of *your* ancestors is aimed not at the entire audience but at those who are not believing the gospel.[87] Barrett even notes that those who are persuaded by the message are listed first, and he explains that this is partly because Luke "is at pains not to represent all Jews as unbelieving."[88] Further, Tannehill says that Paul has far from given up entirely, for he assumes the very role of Isaiah as one who goes and speaks to this blind people nevertheless. Paul "must not abandon the disobedient Jews but must speak to them about their disobedience."[89] Paul is not dismissing the Jewish people wholesale and excommunicating them from eligibility for the kingdom of God; rather, Paul is using this harsh quotation from Isaiah as a weapon, a way of throwing the responsibility into the very laps of those who are rejecting the gospel and are voluntarily blind.

The Isaiah quote, then, is at least in part a means of justifying the Gentile mission. After quoting Isaiah, Paul makes this point clearly: "Let it be known to you then that this salvation of God has been sent to the Gentiles; they will listen" (28:28). A number of commentators speak to the annunciation of the Gentile mission.[90] What is largely unnoticed, however, is that the concept of blindness has now bracketed Luke's work. That is, the mission of Jesus which began in the synagogue in Nazareth as a mission to heal blind eyes has now come all the way to

724; Barrett, *The Acts of the Apostles: A Shorter Commentary* (New York: T&T Clark, 2002), 425; Johnson, *Acts*, 476; and Dennis Hamm, "Sight to the Blind," 121.

[86] Fitzmyer, *Acts*, 795. Most commentators follow this line of thinking, including also Tannehill, *Narrative Unity*, 347; Talbert, *Reading Acts*, 228; and Dunn, *Acts*, 354. To the contrary though, see Hans Conzelmann, *Acts*, 227, who says that this last rejection on the part of the Jews is final, and their opportunity has passed.

[87] Talbert, *Reading Acts*, 228.

[88] Barrett, *Acts*, 424.

[89] Tannehill, *Narrative Unity*, 348.

[90] For the best treatments of the annunciation of the Gentile mission, see the following works: Fitzmyer, *Acts*, 796–97; Talbert, *Reading Acts*, 227–33; Hubertus Waltherus Maria van de Sandt, "Acts 28:28: No Salvation for the People of Israel? An Answer in the Perspective of the LXX," *ETL* 70 (1994): 341–58; and Joseph B. Tyson, "Jews and Judaism in Luke-Acts: Reading as a Godfearer," *NTS* 41 (1995): 19–38.

Rome and has been met by blind eyes. Yet the mission will not fail; it will go to those who will receive it.

Why end with a quote of the apparent failure of the gospel? Why would Luke-Acts end with a statement about eyes that have been intentionally blinded when Jesus' ministry began with a statement about his mission to open blind eyes? Has the gospel message failed to do the very thing Jesus proclaimed that it would do? Has Jesus' mission come all the way to Rome only to ultimately fail to open blind eyes? Indeed not. Perhaps the story ends here in order to once again call the attention of the reader to the fact that blindness to the gospel is a very real possibility. That is, the reader must allow Jesus to open blind eyes lest we be found, like many of the Roman Jews, with eyes blinded to the gospel. It is the responsibility of the one hearing the message to hear, understand, and have his vision healed by the message of Christ and the divine plan of God.

Note that in the end of Acts, "blindness" has shifted to a completely metaphorical level, and this is significant. That is, there is no physical blindness in this text. When blindness first appears in Luke 4, there is a hint of both physical and spiritual blindness in the text. Here, however, the blindness is entirely metaphorical, and this again points us to the real meaning of blindness for this narrative—while Jesus might open the eyes of the physically blind, this is not his primary mission; instead, he is here to open the spiritual eyes, and here at the end of Acts that metaphorical meaning stands separated from the physical layer of meaning that has been interwoven throughout the narrative.

In the end, we are not told what happens to Paul. This is no accident, nor is it a reflection of Luke's ineptitude as an author or his ignorance of the rest of the story. Rather, Luke ends here for a specific reason. Luke Timothy Johnson says it nicely: "the fact that Luke does not find it necessary to tell us these events is a most important clue as to how we should read the conclusion of his work: the point is not the fate of Paul, but the fidelity of God."[91] Johnson is right, and this is exactly how one must understand the Isaiah quotation that draws this narrative to a close. If the people would turn to God—says the prophet, says Jesus, and says Paul—God will open their eyes. Jesus announced his mission in Luke 4 as a mission that is in part directed toward opening blind eyes, and here in the end of Acts the readers is again reminded

---

[91] Johnson, *Acts*, 475.

that God will be faithful to that mission—whoever turns to God and receives the message of Christ will indeed find that spiritual vision has been healed. Those who do not, however, are spiritually blind. Jesus came to heal blind eyes, and Luke reminds the reader again of that mission as the narrative draws to a close.

CHAPTER SEVEN

CONCLUSION

Our study has led us down a long path. We began this work with an exploration of physiognomics, demonstrating that the "physiognomic consciousness" was indeed pervasive throughout the Greco-Roman world in which the New Testament, and specifically Luke-Acts, grew up. We examined the methods of the physiognomists and explored a host of examples in which these conventions drove the characterization in the texts. We then explored the eyes as one specific subset of physiognomic study. It was noted that the eyes were the most important physical marker to the physiognomist. With that being the case, eyes that were blind became all the more terrifying to the ancients. Given the pervasive physiognomic consciousness, it is not surprising that the Greco-Roman world developed something of a literary *topos* for the blind character that equated physical blindness with spiritual blindness. Indeed, we found through examination of multiple examples of blindness that the Greco-Roman auditor would have likely assumed at least three things about a blind character on the sheer basis of being blind, namely, that the blind person was also spiritually blind, the person was likely being punished by the divine world, and that the person was helpless and pitiable.

As we moved through the Jewish and Christian literature, we found two things. First, we found that physiognomic conventions are employed and help to provide characterization, even if at times the physiognomic conventions are employed in rhetorically sly ways that misdirect the reader. Second, we found that the blind *topos* is standard and provides a concrete way of understanding the characterization of the blind person. The only potential exception to the blind *topos* that we find in the biblical literature is Bartimaeus, who seems to shatter the character type as he moves towards the category of the "blind who sees clearly."

We also found that in Luke-Acts, the blind *topos* is standard in every case and provides an interpretive key to the meaning of the text. The narrative of Jesus' public ministry begins with his claim to proclaim sight to the blind, and this text serves as an introduction to Jesus' entire ministry. That is to say that among the things that are defining for the ministry of Jesus is the opening of blind eyes. Read in physiognomic terms, this means that the message of Jesus comes to open our spiritual eyes, and the unfolding narrative is the story of Jesus' life, ministry, and death that collectively serve exactly that function. Jesus' pronouncement that he will open blind eyes, then, serves as a heuristic for understanding the Gospel. As the story progresses, of course, we find further examples, including the unnamed blind man at Jericho, the soon-to-be apostle to the Gentiles, and a false prophet named Bar-Jesus. The narrative of Acts then ends with Paul's proclamation that the gospel will now go to the Gentiles because many of the Jews are blind to the message. The narrative, then, is bracketed by statements about blindness, once again underscoring the interpretive significance of blindness for the whole of Luke-Acts.

By way of conclusion, this project has made at least three significant contributions to the field of biblical studies. First, this project has highlighted the need for modern readers to read with sensitivity toward physiognomics. That is, if ancient auditors listened to these texts with ears sensitive to physiognomic conventions, then it behooves the modern scholar to learn to listen to these texts in the same way. Entire layers of characterization have been missed by failing to be attentive to physiognomics, and as a result we have missed much that is significant to the meaning of these texts. Second, this project has contributed a new understanding of how blindness works as characterization. While some work has been done on this topic in the field of classics, nothing of this sort has yet been done in biblical studies. To outline a character type or *topos*, and to call the attention of the reader to the way in which that *topos* impacts interpretation, is a contribution to the scholarly field. Finally, this project contributes a new interpretive layer to the study of Luke-Acts. While many have noticed the programmatic nature of a text like Luke 4, most attention has been focused on the Lukan theme of the gospel going to the poor and the oppressed. The same also needs to be said of the opening of blind eyes, as both of these elements are programmatic for this gospel. It is the sincere hope of this author that these insights may pay dividends to the biblical scholar who seeks to have eyes to see.

BIBLIOGRAPHY

Physiognomic Handbooks

Aristotle. *Physiognomics*. Pages 84–137 in *Minor Works*. Translated by W. S. Hett. LCL 307. Cambridge: Harvard University Press, 1963.

Polemo. "Polemonis: De Physiognomonia Liber Arabice et Latine." Pages 93–294. *Scriptores Physiognomonici Graeci et Latini*. Edited by Richardus Foerster. Leipzig: Teubner, 1893.

Secondary Resources

Achtemeier, Paul J. "And He Followed Him: Miracles and Discipleship in Mark 10:46–52." *Semeia* 11 (1978): 115–45.

Alexander, Philip S. "Physiognomy, Initiation, and Rank in the Qumran Community." Pages 385–94 in *Geschichte—Tradition—Reflexion*. Edited by H. Cancik, et al. Tubingen: J. C. B. Mohr, 1996.

Allison, Dale C. "The Eye Is the Lamp of the Body (Matthew 6:22–23 = Luke 11:34–36." *New Testament Studies* 33 (1987): 61–83.

Alter, Robert. *The David Story: A Translation with Commentary of 1 and 2 Samuel*. New York: W. W. Norton & Company, 1999.

——. *The Art of Biblical Narrative*. San Francisco: Basic Books, 1981.

Armstrong, A. MacC. "The Methods of the Greek Physiognomists." *Greece and Rome* 5 (1958): 52–56.

Ashton, Mark. "Luke 4:14–30: Freedom for the Oppressed." *Evangel* 16 (1998): 38–41.

Ballók, János. "The Description of Paul in the Acta Pauli." Pages 1–15 in *The Apocryphal Acts of Paul and Thecla*. Edited by Jan N. Bremmer. Kampen, Netherlands: Kok Pharos Publishing House, 1996.

Barré, Michael L. "The Meaning of *pršdn* in Judges 3:22." *Vetus Testamentum* 41 (1991): 1–11.

Barrett, C. K. *The Acts of the Apostles: A Shorter Commentary*. New York: T&T Clark, 2002.

——. *The Acts of the Apostles*. International Critical Commentary. 2 volumes. Edinburgh: T&T Clark, 1994.

——. *The Gospel According to St. John: An Introduction with Commentary and Notes on the Greek Text*. London: S.P.C.K., 1955.

Barton, Tamsyn S. *Power and Knowledge: Astrology, Physiognomics, and Medicine Under the Roman Empire*. Ann Arbor: University of Michigan Press, 1994.

Beasley-Murray, George R. *John*. Word Biblical Commentary 36. Nashville: Thomas Nelson Publishers, 1999.

Beavis, Mary Ann. "From the Margin to the Way: A Feminist Reading of the Story of Bartimaeus." *Journal of Feminist Studies in Religion* 14 (1998): 19–39.

Bergen, Robert D. *1, 2 Samuel*. The New American Commentary 7. Nashville: Broadman and Holman Publishers, 1996.

Bernidaki-Aldous, Eleftheria A. *Blindness in a Culture of Light: Especially the Case of* Oedipus at Colonus *of Sophocles*. New York: Peter Lang, 1990.

Berquist, James A. "'Good News to the Poor': Why Does This Lukan Motif Appear to Run Dry in the Book of Acts?" *Bangalore Theological Forum* 18 (1986): 1–16.

Betz, Hans Dieter. "Matthew vi.22f and Ancient Greek Theories of Vision." Pages 43–56 in *Text and Interpretation: Studies in the New Testament Presented to Matthew Black*. Edited by Enest Best and R. McL. Wilson. Cambridge: Cambridge University Press, 1979.

Betz, Otto. "Die Vision des Paulus im Tempel von Jerusalem—Apg 22, 17–21 als Beitrag zur Deutung des Damaskuserlebnisses." Pages 113–23 in *Verborum Veritas*. Wuppertal: Theologischer Verl. Brockhaus, 1970.

Bock, Darrell L. *Luke*. The IVP New Testament Commentary Series. Downers Grove, Ill: InterVarsity, 1994.

Boling, Robert G. *Judges*. Anchor Bible 6A. Garden City, NY: Doubleday, 1975.

Borchert, Gerald L. *John 1–11*. The New American Commentary 25A. Nashville: Broadman and Holman Publishers, 1996.

Borgen, Peter, and Søren Giversen, eds. *The New Testament and Hellenistic Judaism*. Aarhus: Aarhus University Press, 1995.

Bottéro, J. "Symptômes, signes, écritures." Pages 70–199 in *Divination et rationalité*. Edited by J.-P. Vernant. Paris: Éditions du Seuil, 1974.

Bovon, François. *Evangelium nach Lukas: Luke 1: a commentary on the Gospel of Luke 1:1–9:50*. Hermenia. Minneapolis: Fortress, 2002.

Braun, Willi. "Physiotherapy of Femininity in the *Acts of Thecla*." Pages 209–230 in *Text and Artifact in the Religions of Mediterranean Antiquity: Essays in Honour of Peter Richardson*. Studies in Christianity and Judaism 9. Edited by Stephen G. Wilson and Michel Desjardins. Waterloo, Ont: Wilfrid Laurier University Press, 2000.

Britton, Piers D. G. "The Signs of Faces: Leonardo on Physiognomic Science and the 'Four Universal States of Man.'" *The Society for Renaissance Studies* 16 (2002): 143–62.

Brown, Raymond. *The Gospel According to John I–XII: A New Translation with Introduction and Commentary*. Anchor Bible 29. New York: Doubleday, 1966.

Bruce, F. F. *The Book of Acts*. The New International Commentary on the New Testament. Grand Rapids: Eerdmans, 1956.

Brueggemann, Walter. *First and Second Samuel*. Interpretation. Louisville: John Knox, 1990.

Buxton, R. G. A. "Blindness and Limits: Sophokles and the Logic of Myth." *Journal of Hellenic Studies* 100 (1980): 22–37.

Caird, George Bradford. *Saint Luke*. Westminster Pelican Commentaries. Philadelphia: Westminster, 1978.

Carroll, Robert P. "Blindsight and the Vision Thing: Blindness and Insight in the Book of Isaiah." Pages 79–93 in *Writing and Reading the Scroll of Isaiah: Studies of an Interpretive Tradition*. Edited by Craig C. Broyles and Craig A. Evans. Supplements to Vetus Testamentum 70. Leiden: Brill, 1997.

Carson, D. A. *The Gospel According to John*. Grand Rapids: Eerdmans, 1991.

Celenko, Theodore, editor. *Egypt in Africa*. Indianapolis: Indianapolis Museum of Art, 1996.

Ceresko, Anthony R. "The Identity of 'the blind and the lame' in 2 Samuel 5:8b." *Catholic Biblical Quarterly* 63 (2001): 23–30.

Charlesworth, James H. "The Son of David: Solomon and Jesus (Mark 10:47)." Pages 72–87 in *The New Testament and Hellenistic Judaism*. Edited by Peder Borgen and Søren Giversen. Peabody, Mass: Hendrickson Press, 1997.

Christenson, Eric S. "A Fistful of Shekels: Scrutinizing Ehud's Entertaining Violence (Judges 3:12–30)." *Biblical Interpretation* 11 (2003): 53–78.

Clements, Ronald E. "'Who Is Blind but My Servant?' (Isaiah 42:19): How Then Shall We Read Isaiah?" Pages 143–56 in *God in the Fray: A Tribute to Walter Brueggemann*. Edited by Tod Linafelt and Timothy K. Beal. Minneapolis: Fortress, 1998.

——. "Patterns in the Prophetic Canon: Healing the Blind and the Lame." Pages 189–200 in *Canon, Theology, and Old Testament Interpretation: Essays in Honor of Brevard*

S. Childs. Edited by Gene M. Tucker, David L. Petersen, and Robert R. Wilson. Phildelphia: Fortress, 1988.
——. *Isaiah 1–39*. New Century Bible Commentary. Grand Rapids: Eerdmans, 1980.
Cohen, Kenneth. "King Saul: A Bungler from the Beginning." *Bible Review* 10 (October 1994): 34–39, 56–57.
Conzelmann, Hans. *Acts of the Apostles: A Commentary on the Acts of the Apostles*. Hermeneia. Philadelphia: Fortress Press, 1987.
Cooper, Howard. "'Too Tall by Half'—King Saul and Tragedy in the Hebrew Bible." *Journal of Progressive Judaism* 9 (November 1997): 5–22.
Cotter, Wendy. *Miracles in Greco-Roman Antiquity: A Sourcebook*. New York: Routledge, 1999.
Cousland, J. R. C. "Tobit: A Comedy in Error?" *Catholic Biblical Quarterly* 65 (2003): 535–53.
Craghan, John. *Esther, Judith, Tobit, Jonah, Ruth*. Old Testament Message 16. Wilmington, Del: Michael Glazier, 1982.
Crenshaw, James L. *Samson: A Secret Betrayed, a Vow Ignored*. Atlanta: John Knox Press, 1978.
Culpepper, R. Alan. *Anatomy of the Fourth Gospel: A Study in Literary Design*. Philadelphia: Fortress Press, 1983.
Darr, John. *Herod the Fox: Audience Criticism and Lukan Characterization*. Journal for the Study of the New Testament Supplement Series 163. Sheffield; Sheffield Academic Press, 1998.
Denova, Rebecca. *The Things Accomplished Among Us: Prophet Traditions in the Structural Pattern of Luke-Acts*. Journal for the Study of the New Testament Supplement Series 141. Sheffield: Sheffield Academic Press, 1997.
Derrett, J. Duncan M. "Trees Walking, Prophecy, and Christology." *Studia Theologica* 35 (1981): 33–54.
Deselaers, P. *Das Buch Tobit: Studien zu seiner Entstehung, Komposition und Theologie*. Orbis Biblicus et Orientalis 43. Guttenburg: University Press, 1982.
deSilva, David A. *Introducing the Apocrypha: Message, Context, and Significance*. Grand Rapids: Baker, 2002.
Devereux, G. "The Self-Blinding of Oidipous in Sophokles: *Oidipous Tyrannos*." *Journal of Hellenic Studies* 93 (1973): 36–49.
Dibelius, Martin. *The Book of Acts: Form, Style, and Function*. Edited by K. C. Hanson. Minneapolis: Fortress, 2004.
Di Lella, Alexander A. "The Deuteronomic Background of the Farewell Discourse in Tobit 14:3–11." *Catholic Biblical Quarterly* 41 (1979): 380–89.
Dowd, Sharyn. *Reading Mark: A Literary and Theological Commentary on the Second Gospel*. Macon, GA: Smyth and Helwys, 2000.
Dragga, Sam. "In the Shadow of the Judges: The Failure of Saul." *Journal for the Study of the Old Testament* 38 (June 1987): 39–46.
Dunn, James D. G. *The Acts of the Apostles*. Valley Forge, PA: Trinity Press International, 1996.
Edelman, Diana. "Saul's Battle Against Amaleq." *Journal for the Study of the Old Testament* 35 (June 1986): 71–84.
Eiesland, Nancy L. *The Disabled God: Toward a Liberation Theology of Disability*. Nashville: Abingdon Press, 1994.
——, and Don E. Saliers, eds. *Human Disability and the Service of God: Reassessing Religious Practice*. Nashville: Abingdon Press, 1998.
Elliott, John H. "The Evil Eye and the Sermon on the Mount: Contours of a Pervasive Belief in Social Scientific Perspective." *Biblical Interpretation* 2 (1994): 51–84.
Eslinger, Lyle M. *Kingship of God in Crisis: A Close Reading of 1 Samuel 1–12*. Bible and Literature Series 10. Decatur, GA: Almond Press, 1985.

Esser, Albert. *Das Antlitz Der Blindheit in der Antike: Dei Kulturellen und Medizinhistorischen Ausstrahlungen des Blindenproblems in den Antiken Quellen*." Leiden: E. J. Brill, 1961.

Evans, Craig A. *Mark 8:27–16:20*. Word Biblical Commentary 34b. Nashville: Thomas Nelson Publishers, 2001.

——. *Luke*. New International Biblical Commentary 3. Peabody, Mass: Hendrickson, 1990.

——. *To See and Not Perceive: Isaiah 6:9–10 in Early Jewish and Christian Interpretation*. Journal for the Study of the Old Testament Supplement Series 64. Sheffield: Sheffield Academic Press, 1989.

Evans, Elizabeth C. *Physiognomics in the Ancient World*. Transactions of the American Philosophical Society 59. Philadelphia: The American Philosophical Society, 1969.

——. "Literary Portraiture in Ancient Epic: A Study of the Descriptions of Physical Appearance in Classical Epic." *Harvard Studies in Classical Philology* 58 (1948): 189–217.

——. "Galen the Physician as Physiognomist." *Transactions and Proceedings of the American Philological Association* 76 (1945): 287–98.

——. "The Study of Physiognomy in the Second Century A.D." *Transactions and Proceedings of the American Philological Association* 72 (1941): 96–108.

——. "Roman Descriptions of Personal Appearance in History and Biography." *Harvard Studies in Classical Philology* 46 (1935): 43–84.

Evans, Mary J. *1 and 2 Samuel*. New International Biblical Commentary. Peabody, Mass.: Hendrickson, 2000.

Exeogu, Ernest M. "Surely We Are Not Blind, Are We": An African Theological Reading of the Story of the Healing of the Man Born Blind, John 9:1–41." Pages 1–15 in *Society of Biblical Literature Seminar Papers*, 2003. Society of Biblical Literature Seminar Papers 30. Chico, Calif.: Scholars Press, 2003.

Finkel, Asher. "Jesus' Preaching in the Synagogue on the Sabbath (Luke 4:16–28)." Pages 325–41 in *The Gospels and the Scriptures of Israel*. Edited by Craig A. Evans and W. Richard Stegner. Journal for the Study of the New Testament Supplement Series 104. Sheffield: Sheffield Academic Press, 1994.

Fitzmyer, Joseph A. *Tobit*. Commentaries on Early Jewish Literature. New York: Walter de Gruyter, 2003.

——. *The Acts of the Apostles*. Anchor Bible 31. New York: Doubleday, 1998.

——. "The Aramaic and Hebrew Fragments of Tobit from Qumran Cave 4." *Catholic Biblical Quarterly* 57 (1995): 655–75.

——. *The Gospel According to Luke*. Anchor Bible 28–28A. Garden City: Doubleday, 1981–85.

Ford, J. Massyngbaerde. "The Physical Features of the Antichrist." *Journal for the Study of the Pseudepigrapha* 14 (1996): 24–41.

France, R. T. *The Gospel of Mark: A Commentary on the Greek Text*. Grand Rapids: Eerdmans, 2002.

Frisch, Amos. "'For I Feared the People and I Yielded to Them'—Is Saul's Guilt Attenuated or Intensified?" *Zeitschrift für die Alttestamentliche Wissenschaft* 108 no. 1 (1996): 98–104.

Furlani, Giuseppe. "A Short Physiognomic Treatise in the Syriac Language." *Journal of the American Oriental Society* 39 (1919): 289–294.

Gamberoni, Johann. *Die Auslegung Des Buches Tobias: in der griechisch-lateinischen Kirche der Antike und der Christenheit des Westens bis 1600*. Studien zum Alten und Neuen Testaments 21. Munich: Kösel-Verlag, 1969.

Garland, David. *Mark*. The NIV Application Commentary. Grand Rapids: Zondervan: 1996.

Garland, Robert. *The Eye of the Beholder: Deformity and Disability in the Graeco-Roman World*. Ithaca, N.Y.: Cornell University Press, 1995.

Garrett, Susan. *The Demise of the Devil: Magic and the Demonic in Luke's Writings*. Minneapolis: Fortress Press, 1989.

——. "Light on a Dark Subject and Vice Versa: Magic and Magicians in the New Testament." Pages 142–65 in *Religion, Science, and Magic: In Concert and in Conflict*. Edited by Jacob Neusner, et al. New York: Oxford University Press, 1989.

Gaventa, Beverly Roberts. *The Acts of the Apostles*. Abingdon New Testament Commentary. Nashville: Abingdon, 2003.

——. *From Darkness to Light: Aspects of Conversion in the New Testament*. Overtures to Biblical Theology 20. Philadelphia: Fortress, 1986.

Glancy, Jennifer A. "Boasting of Beatings (2 Corinthians 11:23–25)." *Journal of Biblical Literature* 123 (2004): 99–135.

Glasson, Thomas Francis. "The Main Source of Tobit." *Zeitschrift für die Alttestamentliche Wissenschaft* 71 (1959): 275–77.

Gleason, Maud W. *Making Men: Sophists and Self-Presentation in Ancient Rome*. Princeton, Princeton University Press, 1995.

Goulder, Michael Douglas. "Those Outside (Mk 4:10–12)." *Novum Testamentum* 33 (1991): 289–302.

Grant, Coleen C. "Reinterpreting the Healing Narratives." Pages 72–87 in *Human Disability and the Service of God: Reassessing Religious Practice*. Nancy L. Eiesland and Don E. Saliers. Nashville: Abingdon, 1998.

Grant, Robert M. "The Description of Paul in the Acts of Paul and Thecla." *Vigiliae Christianae* 36 (1982): 1–4.

Green, Joel B. *The Gospel of Luke*. The New International Commentary on the New Testament. Grand Rapids: Eerdmans, 1997.

Guelich, Robert A. *Mark 1–8:26*. Word Biblical Commentary 34a. Nashville: Thomas Nelson Publishers, 1989.

Gundry, Robert H. *Mark: A Commentary on His Apology for the Cross*. Grand Rapids: Eerdmans, 1993.

Gunkel, Hermann. *Genesis*. Translated by Mark E. Biddle. Macon, GA: Mercer University Press, 1997.

Gunn, David. *The Fate of King Saul*. Sheffield: JSOT Press, 1980.

Habel, N. "The Form and Significance of the Call Narratives." *Zeitschrift fur die Alttestamentliche Wissenschaft* 77 (1965): 297–323.

Haenchen, Ernst. *John 2: A Commentary on the Gospel of John Chapters 7–21*. Hermeneia. Translated by Robert W. Funk. Philadelphia: Fortress Press, 1984.

——. *The Acts of the Apostles: A Commentary*. Philadelphia: Westminster Press, 1971.

Hamm, Dennis. "Paul's Blindness and Its Healing: Clues to Symbolic Intent (Acts 9, 22, and 26)." *Biblica* 71 (1990): 63–72.

——. "Sight to the Blind: Vision as Metaphor in Luke." *Biblica* 67 (1986): 457–77.

Hanford, William Richard. Deutero-Isaiah and Luke-Acts: Straightforward Universalism?" *Church Quarterly Review* 168 (1967): 141–52.

Harrington, Daniel J. *Invitation to the Apocrypha*. Grand Rapids: Eerdmans, 1999.

Harrill, J. Albert. "Invective against Paul (2 Cor 10:10), the Physiognomics of the Ancient Slave Body, and the Greco-Roman Rhetoric of Manhood." Pages 189–213 in *Antiquity and Humanity: Essays on Ancient Religion and Philosophy Presented to Hans Dieter Betz on His 70th Birthday*. Edited by Adela Yarbro Collins and Margaret M. Mitchell. Tübingen: Mohr Siebeck, 2001.

Harris, J. Rendel. "On the Stature of Our Lord." *Bulletin of the John Rylands Library Manchester* 10 (1926): 112–126.

Hawk, Daniel. "Saul as Sacrifice: The Tragedy of Israel's First Monarch." *Bible Review* 12 (December 1996): 20–25, 56.

Hilgert, Earle. "The Son of Timaeus: Blindness, Sight, Ascent, Vision in Mark." Pages 185–98 in *Reimagining Christian Origins: A Colloquium Honoring Burton L. Mack*.

Edited by Elizabeth A. Castelli and Hal Taussig. Valley Forge, Penn: Trinity Press International, 1996.

Hill, David. "Rejection of Jesus at Nazareth (Luke 4:16–30)." *Novum Testamentum* 13 (1971): 161–80.

Hobart, William Kirk. *The Medical Language of St. Luke*. Grand Rapids, Baker Book House, 1954 (originally printed 1882).

Hodges, Zane Clark. "Blind Men at Jericho." *Bibliotheca Sacra* 122 (1965): 319–30.

Holden, Lynn. *Forms of Deformity*. Journal for the Study of the Old Testament Supplement Series 131. Sheffield: JSOT Press, 1991.

Holleran, J. Warren. "Seeing the Light: A Narrative Reading of John 9." *Ephemerides Theologicae Loveanienses* 69 (1993): 354–82.

Horne, Simon. "'Those Who Are Blind See': Some New Testament Uses of Impairment, Inability, and Paradox." Pages 88–101 in *Human Disability and the Service of God: Reassessing Religious Practice*. Edited by Nancy L. Esland and Don E. Saliers. Nashville: Abingdon Press, 1998.

Howe, E. Margaret. "Interpretations of Paul in the Acts of Paul and Thecla." Pages 33–49 in *Pauline Studies: Essays Presented to Professor F. F. Bruce on His 70th Birthday*. Edited by Donald A. Hagner and Murray J. Harris. Grand Rapids: Eerdmans, 1980.

Humphries, Michael L. "The Physiognomy of the Blind: The Johannine Story of the Blind Man." Pages 229–243 in *Reimagining Christian Origins: A Colloquium Honoring Burton L. Mack*. Edited by Elizabeth A. Castelli and Hal Taussig. Valley Forge, Penn: Trinity Press International, 1996.

Jacoby, A. "Zur Heilung des Blinden von Bethsaida." *Zeitschrift für die neuentestamentliche Wessenschaft* 10 (1909): 185–94.

Jeremias, Joachim. *The Parables of Jesus*. Upper Saddle River, NJ: Prentice-Hall, 1954.

Jobling, David. *1 Samuel*. Berit Olam. Collegville, Minn.: Liturgical Press, 1998.

Johnson, E. S. "Mark 8:22–26: the Blind Man from Bethsaida." *New Testament Studies* 25 (1979): 370–83.

——. "Mark 10:46–52: Blind Bartimaeus." *Catholic Biblical Quarterly* 40 (1978): 191–204.

Johnson, Luke Timothy. *The Acts of the Apostles*. Sacra Pagina 5. Collegeville, Minn: Liturgical Press, 1992.

——. *The Gospel of Luke*. Sacra Pagina 3. Collegeville, Minn: Liturgical Press, 1991.

Just, Felix N. W. "From Tobit to Bartimaeus, from Qumran to Siloam: The Social Role of Blind People and Attitudes Toward the Blind in New Testament Times." Ph.D. diss., Yale University, 1997.

Keller, Marie Noël. "Opening Blind Eyes: A Revisioning of Mark 8:22–10:52." *Biblical Theology Bulletin* 31 (2001): 151–57.

Kelley, Nicole. "The Theological Significance of Physical Deformity in the Psuedo-Clementine *Homilies*." *Perspectives in Religious Studies* 34 (2007): 77–80.

Kiessling, Nicolas K. "Antecedents of the Medieval Dragon in Sacred History." *Journal of Biblical Literature* 89 (1970): 167–77.

Kilgallen, John J. "Acts 13:4–12: The Role of the Magos." *Estudios Bíblicos* 55 (1997): 223–37.

Kim, Jichan. *The Structure of the Samson Cycle*. Kampen, Netherlands: Kok Pharos Publishing House, 1993.

Kimball, Charles. *Jesus' Exposition of the Old Testament in Luke's Gospel*. Journal for the Study of the New Testament Supplement Series 94. Sheffield: Sheffield Academic Press, 1994.

——. "Jesus' Exposition of Scripture in Luke 4:16–30: An Inquiry in Light of Jewish Hermeneutics." *Perspectives in Religious Studies* 21 (1994): 179–202.

Kirtley, Donald J. *The Psychology of Blindness*. Chicago: Nelson-Hall, 1975.

Klein, Ralph. *1 Samuel*. Word Biblical Commentary 10. Waco: Word, 1983.

Klein, William W. "The Sermon at Nazareth (Luke 4:14–22)." Pages 153–72 in *Christian Freedom: Essays in Honor of Vernon C. Grounds*. Edited by Kenneth W. M. Wozniak and Stanley J. Grenz. Lanham, MD: University Press of America, 1986.
Kolasny, Judette M. "An Example of Rhetorical Criticism." Pages 67–77 in *New Views on Luke and Acts*. Edited by Earl Richard. Collegeville, Minn: Liturgical Press, 1990.
Kollmann, Bernd. "Göttliche Offenbarung magisch-pharmakologischer Heilkunst im Buch Tobit." *Zeitschrift für die Alttestamentliche Wissenschaft* 106 (1994): 289–99.
Köstenberger, Andreas J. *John*. Baker Exegetical Commentary on the New Testament. Grand Rapids: Baker Academic, 2004.
Kraus, Fritz Rudolf. *Die Physiognomischen Omina Der Babylonier*. Leipzig: J. C. Hinrichs Buchhandlung, 1935.
Kremer, Jacob. "Die dreifache Wiedergabe des Damaskuserlebnisses Pauli in der Apostelgeschichte: eine Hilfe für das rechte Verständis der lukanischen Osterevangelien." Pages 329–55 in *Unity of Luke-Acts*. Edited by J. Verheyden. Bibliotheca Ephemeridum theologicarum Lovaniensium 142. Leuven: Leuven University Press, 1999.
Kugel, James. "Why Was Lamech Blind?" *Hebrew Annual Review* 12 (1990): 91–103.
Kutsch, E. "Gideons Berufung und Alterbau Jdc 6 11–24." *Theologische Literaturzeitung* 81 (1956): 75–84.
Larkin, William J. *Acts*. IVP New Testament Commentary Series. Downers Grove, Ill.: InterVarsity Press, 1995.
Larson, Jennifer. "Paul's Masculinity." *Journal of Biblical Literature* 123 (2004): 85–97.
Lee, Dorothy A. *The Symbolic Narrative of the Fourth Gospel: The Interplay of Form and Meaning*. Journal for the Study of the New Testament Supplement Series 95. Sheffield: JSOT Press, 1994.
Levin, S. "Isaac's Blindness: A Medical Diagnosis." *Judaism* 37 (1988): 81–83.
Levine, Amy-Jill. "Diaspora as Metaphor: Bodies and Boundaries in the Book of Tobit." Pages 105–17 in *Diaspora Jews and Judaism: Essays in Honor of, and in Dialogue with, A. Thomas Kraabel*. Edited by J. Andrew Overman and Robert S. MacLennan. South Florida Studies in the History of Judaism 41. Atlanta: Scholars Press, 1992.
——. "Tobit: Teaching Jews How to Live in the Diaspora." *Bible Review* 8 (Aug. 1992): 42–51, 64.
Lieu, Judith M. "Blindness in the Johannine Tradition." *New Testament Studies* 34 (1988): 83–95.
Lindars, Barnabas. *Judges 1–5: A New Translation and Commentary*. Edinburgh, Scotland: T&T Clark, 1995.
Loader, William R. G. "Son of David, Blindness, Possession, and Duality in Matthew." *Catholic Biblical Quarterly* 44 (1982): 570–85.
Long, Philips. *The Reign and Rejection of King Saul: A Case for Literary and Theological Coherence*. Atlanta: Scholars Press, 1989.
MacDonald, Dennis. "Tobit and the Odyssey." Pages 11–40 in *Mimesis and Intertextuality in Antiquity and Christianity*. Edited by Dennis MacDonald. Harrisburg, Penn: Trinity Press International, 2001.
Malherbe, Abraham J. "A Physical Description of Paul." Pages 170–75 in *Christians Among Jews and Gentiles: Essays in Honor of Krister Stendahl on his Sixty-fifth Birthday*. Edited by George W. E. Nickelsburg with George W. MacRae. Philadelphia: Fortress Press, 1986.
Malina, Bruce J. and Jerome H. Neyrey. *Portraits of Paul: An Archaeology of Ancient Personality*. Louisville: Westminster John Knox Press, 1996.
Mann, C. S. *Mark: A New Translation with Introduction and Commentary*. Anchor Bible 27. Garden City, N.Y.: Doubleday, 1986.
Marcus, Joel. "A Note on Markan Optics." *New Testament Studies* 45 (1999): 250–56.
Margeurat, Daniel. "Saul's Conversion (Acts 9, 22, 26) and the Multiplication of Narrative in Acts." Pages 127–55 in *Luke's Literary Achievement: Collected Essays*. Edited by

C. M. Tuckett. Journal for the Study of the New Testament Supplement Series 116. Sheffield: Sheffield Academic Press, 1995.

Marshall, Evan. *The Eyes Have It: Revealing Their Power, Messages, and Secrets*. New York: Citadel Press, 2003.

Martin, Clarice. "A Chamberlain's Journey and the Challenge of Interpretation for Liberation." *Semeia* 47 (1989): 105–135.

Martin, Dale B. *The Corinthian Body*. New Haven, CT: Yale University Press, 1995.

Martin, Troy W. "Paul's Argument from Nature for the Veil in 1 Corinthians 11:13–15: A Testicle Instead of a Head Covering." *Journal of Biblical Literature* 123 (2004): 75–84.

Martyn, J. Louis. *History and Theology in the Fourth Gospel*. New York: Harper and Row, 1968.

Marx, Tzvi C. *Disability in Jewish Law*. New York: Routledge, 2002.

Mason, Hugh J. "Physiognomy in Apuleius Metamorphoses 2.2." *Classical Philology* 79 (1984): 307–09.

Mathews, Kenneth A. *Genesis 11:27–50:26*. New American Commentary 1B. Nashville: Broadman and Holman Publishers, 2005.

Matthews, Victor H. *Judges and Ruth*. New Cambridge Bible Commentary. Cambridge: Cambridge University Press, 2004.

McCarter, P. Kyle. *I Samuel*. Anchor Bible 8. Garden City, NY: Doubleday, 1980.

Mayes, A. D. H. *Judges*. Old Testament Guides. Sheffield: JSOT Press, 1985.

Mesk, Josef. "Die Biespiele in Polemons Physiognomonik." *Wiener Studien* 50 (1932): 51–67.

Miscall, Peter D. *1 Samuel: A Literary Reading*. Indiana Studies in Biblical Literature. Bloomington, IN: Indiana University Press, 1986.

Misener, Geneva. "Loxus, Physician and Physiognomist." *Classical Philology* 18 (1923): 1–22.

Mitchell, David T. and Sharon L. Snyder, eds. *The Body and Physical Difference: Discourses of Disability*. Ann Arbor: University of Michigan Press, 1997.

Moloney, Francis J. *The Gospel of Mark: A Commentary*. Peabody: Hendrickson, 2002.

——. *The Gospel According to John*. Sacra Pagina 4. Collegeville, Minn.: Liturgical Press, 1998.

Moore, Carey A. *Tobit: A New Translation with Introduction and Commentary*. The Anchor Bible 40A. New York: Doubleday, 1996.

——. "Scholarly Issues in the Book of Tobit Before Qumran and After: An Assessment." *Journal for the Study of the Pseudepigrapha* 5 (1989): 65–81.

Moore, George Foote. *A Critical and Exegetical Commentary on Judges*. International Critical Commentary. New York: Schribner's Sons, 1903.

Morosco, Robert E. "Matthews Formation of a Commissioning Type-Scene Out of the Story of Jesus' Commissioning of the Twelve." *Journal of Biblical Literature* 103 (1984): 539–56.

Murphy-O'Connor, Jerome. *Paul: A Critical Life*. New York: Oxford University Press, 1996.

Neirynck, Frans. "Luke 4:16–30 and the Unity of Luke-Acts." Pages 357–95 in *Unity of Luke-Acts*. Edited by J. Verheyden. Bibliotheca Ephemeridum theologicarum Lovaniensium 142. Leuven: Leuven University Press, 1999.

Nickelsburg, George, W. E. "Tobit, Genesis, and the *Odyssey*: A Complex Web of Intertextuality." Pages 41–55 in *Mimesis and Intertextuality in Antiquity and Christianity*. Edited by Dennis MacDonald. Harrisburg, Penn: Trinity Press International, 2001.

——. "Tobit and Enoch: Distant Cousins with a Recognizable Resemblance." Pages 54–68 in *SBL Seminar Papers, 1988*. Society of Biblical Literature Seminar Papers 27. Atlanta: Scholars Press, 1988.

Nolland, John. *Luke 1–9:20*. Word Biblical Commentary 35A. Dallas: Word Books, 1989.

Nolland, John. *Luke 18:35–24:53*. Word Biblical Commentary 35B. Dallas: Word Books, 1993.
Nowell, Irene. "The Narrator in the Book of Tobit." Pages 27–38 in *SBL Seminar Papers* 1988. Society of Biblical Literature Seminar Papers 27. Atlanta: Scholars Press, 1988.
Olyan, Saul M. "'Anyone Blind or Lame Shall Not Enter the House': On the Interpretation of 2 Samuel 5:8b." *Catholic Biblical Quarterly* 60 (1998): 218–27.
Otzen, Benedikt. *Tobit and Judith*. Guides to the Apocrypha and Pseudopigrapha. New York: Sheffield Academic Press, 2002.
Parsons, Mikeal C. *Body and Character in Luke and Acts: The Subversion of Physiognomy in Early Christianity*. Grand Rapids: Baker Academic Press, 2006.
——. "'Bound by Satan, Behold These Ten and Eight Years': The Symbolism of the Length of the Bent Woman's Illness (Luke 13:10–17) in P45." *Journal of Higher Criticism*. Forthcoming.
——. "'Short in Stature': Luke's Physical Description of Zacchaeus." *New Testament Studies* 47 (2001): 50–57.
Pao, David W. *Acts and the Isaianic New Exodus*. Wissenschaftliche Untersuchungen zum Neuen Testament 130. Tübingen: Mohr Siebeck, 2000.
Pervo, Richard I. "A Hard Act to Follow: *The Acts of Paul* and the Canonical Acts." *Journal of Higher Criticism* 2 (1995): 3–32.
——. *Luke's Story of Paul*. Minneapolis: Fortress, 1990.
Petersen, Norman R. "The Composition of Mark 4:1–8:26." *Harvard Theological Review* 73 (1980): 185–217.
Pilch, John J. "Paul's Ecstatic Trance Experience Near Damascus in Acts of the Apostles." *Hervormde Teologiese Studies* 58 (2002): 690–707.
Polzin, Robert. *Samuel and the Deuteronomist: A Literary Study of the Deuteronomic History*. Indiana Studies in Biblical Literature. Bloomington, IN: Indiana University Press, 1989.
——. *Moses and the Deuteronomist: A Literary Study of the Deuteronomic History*. New York: Seabury Press, 1980.
Preuschen, E. "Paulus als Antichrist." *Zeitschrift fur die Neutestamentlich Wissenschaft* 2 (1901): 169–201.
Rabenau, Merten. *Studien zum Buch Tobit*. Beihefte zur Zeitschrift für die alttestamentliche Wissenschaft 220. Berlin: Walter de Gruyter, 1994.
Reader. William W. *The Severed Hand and the Upright Corpse: The Declamations of Marcus Antonius Polemo*. SBL Texts and Translations 42. Atlanta: Scholars Press, 1996.
Resseguie, James L. "John 9: A Literary-Critical Analysis." Pages 115–22 in *The Gospel of John as Literature: An Anthology of Twentieth-Century Perspectives*. Edited by Mark W. G. Stibbe. Leiden: Brill, 1993.
Ricciotti, Giuseppe. *Paul the Apostle*. Translated by Alba I. Zizzamia. Milwaukee: Bruce, 1953.
Robbins, Vernon K. *New Boundaries in Old Territory: Form and Social Rhetoric in Mark*. Emory Studies in Early Christianity 3. Edited by David B. Gowler. New York: Peter Lang, 1994.
Rordorf, Willy and Peter W. Dunn. "Paul's Conversion in the Canonical Acts and in the Acts of Paul." *Semeia* 80 (1997): 137–144.
Rosenblatt, Marie Eloise. "Recurring Narration as a Lukan Literary Convention in Acts: Paul's Jerusalem speech in Acts 22:1–21." Pages 94–105 in *New Views on Luke and Acts*. Edited by Earl Richard. Collegeville, Minn: Liturgical Press, 1990.
Roth, S. John. *The Blind, The Lame, and the Poor: Character Types in Luke-Acts*. Journal for the Study of the New Testament Supplement Series 144. Sheffield: Sheffield Academic Press, 1997.
Sanders, James A. "Isaiah 61 to Luke 4." Pages 75–106 in *Christianity, Judaism and Other Greco-Roman Cults*. Edited by Jacob Neusner. Studies in Judaism in Late Antiquity 12. Leiden: Brill, 1975.

Sandnes, Karl Olav. *Belly and Body in the Pauline Epistles*. Cambridge: Cambridge University Press, 2002.

Sandt, Hubertus Waltherus Maria van de. "Acts 28:28: No Salvation for the People of Israel? An Answer in the Perspective of the LXX." *Ephemerides theologicae lovanienses* 70 (1994): 341–58.

Schnackenburg, Rudolf. *The Gospel According to John*. 2 volumes. New York: Seabury Press, 1980.

Schneemelcher, Wilhelm, ed. *New Testament Apocrypha II: Writings Related to the Apostles; Apocalypses and Related Subjects*. English translation edited by R. McL. Wilson. Philadelphia: Westminster, 1964. Rev. Ed. Louisville: Westminster/John Knox, 1992.

Schneider, Tammi J. *Judges*. Berit Olam: Studies in Hebrew Narrative and Poetry. Collegeville, Minn: Liturgical Press, 1985.

Schweizer, Eduard. *The Good News According to Luke*. Translated by David E. Green. Atlanta: John Knox Press, 1984.

Seng, Herbert. *Die Heilungen Jesu in medizinischer Beleuchtung*. 2d. ed. Aufl. Schwerin: F. Bahn, 1926.

Skemp, Vincent. "Adelfoj and the Theme of Kinship in Tobit." *Ephemerides theologicae Lovanienses* 75 (1999): 92–103.

Sloan, Robert B. *The Favorable Year of the Lord: A Study in Jubilary Theology in the Gospel of Luke*. Austin, Schola Press, 1977.

Snowden, Jr., Frank M. "The Physical Characteristics of Egyptians and Their Southern Neighbors: The Classical Evidence." Pages 106–08 in *Africa in Egypt*. Edited by Theodore Celenko. Indianapolis: Indianapolis Museum of Art: 1996.

Soggin, J. Alberto. *Judges: A Commentary*. The Old Testament Library. Philadelphia: Westminster Press, 1981.

Soll, Will. "Misfortune and Exile in Tobit: the Juncture of a Fairy Tale Source and Deuteronomic Theology." *Catholic Biblical Quarterly* 51 (1989): 209–31.

Spencer, F. Scott. *Acts*. Readings, A New Biblical Commentary. Sheffield: Sheffield Academic Press, 1997.

Spencer, Richard A. "The Book of Tobit in Recent Research." *Currents in Research* 7 (1999): 147–80.

Staley, Jeffrey L. "Stumbling in the Dark, Reaching for the Light: Reading Character in John 5 and 9." *Semeia* 53 (1991): 55–80.

Steinhauser, Michael G. "The Form of the Bartimaeus Narrative." *New Testament Studies* 32 (1986): 583–95.

Stern, Philip D. "The 'Blind Servant' Imagery of Deutero-Isaiah and Its Implications." *Biblica* 75 (1994): 224–32.

Sternberg, Meir. *The Poetics of Biblical Narrative: Ideological Literature and the Drama of Reading*. Bloomington, Ind: Indiana University Press, 1985.

Stock, Augustine. "Hinge Transitions in Mark's Gospel." *Biblical Theology Bulletin* 15 (Ja 1985): 27–31.

Strawn, Brent A. *What is Stronger Than a Lion? Leonine Image and Metaphor in the Hebrew Bible and the Ancient Near East*. Orbis Biblicus et Orientalis 212. Göttingen: Vandenhoeck & Ruprecht, 2005.

Strelan, Rick. "Who Was Bar Jesus (Acts 13, 6–12)?" *Biblica* 85 (2004): 65–81.

Talbert, Charles. *Reading Acts :A Literary and Theological Commentary on the Acts of the Apostles*. Macon, GA: Smyth & Helwys, 2005.

——. *Reading John: A Literary and Theological Commentary on the Fourth Gospel and the Johannine Epistles*. New York: Crossroad, 1994.

——. *Reading Luke: A Literary and Theological Commentary on the Third Gospel*. New York: Crossroad: 1982.

Tannehill, Robert. *Luke*. Abingdon New Testament Commentaries. Nashville: Abingdon, 1996.

——. *The Narrative Unity of Luke-Acts: A Literary Interpretation.* 2 vols. Foundations and Facets. Philadelphia: Fortress, 1986–90.

——. "The Mission of Jesus According to Luke 4:16–30." Pages 51–75 in *Jesus in Nazareth.* Edited by Erich Grässer, et al. Beiheft zur Zeitschrift für die neutestamentliche Wissenschaft und die Kunde der älteren Kirche 40. Berlin: de Gruyter, 1972.

Tatum, W. Jeffrey. "The Regal Image in Plutarch's Lives." *The Journal of Hellenic Studies* 116 (1996): 135–51.

Todorov, Vladislav. "Introduction to the Physiognomy of Ruins." *Yale Journal of Criticism* 6 (1993): 249–57.

Tolbert, Mary Ann. *Sowing the Gospel: Mark's World in Literary-Historical Perspective.* Minneapolis: Fortress, 1989.

Torrey, Charles C. "'Nineveh' in the Book of Tobit." *Journal of Biblical Literature* 41 (1922): 237–45.

Tuckett, Christopher M. "Luke 4:16–30, Isaiah, and Q." Pages 343–54 in *Logia: Les Paroles de Jésus: The Sayings of Jesus: Mémorial Joseph Coppens.* Edited by Joël Delobel, et al. Leuven, Belgium: Leuven University Press, 1982.

Tyson, Joseph B. "Jews and Judaism in Luke-Acts: Reading as a Godfearer." *New Testament Studies* 41 (1995): 19–38.

Van de Sandt, Huub. "Acts 28, 28: No Salvation for the People of Israel? An Answer in the Perspective of the LXX." *Ephemerides theologicae Lovaneinses* 70 (1994): 341–58.

Vargon, Shmuel. "The Blind and the Lame." *Vetus Testamentum* 46 (1996): 498–514.

Von Dobshütz, E. *Der Apostel Paulus: II. Seine Stellung in der Kunst.* Halle: Buchhandlung des Waisenhauses, 1928.

Von Premerstein, A. "Das Attentat Der Konsulare auf Hadrian im Jahre 118 n. Chr." *Klio Beiheft* 8 (1908): 46–71.

Von Schumann, H. *Traüme der Blinden.* Basel: S. Karger Co, 1959.

Wallach, Luitpold. "The parable of the Blind and the Lame: A Study in Comparative Literature." *Journal of Biblical Literature* 62 (1943): 333–39.

Walz, Clark A. "The Cursing Paul: Magical Contests in Acts 13 and the New Testament Apocrypha: Acts 13:6–12." Pages 167–82 in *Mission in Acts: Ancient Narratives in Contemporary Context.* Edited by Robert L. Gallagher and Paul Hertig. American Society of Missiology Series 34. Maryknoll, NY: Orbis Books, 2004.

Watts, John D. W. *Isaiah 1–33.* Word Biblical Commentary 24. Waco, TX: Word Books, 1985.

Webb, Barry G. *The Book of Judges: An Integrated Reading.* Journal for the Study of the Old Testament Supplement Series 46. Sheffield: JSOT Press, 1987.

Wendling, E. *Die Entstehung des Marcus Evangeliums.* Tübingen: Mohr, 1908.

Wenham, Gordon J. *Genesis 16–50.* Word Biblical Commentary 2. Dallas: Word Books, 1994.

Williams, Benjamin E. *Miracle Stories in the Biblical Book Acts of the Apostles.* Mellen Biblical Press Series 59. Lewiston, NY: E. Mellen Press, 2001.

Witherington, Ben. *The Gospel of Mark: A Socio-Rhetorical Commentary.* Grand Rapids: Eerdmans, 2001.

——. *The Acts of the Apostles: A Social-Rhetorical Commentary.* Grand Rapids: Eerdmans, 1998.

Witherup, Ronald D. "Functional Redundancy in the Acts of the Apostles: A Case Study." *Journal for the Study of the New Testament* 48 (1992): 67–86.

Wrede, William. *The Messianic Secret.* Translated by J. C. G. Greig. Cambridge: J. Clarke, 1971.

Wynn, Kerry H. "Johannine Healings and the Otherness of Disability." *Perspectives in Religious Studies* 34 (2007): 61–75.

Zimmermann, Frank. *The Book of Tobit: An English Translation with Introduction and Commentary.* New York: Harper and Brothers, 1958.

INDEX OF SUBJECTS AND AUTHORS

INDEX OF SCRIPTURE